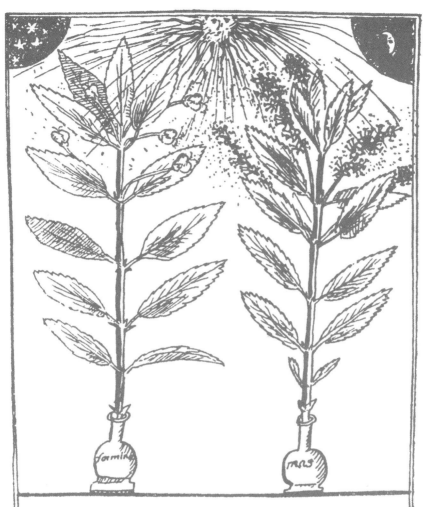

Nature's Body

*Gender in the Making
of Modern Science*

LONDA SCHIEBINGER

BEACON PRESS • BOSTON

Beacon Press
25 Beacon Street
Boston, Massachusetts 02108-2892

Beacon Press books
are published under the auspices of
the Unitarian Universalist Association of Congregations.

99 98 97 96 95 94 93   8 7 6 5 4 3 2 1

Text design by Martine Bruel

Library of Congress Cataloging-in-Publication Data

Schiebinger, Londa.
    Nature's body : gender in the making of modern science /
  Londa Schiebinger.
       p.   cm.
    Includes bibliographical references (p.) and index.
    ISBN 0-8070-8900-1
    1. Sex differences—History—18th century. 2. Science—
History—18th century. 3. Natural history—History—18th century.
4. Anthropology—History—18th century. I. Title.
    QP81.5.S35   1993
    574'.094'09033—dc20   92-45026
                           CIP

For Geoffrey and Jonathan

Contents

Acknowledgments

I wish to thank the Guggenheim Foundation, the Rockefeller Foundation, and the National Science Foundation for their generous support during the researching and writing of this book. I would also like to thank the Josephine Berry Weiss Endowment and the Institute for the Arts and Humanistic Studies at Pennsylvania State University for their kind support in providing both release time and travel monies. Among my colleagues, I am especially grateful to Paul Harvey for coining numerous Latin phrases that rival Linnaeus's own. I also thank Hans-Dieter Sues, Sandra Harding, Anne Fausto-Sterling, Susan Koslow, and the readers for Beacon Press for their helpful comments, and Deborah Hamilton for collecting research materials. Sections of chapters 1, 2, 3, and 4 include materials from essays that originally appeared in *The American Historical Review*, *Eighteenth-Century Studies*, and two volumes edited by Marina Benjamin, *Science and Sensibility* and *A Question of Identity*.

Robert Proctor remains a source of invaluable expertise, but more than that he has been my companion in our many intellectual odysseys. Finally, I dedicate this book to our young sons.

Introduction

> The *stylus* of the female [plant] is the vagina while the vulva and
> the mons Venus . . . correspond to the *stigma*. Thus the uterus,
> vagina, and vulva make up the *pistil*—the name that modern
> botanists give to all the female parts of plants. . . . As far as we
> men are concerned, a quick look is enough: sons of Priapus,[1]
> spermatic animals, our stamen is rolled as in a cylindrical tube.
> The *stamen* is the penis, and the sperm is our fecundating
> powder.
>
> Julien Offray de La Mettrie, *L'homme plante*, 1748

*F*rom Aristotle through Darwin to Freud and beyond, nature
has been infused with sexuality and gender. Carl Linnaeus, the
greatest taxonomist of his age, imagined that plants have vaginas
and penises and reproduce on marriage beds. Aristotle in the ancient world thought that the male cuttlefish courageously defends
his female when under siege. (The female, by contrast, "runs away,"
leaving the male to fend for himself because, as Aristotle tells us, nature has not armed females with weapons for combat.) Pliny taught
that the hyena is bisexual, becoming male and female in alternate
years such that the female bears offspring without a male.[2]

Gender traits ascribed to plants and animals change with shifting notions of masculinity and femininity in Western culture. For
Aristotle, writing long before the historical rise of the passionless
female, mares were sexually wanton, said to "go a-horsing" to satisfy
their unbridled appetites.[3] If not impregnated by a stallion, these
dissolute females would be fertilized by the wind. By the eighteenth
century, females throughout nature—with the exception of Erasmus Darwin's lusty flowers—were said to evince a patient modesty.
Even among insects, females were thought to "repel the first [sex-

ual] attacks of the males" and in so doing win the respect of their paramours.[4]

Analogies to sex were drawn across the kingdoms of nature. When Julien Offray de La Mettrie described his *L'homme plante* ("man, the plant"), it was often a woman he depicted: the calyx was the trunk of her body ornamented with clothes "which she sheds every night"; her "nectaries" (breasts) were "round and globular, soft, white, and smooth to the touch."[5] Hegel continued this association between plants and women in his *Philosophy of Right*. Men, he wrote, are like animals, active and combative; women, by contrast, are like plants, essentially placid.[6]

My purpose in this book is to explore how gender—both the real relations between the sexes and ideological renderings of those relations—shaped European science in the eighteenth century, and natural history in particular. Crucial to our story is that, in the seventeenth and eighteenth centuries, Europeans who described nature were almost exclusively male. Female naturalists were a rare breed, female taxonomists even rarer. Why were so few scientists women? Conservatives and liberals have tried to explain how and why science is what David Noble has described as a "world without women."[7] Many have located the problem in women. Since the eighteenth century, conservatives have focused on women's smaller or less specialized brains, their raging hormones, or faulty genes.[8] Liberals have wanted to improve women's education and scientific self-esteem in an attempt to make them more "fit" for science.

Increasingly, however, we are beginning to understand that the problem may not lie with women but with the broader culture and ethos of science. A decade of scholarship has explored how various aspects of the modern sciences—their cultures, methods, world views, and priorities—have served to hold women at a distance.[9] Carolyn Merchant's *Death of Nature* showed that from ancient to modern times, nature—the object of scientific study—has been conceived as female.[10] Evelyn Fox Keller elucidated the masculine face of science, showing how the coupling of a historically female nature and male science has formed a central metaphor of scientific discovery.[11] My previous book, *The Mind Has No Sex?*, analyzed how women insinuated themselves into scientific circles at the dawn of modern science, and how the multifaceted culture of modern science came to exclude women and something defined as "the feminine" from its ideals and practices. At the core of modern science lies a self-reinforcing system whereby the findings of science (crafted in institutions from which women were excluded) have been used to justify their continued absence.[12]

This book is about how the politics of participation molds scientific knowledge. The question of women engaging in science is not just a question of equality—whether all people should have an equal opportunity to pursue careers of their choosing. Nor is it a question of "manpower," having enough scientists to sharpen a chosen nation's competitive edge, as it is often discussed today. It is a question of knowledge. Only recently have we begun to appreciate that who does science affects the kind of science that gets done. How, then, has our knowledge of nature been influenced by struggles determining who is included in science and who is excluded, which projects are pursued and which ignored, whose experiences are validated and whose are not, and who stands to gain in terms of wealth or well-being and who does not?[13]

Here we investigate natural history. As strange as it may seem in our own high tech–big science world, natural history was one of the premier sciences of the eighteenth century. It was also popular. A cabinet of natural history, containing any number of curiosities— perhaps the brains and genitalia of both sexes, a skeleton, embryos at different stages of development, or a monstrous fetus—was a prized possession of members of the cultivated leisured classes. Wealthy patrons established botanical gardens, menageries, and museums. The Duchess of Queensbury in England went so far as to have a dress designed to give her the appearance of a walking botanical garden.[14] Natural history books were widely read; the initial printing of Buffon's voluminous *Histoire naturelle* sold out in six weeks. Naturalists were accorded a new respect. Linnaeus was the first man of letters awarded the Swedish title "Knight of the Order of the Polar Star," an honor usually reserved for military men.[15]

Eighteenth-century natural history is often portrayed in this innocent light, but it was also big business, an essential component of Europe's commercial and colonial expansion. Natural history cabinets groaned with scientific spoils collected from around the globe—Egyptian mummies extracted from their tombs, exotic animals and peoples brought to fill European menageries. These large private collections epitomized the huge fortunes amassed in this period in European capitals.[16] Naturalists collected nature's bounty with self-professed disinterest but also with an eye toward profit. Voyages, financed by trading companies such as the Parisian *Compagnie des Indes* (whose headquarters today house the Bibliothèque Nationale), had to be profitable to be feasible. As described by a naturalist of the day, men of science competed with one another to discover some previously unknown island that might contain new and exotic spices to add to the riches of Indian cargoes.[17]

As we shall see, gender was to become one potent principle organizing eighteenth-century revolutions in views of nature, a matter of consequence in an age that looked to nature as the guiding light for social reform. Linnaeus, for example, based his botanical taxonomy on the sexuality of plants. His famous "Key to the Sexual System" spoke of the "nuptials" of living plants, stamens and pistils as husbands and wives, heterosexual (but, significantly, not homosexual) liaisons among flowers, and hermaphroditic and androgynous plants. In so doing, he gave male parts priority over female parts in determining the status of the organism in the plant kingdom's taxonomic hierarchy. Chapter 1 examines the social and political circumstances surrounding this sexualization of plants in the seventeenth and eighteenth centuries, and how certain key divisions Linnaeus devised as the basis of his botanical taxonomy came to recapitulate the sexual hierarchy of Western Europe.

Next we explore how sexual categories were insinuated into the animal kingdom. Chapter 2 tells the remarkable story of the origins of the term *Mammalia* (mammals), coined in 1758 and coincident with the starting point of modern zoological nomenclature. In his revolutionary classification of the animal kingdom Linnaeus devised this term, meaning literally "of the breast," to incorporate humans within the class of vertebrates, which includes apes, monkeys, cows, whales, camels, and all other animals with hair, three ear bones, and a four-chambered heart. In so doing, the father of modern taxonomy brought an unseemly focus to bear on the female mammae as the icon of that class. Why Linnaeus called mammals *mammals*, I argue, had less to do with the uniqueness and universality of the female breast than with eighteenth-century politics of wet-nursing and maternal breast-feeding, population growth, and the contested role of women in both science and society.

Chapter 3 moves from mammals to *Primates*, another term coined by Linnaeus. European naturalists were bemused when they first encountered the great apes of Africa and Asia in the seventeenth and eighteenth centuries. Their first and later glimpses of these our closest relatives were highly anthropomorphized and also highly gendered. Female apes were transported from Africa clad in sheer silks and reputed to be sensitive when their "modesty" was violated by the inspection of their private parts. Male apes, by contrast, were seen as wild, lascivious, and given to violent acts of interspecies rape. This chapter investigates how gender influenced the search for those characteristics separating humans from beasts.

Race also became a significant factor in the search for a clear and distinct line dividing humans from brutes. European naturalists tended to describe apes more sympathetically than they did Africans, highlighting the human character of apes while emphasizing the purported simian qualities of Africans. While European naturalists anxiously attempted to assimilate apes into human culture, they distanced themselves from the peoples of Africa. Edward Long, for example, did not think "that an oran-outang husband would be any dishonor to an Hottentot female."[18] Africans were often described as apes; at different times both were cast as "missing links" in the great chain of being. This provided a convenient rationale for slavery; it also led Europeans to treat in similar ways the Africans and great apes brought to Europe for scientific investigation. Both were exhibited in menageries and coffeehouses. Both were given classical names: "César," the baboon, and "the Hottentot Venus" both bore this ironic mark of grandeur. Upon death, apes and Africans were both commonly bequeathed to natural history museums to be dissected and displayed. (Natural history museums still often include "primitives"—but rarely Europeans—within their collections.) The great French naturalist Georges Cuvier anatomized the Hottentot Venus (a woman from the south of Africa) in 1815 and presented her celebrated genitalia to the men of science at the Museum of Natural History in Paris. For a time, apes were even enlisted as slaves to work in European mines.

Chapter 4 examines eighteenth-century attempts to classify humans. Much has been written about race; here we explore how gender shaped studies of race. This chapter tells how, in the seventeenth and eighteenth centuries, a sex-linked characteristic, the male beard, was used to differentiate the races. We see further how notions of female beauty (mediated, so it appears, by the white slave trade) led Johann Blumenbach, widely recognized as the father of physical anthropology, to coin the term *Caucasian* in the 1790s. We also look at one of the most extraordinary ways in which sex bore on race: in the power ascribed to women to shape racial characteristics. Odd as it may sound today, women at this time were said to mold the very bodies that anatomists studied.

Chapter 5 explores the politics of eighteenth-century anatomy, examining how power struggles within Europe and its colonies influenced the way anthropologists studied race and gender. It is significant that in this period scientific debate surrounding *race* focused on *males* in much the same way that males took center stage in struggles for political representation. At the same time discussion of *sexual difference* in this period tended to be confined to the study of middle-class *Europeans*. While women of other races did not escape the prurient eye of the European anthropologist, one rarely finds comparisons of females across racial lines. In a sense there was no need to refine distinctions between females. In the eyes of European law "woman" was a universal—all women, regardless of age, class, or race, were disenfranchised. By the late eighteenth century, many natural historians were postulating a universal reproductive woman, and indeed it was reproductive politics—the perceived need to produce greater populations in both

Europe and the colonies—that animated government legislation and medical inquiry. For men, by contrast, representation in government came to be determined by overly refined distinctions in physical characteristics, such as physical strength, skin color, or intelligence.

While this study focuses on gender, it also looks at how assumptions about class influenced European naturalists. Europeans often envisioned the anthropoid apes arriving in their capital cities as "upper-class" ladies and gentlemen. "Madame Chimpanzee" and César de Malaca, the baboon, were given titles of respect along with European educations. At the same time, blackness (the color of Africans) was seen as the characteristic of lower-class peoples who, because they worked for a living, were exposed to the disfiguring rays of the sun. (Africans were commonly thought to have degenerated from a primitive whiteness through the action of the sun.) It was also the Europeans' sexual parts—the scrotum in the male and the areola and pudendum in the female—that were considered to be the blackest and therefore most vile of all bodily parts.

One critical question in this period was who would do science, as we shall see in Chapter 6. The eighteenth century saw experiments in the education of European women and African men designed to discover whether these people could become scientists. Toward the end of the century, anatomists, anthropologists, and natural historians, working under the banner of scientific neutrality, declared that, by nature, peoples with compressed crania (which included women of all races) or black skin were incapable of pursuing academic science. The claim that science was gender and race neutral perpetuated a system in which those who might have brought new perspectives to the study of nature were barred from the enterprise at the outset, and the findings of science crafted in their absence were used to justify their continued exclusion.

This system held consequences not only for women and non-European men but also for science and knowledge more generally. At least since the eighteenth century, the peculiar form of inquiry called science in the West has distanced itself from what was conceived to be the "feminine." Women—and also a consistent set of values they came to represent—were expelled from modern science. Significantly, too, this was the era that saw the cradle of civilization—the birthplace of Europe's arts and sciences—moved in the European mind and mythos from Mesopotamia and northern Africa to Greece. Europeans disavowed the Afroasiatic origins of Western sciences, as documented in Martin Bernal's recent and explosive *Black Athena*.

The project to uncover gender in science is not and should not be viewed as antiscientific. It is no longer fashionable to argue that science is value neutral, but many are still led to believe that scientists simply decipher laws from the great encrypted book of nature. Nature, after all, is infinitely rich, and there is much we do not know about it. What we do know is influenced by our history and our values. Science is a product of society. The goal of uncovering how gender influences the structure and polity of science extends the process of critique that persuades us to affirm certain knowledge and practices over others by rendering conscious the unconscious in our assumptions, priorities, and methods.

Of course, much more could be written about sex and gender than is included in the pages that follow. Rather than amplify every example of gender in eighteenth-century conceptions of nature, I have chosen to elaborate several representative cases as they arose in a particular time and place. My purpose is to present selected episodes in the political history of science—that is, examples of how implicit and explicit power relations structure the priorities and practices of science. In many of the episodes, the individuals involved may well have been innocent of the broader implications of their actions. There is no evidence, for instance, that Linnaeus intentionally chose a gender-charged term when he named mammals *mammals*. He may have done so naively, but not arbitrarily. As we shall see, he was led to his innovation in response to the world of human interests and the political tensions surrounding him. That scientists might be unaware of the implications of their work does not make them any less mediators or marketeers of political ideas; for many this is a studied innocence. We need to appreciate better the contingencies of scientific knowledge, and especially what is foregone in the choice of one particular course over another. This is why the political history of science asks: Why do we know this and not that? Who gains from knowledge of this and not that?[19]

Finally, I have chosen to analyze sex and gender in eighteenth-century science not because these categories are natural, but because power and privilege continue to follow gender lines—even if not as starkly as was once the case. The categories anthropologists chose did not emerge from nature in some disinterested way but were woven deeply into the fabric of eighteenth-century society. The preoccupation with racial and sexual difference arose alongside and in step with broader movements in Enlightenment Europe. This era of democratic awakenings brought with it the "woman question," the question of women's rights. The Enlightenment challenge that all people are by nature equal was met in conservative quarters with the search for natural differences. At the same time that naturalists were inscribing into nature parochial mores and fantasies, they were also looking to nature for solutions to questions about sexual and racial equality. Nature and its laws spoke loudly in this age of Enlightenment, where philosophes attempted to set social convention on a natural basis. Natural law (as distinct from the positive law of nations) was held to be immutable, given by God or inherent in the material universe.

Eighteenth-century politics became body politics *par excellence*.[20] Scientists, with their privileged knowledge of nature, became consecrated priests of the new secular order, intermediaries between the laws of nature and of states. They took up the task of uncovering differences imagined as natural to bodies and hence foundational to societies based on natural law. The intense inquiry into the exact nature of sexual difference sparked the eighteenth-century revolution in scientific understanding of sexuality and sexual temperament that I have described elsewhere.[21] Thus the great public dramas of the eighteenth century—the struggle for enfranchisement and the abolition of slavery—exposed the Janus-face of *nature* destined to plague democratic orders for the next two hundred years: inclusion in the polis rested on notions of *natural* equalities, while exclusion from it rested on notions of *natural* differences.

Ours is a culture obsessed with difference. In order to understand this obsession, we must unearth its origins and its history. Why are so many still so averse to diversity—in physique, points of view, and ways of living? As the French political pamphleteer Olympe de Gouges remarked in regard to race: "Human color is nuanced, as it is in all the animals, plants, and minerals that nature has produced. . . . All is varied and that is the beauty of nature. Why then destroy her work?"[22]

1

The Private Lives of Plants

In her wane beauty, Ninon won
With fatal smiles her gay unconscious son.—
Clasp'd in his arms she own'd a mother's name,—
"Desist, rash youth! restrain your impious flame,
"First on that bed your infant form was press'd,
"Born by my throes, and nurtured at my breast."
Back as from death he sprang, with wild amaze
Fierce on the fair he fix'd his ardent gaze;
Dropped on one knee, his frantic arms outspread,
And stole a guilty glance toward the bed;
Then breath'd from quivering lips a whisper'd vow
And bent on heaven his pale repentant brow;
"Thus, thus!" he cried, and plung'd the furious dart,
And life and love gush'd mingled from his heart.

Erasmus Darwin, *The Loves of the Plants*, 1789

*H*ermaphroditic plants "castrated" by unnatural mothers. Trees and shrubs clothed in "wedding gowns." Flowers spread as "nuptial beds" for a verdant groom and his cherished bride. Are these the memoirs of an eighteenth-century academy of science, or tales from the boudoir?

These are, in fact, some of the categories developed by Carl Linnaeus, the father of modern botany, and his disciples in their attempts to understand the sexuality of plants. Plant sexuality was not incidental to but indeed lay at the heart of the eighteenth-century revolution in the study of the plant kingdom. From the Middle Ages through the Renaissance botany was studied for one primary reason: plants were used as medicines. In the eighteenth century, however, focus shifted from the medicinal virtues of plants to finding abstract and universal methods of classification. Paradoxically, this "scientization" of botany coincided with an ardent "sexualization" of plants.

Why did the study of plant sexuality become a priority of the botanical sciences in the eighteenth century? More important, why did sexuality become the key to classification? The story that follows draws on two rarely juxtaposed transformations in early modern Europe: the scientific revolution and the revolution in sexuality and gender. The much-celebrated scientific revolution began in the sixteenth century with the innovations of men like Copernicus, author of the modern heliocentric universe, Galileo, inventor of a modern physics, and Vesalius, widely regarded as the father of modern anatomy. Historians, in treating this profound and far-reaching revolution, have tended to scrutinize developments both internal to the scientific community (new institutions, new methods, new foundations and conceptions of nature) and external to it (struggles with church and state, spurs from technology and warfare).[1] Seldom, however, have historians brought the revolution in science to bear on another fundamental transformation of European society in this period: the revolution in sexuality and gender, the remaking of relations between men and women that began in the late seventeenth century and culminated in the French Revolution. Historians have described changing views of men and women, of husbands and wives in relation to childbearing and rearing, of the family and of the state, but rarely have they examined how these changes affected the making of modern science. As we shall see, the revolutions in science and sexuality cannot be understood in isolation, for they share an intimate history.

What bearing, then, did the "scientization" of botany have on the "sexualization" of plants, and vice versa? Botanists praised Linnaeus for creating a new language for botany. Linnaeus's nomenclature was indeed precise and convenient; Rousseau judged its value to botanists to be as great as the creation of algebra was for mathematicians.[2] The notion that plants are sexual did not arise uncontested, however. Great debates erupted in the late eighteenth and early nineteenth centuries over the scientific and moral propriety of what Erasmus Darwin (grandfather of Charles) called "the loves of the plants." Yet it is important to point out that these self-appointed censors missed the sexualists' most glaring impropriety—that of reading the laws of nature through the lens of social relations.

It is possible to distinguish two levels in the sexual politics of early modern botany—the *implicit* use of gender to structure botanical taxonomy and the *explicit* use of human sexual metaphors to introduce notions of plant reproduction into botanical literature. I turn first to the most important aspect of sexual politics in early modern botany—the way in which unarticulated notions of gender structured Linnaean taxonomy. In the uproar that surrounded the introduction of notions of sexuality into botany, no one noticed that Linnaeus's taxonomy, built as it was on sexual difference, imported into botany traditional notions about sexual hierarchy. Second, I explore the origins and implications of the vivid sexual language employed by Carl Linnaeus and Erasmus Darwin. Investigating the specific circumstances surrounding the reception of each of these botanists in England deepens our understanding of how science interacts with changing attitudes toward women and female sexuality, the stability of church and state, and the importance attributed to sex. Indeed, as we shall see, the sexual politics of botany in the eighteenth century cut deeply into the political landscape, having ultimately to do with the European-wide revolution in scientific views of sexual difference that took place in the upheavals leading up to the American and French revolutions.

The Search for New Methods of Classification

Within medieval cosmology, plant classification generally emphasized the usefulness of plants as foods and medicines to human beings. By the seventeenth century, botany still remained closely allied with medicine. Herbal texts, often arranged alphabetically, classified plants according to their use; each entry included a description of a plant's appearance and its varieties, the season and place it could be collected, the parts to be used, and methods for preserving it. Also included were a plant's degrees of heat and moisture, its powers against particular ailments, dosages, and methods of prep-

aration and administration.[3] Knowledge of plants at this time was local and particular, derived from direct experience with plants in agriculture, gardening, or medicine, or from knowledge handed
down based upon that experience.

In the seventeenth century, academic botanists began to break
their ties with medical practitioners. New plant materials from the
voyages of discovery and the new colonies flooded Europe (the
number of known plants quadrupled between 1550 and 1700) at
the same time that an emphasis on observation increased discord
between ancient texts and modern knowledge. The proliferation of
knowledge required new methods of organization.[4] Emphasis in
classification turned from medical application to more general and
theoretical issues of pure taxonomy, as botanists sought simple
principles that would hold universally.[5]

Though botanists agreed that a new taxonomy was desirable,
few agreed on a system. By 1799, when Robert Thornton published
his popular version of the Linnaean system, he counted fifty-two different systems of botany; the "system-madness," one botanist complained, was truly "epidemical."[6] Botanists based their taxonomies
on different parts of the plant. In England, John Ray developed a system for establishing genera based on the flower, calyx, seed, and
seed coat; in France, the great Joseph Pitton de Tournefort defined
genera principally by the characteristics of the corolla and fruit. Sébastien Vaillant and Linnaeus were early advocates of classification
by sexual differences. Others, including Albrecht von Haller, continued to argue that geography was crucial to an understanding of
plant life and that development as well as appearance should be
represented in taxonomy.

Despite the number and variety of systems, Linnaeus's sexual
system was widely adopted after 1737 and until the first decades of
the nineteenth century was generally considered the most convenient system of classification. Linnaeus's system, as set out in his first
major publication, *Systema naturae* (1735), was based on the difference between the male and female parts of flowers (FIG. 1.1). Linnaeus divided the vegetable world (as he called it) into *classes*
based on the number, relative proportions, and position of the male

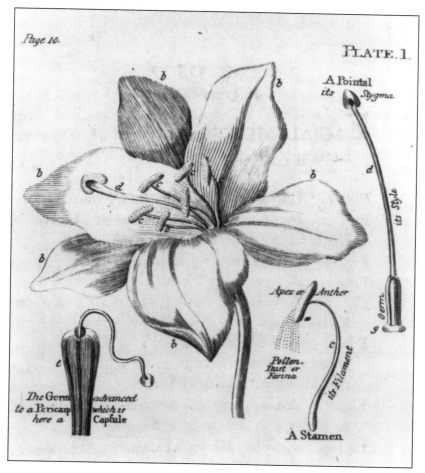

FIG. 1.1. The English woman of letters, Priscilla Wakefield, nicely illustrated the parts of a hermaphroditic flower (a flower with both male and female parts) in her *Introduction to Botany* (London, 1796), plate 1. Letter "b" shows the petals. Letter "c" refers to the male stamen with its pollen producing "anther." Letter "d" refers to the female pistil (she calls it a "pointal") with its stigma, style, and germ (ovary). Courtesy of the Princeton University Library.

parts or stamens (FIG. 1.2). These classes were then subdivided into some sixty-five *orders* based on the number, relative proportions, and positions of the female parts or pistils. These were further divided into *genera* (based on the calyx, flower, and other parts of the

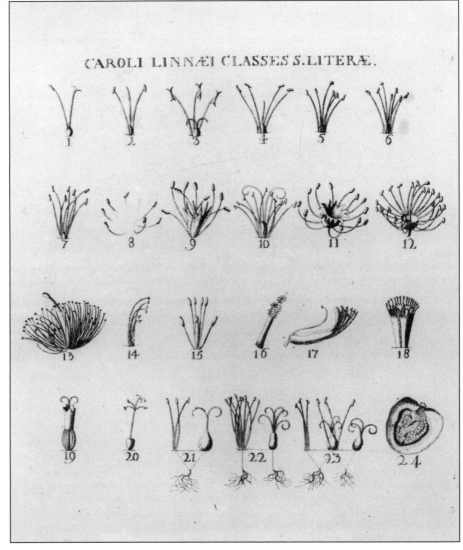

FIG. 1.2. "Carl Linnaeus's Classes or Letters." Georg Ehret, a well-known eighteenth-century botanical artist, drew these stamen and pistils to illustrate Linnaeus's sexual system. Printed with Linnaeus's *Systema naturae* beginning with the second edition (1737).

fruit), *species* (based on the leaves or some other characteristic of the plant), and *varieties.*

One might argue that Linnaeus based his system on sexual difference because he was one of the first to recognize the biological importance of sexual reproduction in plants. For this reason, he considered the stamens and pistils "the very essence of the flower."[7] But the success of Linnaeus's system did not rest on the fact that it was "natural," that it captured true affinities between organisms. Indeed Linnaeus readily acknowledged that it was highly artificial.[8] Though focused on reproductive organs, his system did not capture fundamental sexual functions. Rather, it focused on purely morphological features (that is, the number and mode of unions)—exactly those characteristics of the male and female organs *least* important for their sexual function.[9]

In view of this, it is striking that Linnaeus chose to highlight the sexual parts of plants at all. Furthermore, it is important to point out that Linnaeus devised his system in such a way that the number of a plant's stamens (or male parts) determined the *class* to which it was assigned, while the number of its pistils (the female parts) determined its *order*. In the taxonomic tree, class stands above order. In other words, Linnaeus gave male parts priority in determining the status of the organism in the plant kingdom. There is no empirical justification for this outcome; Linnaeus simply brought traditional notions of gender hierarchy whole cloth into science. He read nature through the lens of social relations in such a way that the new language of botany incorporated fundamental aspects of the social world as much as those of the natural world. Although today Linnaeus's classification of groups above the rank of genus has been abandoned, his binomial system of nomenclature remains, together with many of his genera and species.[10]

But the debate surrounding Linnaeus's notions of plant sexuality did not focus on his fundamental (mis)reading of the laws of nature. No one at that time or since for that matter has objected to this flaw in his system. Instead, debate has centered on scientific and moral questions surrounding the nature of plant sexuality and the

18   language Linnaeus and his disciples used to describe the loves of the plants.

Plant (Hetero)sexuality

Since at least the eighteenth century, ours has been a culture compelling two sexes, even though the canonical chromosomal sex of humans—the XX female and XY male—is not as rigid as we sometimes think. It is important to keep in mind that in the United States sexually ambiguous babies are sometimes "fixed" at birth. (Endocrinologists make these babies mostly into girls; urologists make mostly boys.)[11] Our culture is so invested in notions of fixed sexuality that individuals of ambiguous sex (with testicular feminization syndrome, for example) have been barred from competing in the Olympic games.[12]

Today it is recognized that many plants reproduce sexually. Plants (and plant parts) are also typed as male and female. But what does it mean to call a plant female or male? How did botanists in early modern Europe address this question?

As extraordinary as it seems today, it was not until the late seventeenth century that European naturalists began to recognize that plants reproduce sexually.[13] The ancients, it is true, had some knowledge of sexual distinctions in plants. Theophrastus knew the age-old practice of fertilizing date palms by bringing male flowers to the female tree. Peasants working the land also recognized sexual distinctions in trees such as the pistachio. Some in the ancient world ascribed sex to plants based on appearance alone. Pliny remarked that male frankincense is so called from its resemblance to the testes.[14] Plant sexuality, however, was not the focus of interest in the ancient world. An eighteenth-century observer charged that the ancients were ignorant of what he considered the essential nature of sexuality in plants: they called, for example, the seed-bearing plant "the male," and the barren plant "the female."[15]

As late as the Renaissance, botanists gave names to what we today call the sexual parts of flowers that were not associated in any way with reproduction. The male organ was called the *stamen*, a Latin word denoting the warp thread of a fabric. The female organ was called the *pistil*, a term suggesting the resemblance of those flower parts to a pestle.[16] Even the sixteenth-century revival of botany brought no immediate revival of interest in the sexual nature of plants.[17] Until the seventeenth century most botanists discounted the entire notion of plant sexuality as just another fable.

Plant sexuality exploded onto the scene in the seventeenth and eighteenth centuries. Everyone wanted to claim the honor of having discovered sexuality in plants. In France, Sébastien Vaillant and Claude Geoffroy tussled over priority.[18] In England, Robert Thornton complained that the honor of this discovery was always given to the French, though properly it belonged to the English. Linnaeus, always keen to reap his due reward for scientific innovation (and not, in fact, the first to describe sexual reproduction in plants), claimed that it would be difficult and of no utility to decide who first discovered the sexes of plants.[19]

Systematic investigations into the sexuality of plants became a priority for naturalists late in the seventeenth century. Interest in assigning sex to plants ran ahead of any real understanding of fertilization, or the "coitus of vegetables," as it was sometimes called.[20] Botanists distinguished certain parts of plants as male and female, Claude Geoffroy reported, "without knowing well the reason."[21] They developed their notions of plant sexuality from their knowledge of animals. This was true of Nehemiah Grew, who was the first to identify the stamen as the male part in flowers. In his 1682 *Anatomy of Plants*, Grew reported that Sir Thomas Millington, a distinguished physician, had suggested to him that "the attire" (Grew's term for the stamen) performs the function of the male in reproduction. In quiet prose Grew carefully worked out his analogies between plant and animal parts:

> The blade (or stamen) does not unaptly resemble a small penis, with the sheath upon it, as its praeputium [prepuce]. And the . . . several thecae, are like so many little testicles. And the globulets [pollen] and other small particles upon the blade or

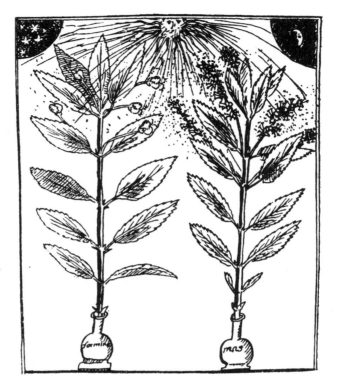

FIG. 1.3. "Love attacks the herbs themselves": sexual relations between a female (left) and a male (right) plant as portrayed in Linnaeus's *Praeludia sponsaliorum plantarum* (1729), in *Smärre Skrifter af Carl von Linné*, ed. N. H. Lärjungar and T. Fries (Uppsala: Almquist & Wiksell, 1908).

> penis . . . are as the vegetable sperme. Which as soon as the penis is erected, falls down upon the seed-case or womb, and so touches it with a prolific virtue.

Thus Grew ascribed maleness to the "blade" of plants because it looked and functioned like the penis of animals. In a moment of unbridled enthusiasm, Grew declared that sexual dimorphism pervaded the vegetable kingdom, that "every plant is . . . male or female."[22]

By the early part of the eighteenth century, the analogy between animal and plant sexuality was fully developed (FIG. 1.3).[23] Linnaeus, in his *Praeludia sponsaliorum plantarum*, related the terms of comparison: in the male, the filaments of the stamens are the vas deferens, the anthers are the testes, the pollen that falls from them when they are ripe is the seminal fluid; in the female, the stigma is the vulva, the style becomes the vagina, the tube running the length of the pistil is the Fallopian tube, the pericarp is the impregnated ovary, and the seeds are the eggs (see FIG. 1.1).[24] Julien Offray de La Mettrie along with other naturalists even claimed that the honey reservoir found in the nectary is equivalent to mother's milk in humans.[25]

Attributing sexuality to plants involved a revaluation of those parts of the plant that came to be seen as male. The stamen had earlier been thought to be a "superfluous" and "idle" part of flowers. The French botanist Tournefort, still unconvinced at his death in 1708 that plants were sexual, spoke of stamens as *"vaisseaux excretories,"* the most "abject" parts in vegetables; he considered their dust (pollen) a vile excrement spoiling the beauty of the flower. (Karl Ernst von Baer, who discovered the mammalian ovum, expressed similar sentiments when he coined the term *spermatozoa* in the 1820s for what he thought to be parasites in semen.[26]) Tournefort's successors, Geoffroy and Vaillant, both ardent sexualists, insisted that the stamens, now seen as male, were "most noble" and performed an essential role in generation.[27]

Interest in plant sexuality in the early eighteenth century focused on male parts; the identity and nature of female parts went uncontested. Few botanists disputed the notion that the seeds of plants were similar to the eggs of animals and that their seed-producing parts should be called female. Vaillant, in his famous 1717 lecture on plant sexuality, remarked that the idea that the pistil or ovaries are the female organs of plants was too well known to dwell upon.[28]

Most flowers, however, are hermaphroditic with both male and female organs in the same individual. As one eighteenth-century botanist put it, there are two sexes, but three kinds of flowers: male, female, and hermaphrodites or, as they were sometimes called, androgynes. While eighteenth-century botanists enthusiastically embraced sexual dimorphism, conceiving of plants as hermaphroditic was more difficult: they could not or would not recognize an unfamiliar sexual type. In France, Vaillant accused Geoffroy of refusing to refer to plants as hermaphrodites. In England, William Smellie, who rejected the whole notion of sexuality in plants, distanced himself from the term hermaphrodite, noting when using the word that he merely spoke "the language of the system."

Though eighteenth-century botanists were correct to recognize that many plants do reproduce sexually, they gave undue primacy to sexual reproduction and heterosexuality.[29] Linnaeus was so taken with heterosexual coupling that he attributed this form of reproduction to his *Cryptogamia* ("plants that marry secretly," by which he meant ferns, mosses, algae, and fungi)—organisms that display little fixed sexuality let alone long-term relationships. Sexuality characterizes reproduction among the higher organisms but not the earth's majority of organisms. The very fact that nonsexual reproduction is called *a*sexual (a term of nineteenth-century origin expressing the absence of sex, though parthenogenesis had been recognized since the 1740s) reveals the normative preference given to sexual reproduction.[30]

Linnaeus did not, however, stop with simple definitions of maleness and femaleness. Not only were his plants sexed, but they actually became human; more specifically, they became husbands and wives. When Linnaeus introduced new terminology to describe the sexual relations of plants, he did not use the terms stamen and pistil but *andria* and *gynia*, which he derived from the Greek for husband (*aner*) and wife (*gyne*).[31] The names of his classes of plants end in "andria" (*monandria, diandria, triandria*, and so on); his orders end in "gynia" (*monogynia, digynia, trigynia*, and so forth). His text is filled with tender embraces of duly wedded couples:

> The flowers' leaves . . . serve as bridal beds which the Creator has so gloriously arranged, adorned with such noble bed curtains, and perfumed with so many soft scents that the bridegroom with his bride might there celebrate their nuptials with so much the greater solemnity. When now the bed is so pre-

pared, it is time for the bridegroom to embrace his beloved bride and offer her his gifts.[32]

Indeed, his renowned "Key to the Sexual System" is founded on the *nuptiae plantarum* (the marriages of plants), on their union rather than on their dimorphism. Linnaeus saw plants as having sex, in the fullest sense of the term. For him, sexuality in plants was romantic, erotic, sometimes illicit, and sometimes the sanctified expression of love between husband and wife.

Plants were not the only organisms to suffer misplaced anthropomorphism. The enormous influence that gender exerted on definitions of sex in this period can also be seen in the sexing of bees. From the time of Aristotle until the mid-eighteenth century, naturalists spoke of the ruling bee as "the king bee," despite the fact that these "kings" gave birth. Even after Jan Swammerdam correctly identified the genitalia of the queen bee in the 1670s, naturalists persisted in their belief that the ruler of a hive must be a king. To the European mind, a monarch simply was male. In this instance, social function—the act of wielding sovereignty—held greater sway in assigning sex than did the biological act of giving birth. When, in the eighteenth century, entomologists finally dethroned the king bee, they domesticated the newly crowned queen, as Jeffrey Merrick has brilliantly shown, emphasizing her maternal role in order to accommodate their notions about the natural destiny of women.[33]

The Use of Metaphor in Science

Linnaeus's system focused as much on the "nuptials" of living plants as on their sexuality. Before their lawful marriage, trees and shrubs donned "wedding gowns." Flower petals spread as "bridal beds" for a verdant groom and his cherished bride, while the curtain of the *corolla* lent privacy to the amorous newlyweds. This desire on the part of botanists to view plants as highly erotic creatures reached its peak in the work of Erasmus Darwin, one of Linnaeus's many popularizers in England. In his 1789 poem *The Loves of the Plants* an ordinary *Gloriosa superba* repulses the incestuous advances of her son who, clasped in her arms, steals a guilty glance toward the bed of his passion and, quivering, plunges a dagger into his own heart.[34]

Why this melodrama? Why was the discovery of plant sexuality accompanied by the extended use of hypersexual metaphors? This question does not mean to suggest that metaphor is *not* part of science today; metaphors and analogies are themselves constitutive elements of science.[35] The prominent eighteenth-century notion, for example, that nature was a machine gave direction to research, suggested interpretive frameworks, and, in many cases, dictated what counted as proof or explanation. How, then, are we to understand the metaphors and analogies surrounding the discovery of sexuality in plants?

This question of the nature of Linnaeus's and Darwin's sexual metaphors—their social context and implications—has been a topic of debate among historians of science. Some have dismissed them as "charming absurdities."[36] Others have suggested that the Enlightenment was a time of freer sexuality and that attributing sexuality to plants was designed to titillate appreciative audiences.[37] Still others have argued that sexuality was deemed acceptable only if plants observed the mores of eighteenth-century society, having sexual relations only after lawful marriages.[38]

The origins and implications of this imagery are complex. Its use was not bounded nationally: Vaillant, a Frenchman, used it in 1717; the Swede Linnaeus never abandoned it; Charles Bonnet, the Swiss naturalist who discovered asexual reproduction in aphids, also embraced it; the Englishman Erasmus Darwin pushed it to its apogee in the 1780s and 1790s. Nor were there clear political alignments. In England, conservatives, such as the Reverend Richard Polwhele, associated loose sexual imagery with Jacobin free love, and Erasmus Darwin, a radical democrat and atheist, may have tried through his revelations of plant polygamy to subvert the growing tyranny of straitlaced middle-class monogamy.[39] Linnaeus, by contrast, was distinctly conservative in his social attitudes. He wanted his daughters to grow up to be hearty, strong housekeepers, not "fashionable dolls" or bluestockings.

One of the most striking elements of Linnaeus's system is that plant sexuality took place almost exclusively within the bonds of marriage. His "Key to the Sexual System" is founded on the marriages of plants; the plant world is divided into major groups according to the type of marriage each plant has contracted—whether, for example, the marriage was "public" or "clandestine." These two types of marriage, in fact, characterized custom in much of Europe; only in 1753 did Lord Harwicke's Marriage Act do away with clandestine marriages by requiring a public proclamation of banns.[40]

It is significant that Linnaeus focused on marriage when he thought of sexuality. As Lawrence Stone has shown, marriage underwent rapid change throughout the late seventeenth and eighteenth centuries. Upper-class parents and even wealthy peasants no longer routinely arranged unions for their children strictly out of property considerations. Love and affection increasingly became legitimate reasons for weddings. Men and women fell in love and created for themselves elaborate rituals of courtship as the middle-class romance was born.[41] Linnaeus's own marriage followed this pattern. He courted with tender expressions of love a small-town physician's daughter (who also brought a substantial dowry to the union). As he wrote some years later, he left the running of his house entirely to his wife, and concerned himself with the works of nature.[42]

This was also the period of the rise of modern pornography with its emphasis on explicit description of genitalia and romantic encounters. The same forces—the loosening of traditional social controls—leading to Stone's "companionate marriages" also fostered the rise of the pornographic novel with its unique relationship to mechanistic natural philosophy that Margaret Jacob has described.[43] Though all of Linnaeus's plants celebrated nuptials, the majority did not engage in lawful marriages. Only one class of plants—Linnaeus's *monandria*—practiced monogamy. Plants in other classes joined in marriages consisting of two, three, twenty, or more "husbands" who shared their marriage bed (that is, the petals of the same flower) with one wife. Plant husbands of his "class xxiii"—*polygamia*—lived with their wives and harlots, later called

26 concubines, in distinct marriage beds. Each of these "marriages" signified a particular arrangement of stamens and pistils on the flower. *Monandria* had but one stamen or husband on a hermaphroditic flower. *Diandria* had two stamens (or husbands) on a flower with one pistil, and so on.

There is no evidence, however, that Linnaeus, the Swedish country-parson's son, consciously wielded a pornographic pen, though he was sometimes accused of doing so. Raised in an upright, thrifty, Protestant family in rural Sweden, he was conservative in his religious views (all of nature celebrating the glory of its Creator) and in his attitudes toward women. He would not allow his four daughters to learn French for fear they would adopt the liberties of French custom. When his wife placed their daughter Sophia in school, Linnaeus immediately took her out again, stopping what he considered "nonsensical" education. He also refused Queen Louisa Ulrika's offer to receive one of his daughters at court, thinking the court environment apt to corrupt morals.[44] He did, however, allow his eldest daughter to develop a mild interest in botany: Elisabeth Christina contributed a paper to the *Transactions* of the Royal Academy of Science entitled "Remarks on a Luminous Appearance of the Indian Cresses" (or *Tropaeolum*, though she did not use the technical term).

Though we cannot be sure, it seems likely that Linnaeus did not introduce his explicitly sexual imagery as an affront to social custom. He simply tended to see anything female as a wife. He considered "Dame Nature" his second wife and true helpmate.[45] The celebrated botanical illustrator Mademoiselle Basseporte, who worked at the Jardin du Roi in Paris, he called his second wife.[46] Linnaeus called his own wife "my monandrian lily"; the lily signifying virginity and *monandrian* meaning "having only one man."[47]

The notion that plants and animals reproduce within marital relations persisted into the nineteenth century. The term "gamete"—adopted by biologists in the 1860s to refer to a germ cell capable of fusing with another cell to form a new individual—derives from the Greek *gamein*, to marry.[48]

Though Linnaeus's images seem to us incongruous with his

science, they were not completely out of place when he wrote in the mid-eighteenth century. A sharp line had yet to be drawn between scientific writing and poetic imagination. Rhetorical flourish—ornamentation, metaphor, or allegory—was still appreciated in scientific texts and illustrations.[49] Early modern botanists employed a wide variety of images. The sixteenth-century Italian botanist Andrea Cesalpino arranged plants like armies ready for battle in his *De plantis*. Linnaeus, in his *Deliciae naturae*, portrayed nature as a copy of human society with its military and civil classes. Robert Thornton, Erasmus Darwin's contemporary, used Christian imagery, seeing the passion flower as emblematic of the passion of Christ; the leaves were said exactly to resemble the spear that pierced his side, the tendrils appeared to be the cords that bound his hands, and so forth.[50] Moreover, Linnaeus drew much of his sexual imagery directly from the classics.[51] Pliny, for example, had described the passion of love and mutual embrace of the date palms. Erasmus Darwin, too, employed a kind of Ovidian personification by transforming flowers and plants into men and women.[52] In this sense, the fathers of modern botany stood closer to older traditions, being as much the denizens of an earlier era as the heralds of a new one.[53]

We often think of the conspicuous use of metaphor as a thing of the past, but it still pervades science. Mary Willson, plant ecologist and sociobiologist, is a case in point. Willson's plants do not engage in the tender marriages characteristic of Linnaeus's or Erasmus Darwin's. Being more up-to-date, they channel their energies into investment portfolios. Willson's plants judge their "reproductive success" ("RS" in the sociobiological literature), measured against the cost of their mating investment (MI) and parental investment (PI). Willson puts it this way: "The intensity of sexual selection can be indexed by the disparity (as a ratio) of net RS (reproductive success) of breeding males and females, where net RS is measured as benefit to the parents (in present offspring) minus the cost (in reduced numbers or quality of future offspring)." Thus, Willson's plants have "tactics," make "choices," and engage in "conflict."[54] Conscious and unconscious use of metaphor structures ways of thinking about nature. Seeing plants as joined in heterosexual unions or locked in competitive reproductive strategies highlights certain behaviors and characteristics of plant life to the exclusion of others.

Linnaeus and the Botanic Reveries of Erasmus Darwin

By the middle of the eighteenth century, the sexualist metaphor had swept the botanical world, except for France. Linnaeus's system did not flourish there, even though his sexual images came most immediately from the French botanist Sébastien Vaillant, whose provocative lecture on plant sexuality at the Jardin du Roi at six o'clock on a June morning in 1717 had "charmed" some six hundred people of all social ranks.[55] For one thing, French natural history remained vibrant throughout the eighteenth century. The dynasty of naturalists—the brothers Jussieu—took little interest in Linnaeus's artificial system of classification, preferring instead to continue their countryman's (Tournefort's) efforts at developing what they considered a natural system.

Linnaeus also encountered a formidable opponent in Georges-Louis Leclerc, comte de Buffon, director of the Jardin du Roi (now the Jardin des Plantes). Buffon opposed system building generally and ridiculed Linnaeus's system in particular for being too abstract and artificial and for depending on characteristics so minute and inconsequential that a naturalist had to carry a microscope into the field in order to recognize a plant. As for Linnaeus's system of nomenclature, Buffon considered it merely a language, easy to learn and recite but contributing nothing to the knowledge of nature.[56]

Linnaeus took England by storm in the 1750s and 1760s. His sexual system gained easy acceptance in Britain because academic natural history had been in decline since the 1720s; the classificatory advances of John Ray (said to be one of the first to develop a system based on "natural affinities") had persisted since the late seventeenth century but without further development. During this same period, however, natural history—especially entomology, conchology, and eventually botany—became popular among the fashionable. Well-born ladies, including the Duchess of Beaufort, Lady Margaret of Portland, and Mrs. Eleanor Glanville, led the way, collecting rare and exotic plants from all over the world.[57] The royal family (George III, Queen Charlotte, and his mother, Augusta—all botanical enthusiasts) further enhanced the popularity of botany by serving as influential patrons and enlarging the Royal Botanical Gardens at Kew, in London.

It was in this new atmosphere of interest in botany, especially among ladies of the upper classes, that Linnaeus's sexual system gained wide acclaim. *Gentleman's Magazine* lauded his work in 1754. Three popular translations of his prize-winning essay on the sexes of plants were published between 1777 and 1807.[58] The Linnean Society was founded in 1788. The Botanical Society of Lichfield (under the auspices of Erasmus Darwin and with the aid of Samuel Johnson) sponsored a translation of both Linnaeus's *Systema naturae* and *Species plantarum*.

But it was also in Britain that bloody and protracted battles erupted almost immediately over the scientific and moral implications of Linnaeus's sexual system. Antisexualists, especially those working in Edinburgh, attacked Linnaeus's work primarily on empirical grounds. Charles Alston, professor of medicine and botany at the University of Edinburgh, argued in his address to the Philosophical Society in 1754 that there was simply not sufficient data to enable botanists to attribute a prolific role to pollen. The crucial experiment for antisexualists was to discover whether a female plant can produce fertile seeds without coming into contact in any way with the male; this they claimed was indeed the case.[59]

William Smellie, chief compiler of the first edition of the *Encyclopaedia Britannica*, blasted the "alluring seductions" of the analogical reasoning upon which the sexualist hypothesis was founded and argued that it did not hold up to facts of experience. Many animals (he mentioned polyps and millipedes) reproduce without sexual embraces, and if many species of animals are destitute of "all the endearments of love," what, he asked, should induce us to fancy that the oak or mushroom enjoy these distinguished privileges? Neither could Smellie abide the notion that plants might change their sex—that trees that had been female might suddenly assume the robust features peculiar to the male. Nor did he think that nature would leave to chance a matter of such import as reproduction. He felt certain that pollen, flying "promiscuously" aloft, would produce universal anarchy and cover the earth with "monstrous productions."[60]

In addition to his ontological qualms, Smellie denounced Linnaeus for taking his analogy "far beyond all decent limits," claiming that Linnaeus's metaphors were so indelicate as to exceed the most "obscene romance-writer."[61] Smellie's sentiments were shared by other botanists. William Withering, a member along with Erasmus Darwin of the Lunar Society, advocated suppressing "the sexual distinctions in the titles to the Classes and Orders."[62] Some years earlier, in St. Petersburg, Johann Siegesbeck had also found the idea of sexuality in flowers scientifically unconvincing and morally revolting. What man, he fumed, would believe that God Almighty would introduce such "loathsome harlotry" into the plant kingdom?[63] John Amman, another professor of botany in St. Petersburg, objected to Linnaeus's system because the great concourse of husbands to one wife is so "unsuitable to the laws and manners of our people."[64] The Reverend Samuel Goodenough, later Bishop of Carlisle, wrote in 1808 to the founder of the Linnean Society, James Edward Smith, that "a literal translation of the first principles of Linnaean botany is enough to shock female modesty. It is possible that many virtuous students might not be able to make out the similitude of *Clitoria*." Even Goethe thought the innocence of the young, particularly girls, should not be exposed to works setting out the "dogma of sexuality."[65]

In face of such opposition, the authors who popularized Linnaeus's system—John Miller, James Smith, or John Rotheram—made little use of his sexual imagery.[66] Erasmus Darwin, however, brought the Linnaean sexual system to full bloom in his *The Loves of the Plants*, elaborating Linnaeus's ideas in such a way that may well have shocked Linnaeus himself.

Darwin's plants, unlike Linnaeus's, did not limit sexual relations to the bonds of holy matrimony. Rather, they freely expressed every imaginable form of heterosexual union. The fair *Collinsonia*, sighing with sweet concern, satisfied the love of two brothers by turns. The *Meadia* (an ordinary cowslip) bowed with "wanton air," rolled her dark eyes, and waved her golden hair as she gratified each of her five beaux. Three youthful swains succumbed to the riper years of the *Gloriosa*.[67] For Darwin, sex was not just the mechanism for improving and diversifying the stock of living organisms: it was also the purest source of happiness—"the cordial drop in the otherwise vapid cup of life."[68]

To the modern reader, Darwin's poetry seems arcane and overdrawn. Though Anna Seward, a close friend and well-known poet, praised *The Botanic Garden* for establishing a new poetic form by adapting scientific discoveries to heroic verse, Darwin's poetry was not new, nor was it esoteric or unusual.[69] The eighteenth century abounded with didactic poems on raising hops, sugar cane, gardening, and the like.[70] Botany, too, figured as the subject of elaborate poems; one reviewer of Darwin's *Loves of the Plants* even suggested that Darwin might be guilty of plagiarizing Monsieur de la Croix's *Connubia florum*.[71]

Darwin was also content to cash in on the botany craze. To James Watt and the industrialists of the Lunar Society, Darwin justified his seemingly frivolous endeavor saying that "*The Loves of the Plants* pays me well, and . . . I write for pay, not for fame."[72] At the same time, Darwin feared the "professional danger" of writing poetry. He first published *The Loves of the Plants* anonymously in 1789 because, as he wrote his publisher, he thought that it might injure his lucrative medical practice.[73] Darwin had suggested initially that Anna Seward write the poetry, a genre then considered more appropriate to a woman, while he supply elaborate scientific notes in prose. Seward, however, declined, objecting that she did not know enough about botany and that the enterprise was not "strictly proper for a female pen" (she does not say why).[74]

Darwin finally undertook the task himself (though he did incorporate some of Seward's verse without acknowledging it as hers). Darwin's stated purpose in writing these poems was to enlist "imagination under the banner of science."[75] Though Seward judged *The Loves of the Plants* appropriate for philosophers (for whom the extensive notes would provide the prime interest), Darwin intended the poem for a popular audience, fine ladies and gentlemen who would be drawn to the charms of poetry. This was also true of his later work. When preparing his *Economy of Vegetation*, he asked James Watt for some "gentlemanlike facts" (that is, agreeable facts and not "abstruse calculations, only fit for philosophers") about his steam engine.[76]

The fact, then, that Darwin set science to verse was not completely out of step with eighteenth-century expectations. But how was his erotic verse received? It is difficult to say exactly what Darwin's own intentions were in this regard. He could hardly have been unaware that the overtly erotic scenes would appeal to a wider public already fond of steamy romances. Yet, in his *Commonplace Book*, Darwin expressed his belief that Linnaeus's sexual terminology could be translated without evoking indecent ideas.[77] Anna Seward also defended Darwin against charges of indelicacy: "If *The Botanic Garden* is to be judged immodest," she wrote, "the impurity is in the imagination of the reader, not on the pages of the poet." For her, the sexual nature of plants was simply a matter of fact. As it was, Darwin's poetry was criticized at the time for lacking "sensation"; while it delighted the imagination, it was said not to excite deeper emotions.[78]

But this is not the entire story. Darwin was not the conservative that Linnaeus was. He was a founding member of the Lunar Society of Birmingham, where about half the men involved were Dissenters, and he was himself an atheist. Members, such as Joseph Priestley and Josiah Wedgewood, fostered innovation in industry and advocated liberty, equality, and leadership for the middle classes in politics. (The working classes were to supply an orderly and well-disciplined work force for the new factory system.)[79] Darwin himself supported the abolition of the slave trade, religious freedom, freedom of the press, and, like most members of the Lunar Society, welcomed the French Revolution.[80] Darwin also chose as his publisher Joseph Johnson, who was to become well known for disseminating radical literature, including the works of Joseph Priestley, Thomas Paine, William Godwin, and Mary Wollstonecraft.

Remarkably, neither Darwin's style nor his politics disturbed the public when his *Loves of the Plants* first appeared in 1789. The two hundred-page poem was greeted with enthusiasm and favorably reviewed in both the Whig *Monthly Review* and the Tory *Critical Review*.[81] Similarly his *Botanic Garden* and *Zoonomia* (a medical treatise and an early systematic statement of the theory of evolution) met with success, and for a time Darwin was one of the most widely read poets in England.

This initial indifference to Darwin's unorthodox scientific, religious, and political opinions has been explained as resulting from the relative political stability that England had enjoyed since the 1750s.[82] In this atmosphere mild expression of unorthodox opinion by men of the gentry and professional classes could safely be tolerated. As Roy Porter has argued, the Enlightenment had also ushered in more tolerant views of human sexuality.[83] Sex was no longer seen as a sin or vice, but as part of the economy of nature—a natural impulse that should find free expression. Free love was not only discussed among elites, it was practiced: pornographic journals began appearing from the 1770s; erotic novels proliferated; men of substance walked in public with their mistresses; and bastards grew up as accepted members of the family (though without inheriting the family name or property). Fanny Hill even spoke of the penis as a "sensitive plant." Sexuality expressed within the bounds of upper-class sensibility and decorum could be tolerated because it did not pose a serious threat to social order.[84]

The French Revolution shattered this calm. Members of the Lunar Society were violently attacked in the Birmingham Riots of 1791 for their open expression of support for the revolution. Priestley's and Withering's houses were sacked. Thereafter the society was disbanded and members sought to distance themselves from politics.[85] As church and state increasingly felt endangered, the official reaction to Darwin's work changed. The year 1798 saw the publication of *The Loves of the Triangles* (written in mock Darwinian verse) in the *Anti-Jacobin*, a semiofficial weekly, controlled by George Canning, foreign undersecretary in Pitt's government. In this poem Darwin was attacked for being among other things an advocate of free love—a tendency that conservatives saw as threatening to undermine English society in the same way that it had French society.[86] Darwin, under the cover of poetic license, may well have been advocating the free love that he himself practiced after the death of his first wife. Darwin had two illegitimate daughters, Susan and Mary Parker (as the result of a liaison with an unidentified woman) whom he and his second wife raised on equal terms with their other children.

Certainly the Reverend Richard Polwhele, writing shortly after the French Revolution, asserted that the open teaching of the sexual system in botany encouraged unauthorized sexual unions. For him democratic tendencies, liberated and irreligious women, and free love all threatened to corrupt English society. In *The Unsex'd Females*, Polwhele attacked that Amazonian band of "female Quixotes of the new philosophy" for adopting the sentiments and manners of republican France, singling out Mary Wollstonecraft as the prophetess of the movement. In a striking passage, Polwhele exploited the full potential of botanical allegory, which he so despised, in order to paint for the reader a vivid picture of Wollstonecraft's "disgraceful" life:

> But hark! lascivious murmurs melt around;
> And pleasure trembles in each dying sound.
> A myrtle bower, in fairest bloom array'd
> To laughing Venus streams the silver shade . . .
> Bath'd in new bliss, the Fair-one [Wollstonecraft] greets the
>   bower
> And ravishes a flame from every flower;
> Low at her feet inhales the master's sighs,
> and darts voluptuous poison from her eyes.
> Yet, while each heart pulses, in the Paphian grove,
> Beats quick to Imlay and licentious love.[87]

Polwhele was willfully ambiguous in the poem; the reader is left uncertain whether Wollstonecraft actually became one of Darwin's "adulterous" plants or if her libertine relations simply took place in the heaving floral bower.

In any case the message was clear: association with plants leads to licentious love. In his notes Polwhele explained how Wollstone-craft's liaisons in England with Henry Fuseli, the well-known painter who provided several illustrations for Darwin's *Botanic Garden*, and in France with the American writer Gilbert Imlay led her to attempt suicide from which she was rescued by William God-win, only to die soon thereafter in childbirth. An early death, in Pol-whele's view, was a just end to a dissolute life. Our botanizing girls, he wrote, are worthy disciples of Miss Wollstonecraft. These "un-sex'd females," sworn enemies to blushes, he lamented, throw aside their modesty—that "brilliant ornament" of their sex.[88]

Though Erasmus Darwin was a democrat and materialist, it should be pointed out that his radicalism with respect to women was measured. His *Plan for the Conduct of Female Education*, writ-ten for the school set up by his illegitimate daughters at Ashbourne, was in step with the new middle-class prescriptions of sexual com-plementarity which advocated distinct roles for men and women in society.[89] Like Rousseau, Europe's leading advocate of sexual com-plementarity, and Madame Genlis, whose works he recommended to his readers, Darwin held that the female character should possess mild and retiring virtues rather than bold and dazzling displays. Darwin emphasized that female learning and refinements were not to lead to professional employment, but were to be directed toward enhancing the home life of prospective husbands. Darwin's one stroke of innovation was his insistence on physical education for girls.[90] For the most part, however, his girls were to be schooled to be good wives—cheerful, deeply moral, and respectful of religion.

Though the Polwheles of the world taught that Linnaeus's bo-tanical system was inherently dangerous, it was considered a threat to the social order only when combined (as in the case of Erasmus Darwin) with radical politics.[91] Consider the example of Robert Thornton, a contemporary of Darwin, whose "Cupid Inspiring the Plants with Love" appears on the cover of this book. Characterizing himself as a patriot and "lover of social order," Thornton published his *New Illustration of the Sexual System of Carolus von Linnaeus* in 1799 as a challenge to French ascendancy in the fine arts.[92] Though Thornton made ample use of Darwin's poetry, his project enjoyed royal patronage. It was dedicated to Queen Charlotte, and many of the plates were done by the king's own engravers. Thornton's book sold well until 1808 when royal illness and old age rather than political reaction brought an end to enthusiasm for botany and popular tastes began turning toward the new science of chemistry.

In the pre-Victorian era, plants were stripped of sexuality, especially for women of the middle classes. Priscilla Wakefield's 1796 *Introduction to Botany* is interesting in this regard. In these letters on botany written to her sister, she traced the canonical analogy between plants and animals from the bark serving as "skin" to sap as the plant's "blood," but completely desexualized the plant. The anther (the male part) did not resemble a penis but a "kind of a box" that opened when ripe. Fertilization between plants was reduced to "communication." Wakefield allowed only that the seed resembled the eggs of animals. In another place in her *Introduction to Botany*, Wakefield remarked that male and female orchids were distinguished from one another "but without any reason for that distinction."[93]

As I have discussed elsewhere, botany—more than any other field of science—was considered appropriate for ladies. In some cases the identification of women with flowers was so overwhelming that, by the nineteenth century, botany had become known as the feminine science *par excellence*. It should be remembered that though ladies of the middle and upper classes botanized, they primarily collected and dried plants, perhaps corresponded with leading botanical figures, and prepared illustrations for publication. They were not taxonomists, nor among those shaping the future course of the science. Ann Shteir has pointed out that looking at women's work in botany takes us into the domestic sphere; women botanized in their kitchens and around their breakfast tables.[94] Botany, when prescribed for women, was to provide pleasure and instill virtue; it was, in other words, to be enjoyed as an amateur pursuit appropriate for women's leisure hours. Wakefield herself advocated botany as a natural branch of religion leading to the greatest appreciation of God and his universe.

The Scientific Revolution in Views of Sexual Difference

Much attention has been focused on the politics of the overt sexual imagery used by Linnaeus and Darwin. These tales are intriguing, but they divert attention from the heart of our story: the broader political trends that induced botanists to set as a priority the investigation of sexual difference in plants in the eighteenth century. Why did the preoccupation with sexual difference—a project that would carry forward into the nineteenth century—emerge in the late seventeenth and eighteenth centuries?

The recognition of sexual reproduction in plants was pushed first and foremost by developments in zoology. This was a period of keen interest in theories of generation with debates raging between preformationists and epigenesists, ovists and homunculists. Botanists, committed to finding uniform laws of nature, increasingly drew analogies between plant and animal life and thus transferred their fascination with animal sexuality onto plants.

Yet there are broader contexts worth considering. Eighteenth-century interest in plant sexuality coincided with a keen interest in the exact differentiation of sexual character in animals and humans. Both botany and anatomy were branches of medicine as taught at the early modern university. But more than that, both were subject to the imperative to find and analyze sex (and gender) differences that dominated scientific communities in the late seventeenth and eighteenth centuries.[95] Historians have come to recognize this period as a time of profound transformation in the science of sexuality and sexual temperament. Thomas Laqueur has argued that the older Galenic "one sex" model, in which women were conceived as essentially the same as men but merely less perfect versions, gave way to the new "two sex" model, a model of radical biological divergence.[96] Laqueur has focused primarily on changing views of male and female sexual organs, but the revolution in sexual science was more fundamental, marked by a methodological rupture in explanations of sexual difference. At long last, ancient theories of sexuality—the Aristotelian/Galenic theory of humors and biblical accounts—were overturned by modern materialistic theories that grounded sexual difference in the fabric of the human body.

Ironically, this does not mean that the content of medical views of female nature changed in every instance. In many cases, ancient prejudices were merely translated into the language of modern science. What did change were basic understandings of the origin and character of sexual differences. In the ancient world, sexual difference had been explained in terms of cosmic principles. Everything in the universe had a temperament (sexual or otherwise). Things hot and dry—the sun, for example—were considered masculine, while things cold and moist—like the moon, or Western regions of the earth—were thought of as feminine. Differences between the two sexes were reflections of a set of dualistic principles which penetrated the cosmos as well as the bodies of men and women. As Aristotle put it, maleness and femaleness were cosmic principles, and the organs of reproduction were mere instruments.[97]

The new science of sex, by contrast, was materialistic. Anatomists and physiologists developed and deployed new methods for weighing and measuring sexual difference. Anatomists and medical doctors investigated the body as a whole—each bone, organ, hair of the head, and nerve—for telltale signs of sexual differences. This new emphasis on understanding sexual difference in terms compatible with modern materialism was epitomized in the illustrations of distinctively female skeletons that sprang up throughout Europe between the 1730s and 1790s to display the essential differences between female and male anatomy.[98]

Ancient doctrines of sexuality had claimed to reveal women's place in the cosmic and social order. So, too, did modern scientific theories. The grounding of sexual difference in the body played to Enlightenment sensibilities that *nature* prescribed the laws of society. The role of each sex was thought to be inscribed in nature. Thus the new anatomy of sexual difference buttressed the doctrines of sexual complementarity and republican motherhood, two of the ideologies that emerged as often unrecognized girders of the emancipatory liberalism animating the American and French revolutions.

Complementarity provided an important ideological resolution to the new question of rights for women. The doctrine of sexual complementarity, which taught that men and women are not physical and moral equals but complementary opposites, functioned as an important supplement to nascent liberalism, making inequalities seem natural while satisfying the needs of European society for a continued sexual division of labor. This ideology appealed especially to middle-class women because it presented a positive image of the newly domesticated woman. The private, caring woman emerged as a foil to the public, rational man.[99]

It was, therefore, not by chance or genius alone that Linnaeus's system gained such currency in the eighteenth century, amidst upheavals surrounding the nature and definition of sexuality and sexual roles in that century. Linnaeus focused on sexuality as his principal taxonomic division because he saw the sex organs as the most important organs of the plant. He saw plants in this way because he viewed them through an eighteenth-century lens. The new botanical sciences thus went hand in hand with the making and remaking of sexuality in the Enlightenment. Sexual images were prominent in botanists' language at the same time that botanical taxonomy recapitulated the most prominent and contested aspects of European sexual hierarchy.

2

Why Mammals Are Called Mammals

A certain Chinese encyclopedia divides animals into: (a) belonging to the Emperor, (b) embalmed, (c) tame, (d) sucking pigs, (e) sirens, (f) fabulous, (g) stray dogs, (h) included in the present classification, (i) frenzied, (j) innumerable, (k) drawn with a very fine camel's-hair brush, (l) *et cetera*, (m) having just broken the water pitcher, (n) that from a long way off look like flies.

Jorge Luis Borges, *Other Inquisitions*, 1952

*I*n 1758, in the tenth edition of his *Systema naturae*, Carolus Linnaeus introduced the term *Mammalia* into zoological taxonomy.[1] Linnaeus devised this term—meaning literally "of the breast"—to distinguish the class of animals embracing humans, apes, ungulates, sloths, sea cows, elephants, bats, and all other organisms with hair, three ear bones, and a four-chambered heart. In so doing, he idolized the female mammae as the icon of that class.

When examining the evolution of Linnaean nomenclature, historians of science have tended to confine their study to developments within the scientific community. They trace the history of classification from Aristotle through the leading naturalists of the sixteenth and seventeenth centuries, the Swiss Conrad Gesner and the English John Ray, culminating ultimately with the triumph of Linnaean systematics.[2] Linnaeus's nomenclature is taken more or less for granted as part of his foundational work in zoology. No one has grappled with the social origins or consequences of the term *Mammalia*. Certainly, no one has questioned the gender politics informing Linnaeus's choice of this term.

It is also possible, however, to see the Linnaean coinage as a political act. The presence of milk-producing mammae is, after all, but one characteristic of mammals, as was commonly known to eighteenth-century European naturalists. Furthermore, the mammae are "functional" in only half of this group of animals (the females) and, among those, for a relatively short period of time (during lactation) or not at all. As we shall see, Linnaeus could indeed have chosen a more gender-neutral term, such as *Aurecaviga* (the hollow-eared ones) or *Pilosa* (the hairy ones—although as we will see in chapter 4, the significance given hair, and especially beards, was also saturated with gender).

In what follows we consider first the emergence of the Linnaean term from natural history in order to understand naturalists' concerns as they devised categories for classification. What alternatives were available to Linnaeus as he thought about how to join humans to the animal kingdom, and how did other naturalists react? Crucial to my argument is the fact that Linnaeus could have derived a term from a number of equally unique, and perhaps more universal, characteristics of the class he designated mammals.

To appreciate more fully the meaning of Linnaeus's term requires a foray into the cultural history of the breast. Even though Linnaeus's term may have been new to zoology, the female breast evoked deep, wide-ranging, and often contradictory currents of meaning in Western cultures. But, as we shall see, there were also more immediate and pressing political trends that prompted Linnaeus to focus scientific attention on the mammae. Linnaeus venerated the maternal breast at a time when doctors and politicians had begun to extol the virtues of mother's milk (Linnaeus was a practicing physician and the father of seven children). Eighteenth-century middle- and upper-class women were being encouraged to give up their wet nurses; a Prussian law of 1794 went so far as to require that healthy women nurse their own babies. Linnaeus was involved in the struggle against wet-nursing, a struggle that emerged alongside and in step with political realignments undermining women's public power and attaching a new value to women's domestic roles. Understood in broadest terms, the scientific fascination with the female breast helped to buttress the sexual division of labor in European society by emphasizing how natural it was for fe-

buttress

males—both human and nonhuman—to suckle and rear their own children.

Mammalia—*The Genealogy of a Term*

It has been said that God created nature and Linnaeus gave it order; Albrecht von Haller rather mockingly called him "the second Adam."[3] Carolus Linnaeus, ennobled by the Swedish crown in 1761 as Carl von Linné, was, indeed, the central figure in developing European taxonomy and nomenclature. His *Systema naturae* treated the three classical kingdoms of nature—animal, vegetable, and mineral—growing from a folio of only twelve pages in 1735 to a three-volume work of 2,400 pages in the twelfth and last edition revised by Linnaeus himself in 1766. In the epoch-making tenth edition, Linnaeus gave binomial names (generic and specific) to all the animals known to him, nearly 4,400 species.[4]

Linnaeus divided animals into six classes: *Mammalia*, *Aves*, *Amphibia*, *Pisces*, *Insecta*, and *Vermes*.[5] Although Linnaeus had based important aspects of plant taxonomy on sexual dimorphism (see chapter 1), the term *Mammalia* was the only one of his major zoological divisions to focus on reproductive organs and the only term to highlight a character associated primarily with the female. The names of his other classes came, in many cases, from Aristotle: *Aves* simply means bird; *Amphibia* emphasizes habitat; *Insecta* refers to the segmentation of the body; *Vermes* derives from the red-brown color of the common earthworm. Scientific nomenclature was a conservative enterprise in the eighteenth century; suitable terms tended to be conserved and new terms derived by modifying traditional ones. Linnaeus, however, broke with tradition by creating the term *Mammalia*.

In coining the term mammals, Linnaeus abandoned Aristotle's canonical term, *Quadrupedia*. For more than two thousand years most of the animals we now designate as mammals (along with most reptiles and several amphibians) had been called *quadrupeds*. While Aristotle had never intended to develop a definitive taxonomy, his analytical distinctions set out in his *Historia animalium*

laid the groundwork for European taxonomy. Using a number of di-
agnostics—mode of subsistence, locomotion, and reproduction—
he arranged animals hierarchically along what later would be called
the *scala naturae*. Aristotle began by dividing animals into two
main groups according to the quality of their blood. "Blooded animals" had warm, red blood and superior qualities of "soul"
(*psyche*), sharp senses, great courage, and intelligence; "bloodless
animals" had a colorless liquid analogous to blood but with no essential heat. Quadrupeds, then, formed a major category within
blooded animals and included all animals going on four feet. Aristotle further separated quadrupeds into two groups: (1) viviparous
(bearing live young and including many of the animals we now call
mammals) and (2) oviparous (egg layers, what we now call reptiles
and also some amphibians). Birds formed another group within the
blooded animals; they were bipedal but not erect. Fish, the final
group, were considered imperfect, lacking legs, arms, and wings,
and living in water.[6]

Aristotelian categories and terminology formed the foundation of European natural history until well into the early modern period. Conrad Gesner's influential *Historiae animalium* (1551) employed Aristotle's division of quadrupeds into viviparous and
oviparous by treating each in separate volumes. Within each volume, animals were entered alphabetically. The sixteenth-century
Italian naturalist Ulisse Aldrovandi divided quadrupeds into those
with single hoofs (horses, for example) and those with cloven hoofs
(such as cattle, camels, or goats). Gesner and Aldrovandi continued
the medieval practice of reciting all known information (zoological,
historical, cultural, and mythical) about each particular animal. Aldrovandi in his discussion of the horse, for example, included the
miracles attributed to the creature in various religions, along with
poetic allusions, iconographic representations, and a list of coins
bearing the equine image. Other taxonomic schema, such as the
German pastor Herman Frey's, followed Levitical categories dividing animals into clean (edible) and unclean (inedible).[7]

John Ray, the great seventeenth-century English naturalist,
presented the first serious challenge to Aristotelian classification.

Aristotle's primary division of animals into blooded and bloodless, Ray noted, was not strictly accurate since all organisms have a vital fluid. The division of animals into viviparous and oviparous was similarly flawed because all animals come from eggs (either internal or external to the mother's body). More specific to our theme, Ray was the first to question the appropriateness of the term quadruped. Whales, porpoises, and manatees, he pointed out, shared key features with quadrupeds (red blood, a heart with two ventricles, and lungs) but did not have four feet. In his "Table of Classification," Ray correctly removed these animals from the fishes and grouped them with other viviparous quadrupeds. He also suggested that the term quadruped be dropped.[8]

Naturalists did not immediately act on Ray's suggestions. Linnaeus, in the first edition of his *Systema naturae* (1735), continued to use the traditional term, *Quadrupedia*. He did, however, raise eyebrows and ire by including humans (rather uncomfortably) among quadrupeds. Indeed, it was the question of how to place humans in nature—which Thomas Huxley later called "the question of all questions"—more than anything else that led Linnaeus to abandon *Quadrupedia* and search for something more appropriate.[9] Linnaeus was not, of course, the first in modern times to recognize that humans are animals. In 1555 Pierre Belon had pointed to the similarities in the skeletons of a human and a bird, and in 1699 Edward Tyson had dissected a chimpanzee—his *Homo sylvestris*—revealing the "great affinity" between animal and human anatomy.[10]

In setting humans among quadrupeds, Linnaeus called attention to their hairy bodies, four feet (two for locomotion and two for gripping, as he later explained),[11] and the viviparous and lactiferous nature of the females. On the basis of similarities in their teeth (namely, four incisors) he further included humans in his order *Anthropomorpha* (a term he borrowed from Ray) along with apes, monkeys, and sloths. *Anthropomorpha* was changed to *Primates* only in the 1758 edition.[12]

Linnaeus's ranking of humans among quadrupeds outraged naturalists. They found repugnant his characterization of rational man as a hairy animal with four feet and four incisors. Georges-Louis Leclerc, comte de Buffon, born the same year as Linnaeus and his principal rival, made the obvious point that many of the creatures included among Linnaeus's *Quadrupedia* were not quadrupeds at all: humans have two hands and two feet; bats have two feet and no hands; apes have four hands and no feet; and manatees have only two "hands."[13] Louis Daubenton, Buffon's assistant at the Jardin du Roi, denounced Linnaeus's entire system as "false" and "inaccurate."[14] Finally, many naturalists rejected as heretical the notion that humans were essentially animals. Holy Scripture, after all, clearly taught that man was created in God's image. It should be recalled that while Aristotle had included humans among viviparous quadrupeds, in the course of the Middle Ages scholastics removed humans from nature, emphasizing instead their proximity to angels.[15]

Natural historians before Linnaeus had struggled long and hard with these problems of classification. John Ray, often credited with developing binomial nomenclature (though he did not employ it systematically), had used the term *Vivipara* to unite whales and other aquatic mammals with terrestrial quadrupeds. Within his subcategory *Terrestria*, he suggested the term *Pilosa* (hairy animals) as more comprehensive than *Quadrupedia* and thus more suitable for joining amphibious manatees with land-dwelling quadrupeds.[16] Peter Artedi, Linnaeus's close friend and colleague, had also called attention to hair in his proposed *Trichozoologia*, or "science of the hirsute animal."[17] Linnaeus might well have chosen the more traditional adjective *Pilosa* for his new class of quadrupeds; in Linnaeus's system hair had the same diagnostic value as mammae. All mammals (including whales) have hair, and it is still today considered a distinguishing characteristic of mammals.[18]

But Linnaeus did not draw on tradition; he devised instead a new term, *Mammalia*. In its defense, Linnaeus remarked that even if his critics did not believe that humans originally walked on all fours, surely every man born of woman must admit that he was nourished by his mother's milk.[19] Linnaeus thus called attention to the fact, commonly known since Aristotle, that hairy, viviparous females lactate. Linnaeus also was convinced of the diagnostic value of the teat. As early as 1732, in his *Tour of Lapland*, he had already announced: "If I knew how many teeth and of what peculiar form each animal has, as well as how many udders and where situated, I should perhaps be able to contrive a most natural methodical arrangement of quadrupeds."[20] In the first edition of his *Systema naturae*, he used the number and position of teats or udders to align orders within his class of *Anthropomorpha* (complicating factors being that females and males often have different numbers, and that females of the same species may also vary in the number of their teats).[21] In 1758, Linnaeus finally announced the term *Mammalia* with the words: "Mammalia, these and no other animals have mammae [mammata]." He seemed quite unconcerned that mammae were not a universal character of the class he intended to distinguish. "All females," he wrote on the following page, "have lactiferous mammae of determinate number, as do males (except for the horse)."

Mammalia resonated with the older term *animalia*, derived from *anima*, meaning the breath of life or vital spirit.[22] The new term also conformed to Linnaeus's own rules for zoological terms: it was pleasing to the ear, easy to say and to remember, and not more than twelve letters long.[23] For the rest of his life Linnaeus fiddled with his system, moving animals from order to order, creating new categories and combinations to better capture nature's order. Yet he never rechristened mammals.

The term *Mammalia* gained almost immediate acceptance. There were, however, detractors of note.[24] Buffon scorned the entire project of taxonomy but especially Linnaean taxonomy and nomenclature. For Buffon, the task of the natural historian was to describe each animal precisely—its mode of reproduction, nourishment, customs, and habitat—not to divide nature's bounty into artificial categories with incomprehensible names of Greek or Latin origin. Buffon took particular offense at the prominence Linnaeus gave the breast: "A general character, such as the teat, taken to identify quadrupeds should at least belong to all quadrupeds" (Buffon, like Linnaeus, noted that stallions have no teats).[25] Buffon also complained that Linnaeus's order *Anthropomorpha* lumped together things as different as humans, apes, and sloths. This "violence" was wreaked on the natural scheme of things, he lamented, all because there was "some small relationship between the number of nipples or teeth of these animals or some slight resemblance in the form of their horns."[26]

Other taxonomists, including Felix Vicq-d'Azyr and Thomas Pennant, continued to use the traditional term, *Quadrupedia*. Still others developed their own alternatives. The Frenchman Henri de Blainville in 1816 tried to rationalize zoological nomenclature, re-naming mammals *Pilifera* (having hair), birds *Pennifera* (having feathers), and reptiles *Squammifera* (having scales).[27] In England, John Hunter proposed the term *Tetracoilia*, drawing attention to the four-chambered heart.[28]

These critics met with little success. *Mammalia* was adopted by the English as "mammals," though "mammifers" was also occasionally used, and, as one commentator has suggested, the science treating mammals was rather awkwardly rendered as *mammalogy*, meaning literally "a study of breasts" (and not of breast-bearing animals, which would be more properly *mammology* or *mammalology*).[29] The French devised *mammifères*, or the breast-bearers (not *mammaux*, nicely analogous to *animaux*). The Germans re-focused matters slightly, creating *Säugetiere*, or "suckling animals," which appropriately drew attention away from the breast and highlighted the act of suckling (though no distinction was made between a mother giving suck and a newborn taking milk). Linnaeus's term *Mammalia* was retained even after the Darwinian revolution and is today recognized by the International Code of Zoological Nomenclature.

Honorary Mammals: Males and Monotremes

The word *mamma*—the singular form of *mammae*, designating the milk-secreting organs of the female—probably derives from baby talk, being a reduplicated syllable often uttered by young children, who in many countries are taught to use it as their word for mother.[30] Linnaeus devised the term *Mammalia* from the Latin *mammae*, intending it to refer to the breast or teat itself as much as to its milk-producing aspects. These terms—breast and teat—are somewhat ambiguous. *Teat* sometimes refers to the nipple of a cow, sheep, or goat but also refers to the internal structures of the mammary gland. In humans (and some birds) *breast* refers to the chest area as well as to the milk-producing organ in the female. Today it is the mammary gland with its milk-producing structures that defines the class *Mammalia*. While most mammals have mammary glands (though only rudimentary in males), not all mammals have proper teats.[31] The platypus, classified as a mammal only after considerable debate, has mammary glands but no nipples.

The question of why males have breasts at all has long plagued naturalists. The eighteenth-century medical doctor Louis de Jaucourt addressed this as one of six basic questions about the breast in his article, "Mamelle," for Diderot and d'Alembert's *Encyclopédie*. Jaucourt, who also wrote a well-known entry on "Femme," noted that the particular cast of the human body and its parts answers to nature's need to conserve the species, and that even though some parts, such as male breasts, may be superfluous, nature did not take them away. He was quick to argue that male breasts are not defective, that in many cases milk flows in great abundance from them. That males rarely produce milk was to be traced to the absence of menstrual blood—the source of milk. According to Jaucourt, with the onset of puberty, blood surges throughout the female body causing young women's breasts to "inflate"; the passion of love also experienced at this age causes them to inflate even further. Men do not have menses, the author continued, and therefore their breasts, though anatomically similar to women's, never inflate.[32]

The fanciful notion that males were, indeed, capable of producing milk was popular among naturalists. Aristotle had considered it an omen of extraordinary good fortune when a male goat produced milk in such quantities that cheese could be made from it.[33] Eighteenth-century naturalists reported the secretion of a fatty milky substance—"witch's milk"—from the breasts of male as well as female newborns. Buffon related many examples of the male breast filling with milk at the onset of puberty. A boy of fifteen, for example, pressed from one of his breasts more than a spoonful of "true" milk.[34] John Hunter offered the example of a father who nursed his eight children. This man began nursing when his wife was unable to satisfy a set of twins. "To soothe the cries of the male child," Hunter wrote, "the father applied his left nipple to the infant's mouth, who drew milk from it in such quantity as to be nursed in perfectly good health." (The father also shared with his wife all other domestic duties.) Considering milk production within the bounds of normal male physiology, Hunter dutifully noted that the man "was not a hermaphrodite."[35]

Despite dramatic examples such as these, most naturalists recognized that the male breast was barren. Why, then, did males have breasts at all? Erasmus Darwin suggested that the vestigial male teat lent credence to Plato's theory that mammals had hermaphroditic origins and only later developed into distinct males and females.[36] Late into the nineteenth century, comparative anatomists continued to embrace the notion that some remote progenitor of the vertebrate kingdom had been androgynous.[37] Charles Darwin, following Clémence Royer, suggested that in an earlier age male mammals had aided females in nursing their offspring and that later some patterns of events (such as smaller litters) rendered male assistance unnecessary. The disuse of the organ led to its becoming vestigial.[38] Today, naturalists emphasize that many organs in the male and female, such as the clitoris and penis, and the labia majora and scrotal sac, are identical in the early embryos and only later—after the action of various hormones—develop along different trajectories.[39]

It might also be argued that monotremes (egg-laying mammals, including the duck-billed platypus, the spiny echidna, and two genera of anteaters) should be considered only honorary mammals. Female monotremes have functional mammary glands, but unlike all other mammals they have no nipples. Milk is secreted through numerous pores onto the mother's belly where her babies lap it up.

The platypus, the first of these animals to reach Europe (from

Australia), baffled early nineteenth-century taxonomists. Some naturalists suspected that it had been fabricated by foreign taxidermists, already notorious for their willingness to feed European curiosity by producing "mermaids" from the heads of monkeys sewn to the tails of fish. But the question of whether the platypus was a reptile, bird, mammal, or a completely new class of animal, was not resolved even after George Shaw, working at the British Museum, determined that the skin he received in 1799 (eleven years after Linnaeus's death) was from a genuine animal. Because of its curious melange of characteristics, Johann Blumenbach christened it *Ornithorhynchus paradoxus*.[40]

Shaw, having only a stuffed skin to work with, knew nothing of the platypus's internal structure and classified it as a quadruped (order *Bruta*) for its abundant "beaverlike" fur.[41] Zoologists imagined that this furry animal, like other mammals, bore live young and suckled them. Everard Home, the English anatomist who dissected a female and a male that came to him preserved in alcohol in 1802, found no uterus, no nipples, and no mammary glands (the mammary glands of nonnursing females are in fact so small that they are easily overlooked). From his investigation, Home suggested that the reproductive organs of the female platypus most closely resembled those of ovoviviparous lizards, whose young are produced from eggs that hatch within the females' bodies.

In the taxonomic wars that raged for more than thirty years over the classification of the platypus, the French zoologists Etienne Geoffroy Saint-Hilaire and Jean-Baptiste Lamarck faced off against the German Johann Meckel and his French colleague Henri de Blainville. Meckel and Blainville insisted that the platypus was a mammal, predicting viviparity and the presence of mammary glands. Geoffroy Saint-Hilaire adamantly refused to see it as a mammal, asserting (wrongly) that it lacked mammary glands and predicting (correctly) that it would be found to lay eggs. In 1803 Geoffroy Saint-Hilaire coined the term *Monotremata* ("one-holed"), emphasizing the reptilian structure of the platypus's reproductive tract (females and males have only one opening, the cloaca, for all excretory and reproductive functions; other male mammals have two such openings while females have three). In 1822 Geoffroy Saint-Hilaire established *Monotremata* as a fifth class of vertebrates, ranked alongside mammals, birds, reptiles (including amphibians), and fishes.[42]

The debate continued even after Meckel discovered mammary glands in the platypus in 1824. Geoffroy Saint-Hilaire, still committed to seeing the platypus as something other than a mammal, refused to admit that the glands Meckel found produced milk, arguing instead that they were odoriferous glands similar to those found in shrews and used for attracting mates (milk production was not demonstrated until 1832). After discovering the platypus's mammary glands, Meckel predicted that these animals would also prove to be viviparous, placing them squarely among mammals. It was not until 1884, however, that it was confirmed that platypuses lay eggs like reptiles. Despite its nippleless mammae and ovoviviparity, the platypus is still today classed among mammals—where George Shaw had placed it for its abundant hair in 1799. It is included within an egg-laying subclass of mammals (*Prototheria*) along with the anteater, and distinguished from both marsupial and placental mammals. Thus mammals can be mammals whether or not they have fully developed mammae.

How Significant Are the Mammae?

Were there good reasons for Linnaeus to name mammals *mammals*? This question implies a logic uncharacteristic of the naming process. Names of taxa collect over time, and unless there is a technical problem—as was the case with the term *Quadrupedia*—they pass unchanged from generation to generation. Naturalists also name plants and animals for other than empirical reasons. Pleasing plants or animals are often named after a wife or colleague, while a particularly odious species might be given the name of a professional rival (for instance, *Siegesbeckia*, a small and unpleasant flowering weed that Linnaeus named after Johann Siegesbeck, a critic of his sexual system).[43]

Zoological nomenclature—like all language—is, then, to

some degree arbitrary; naturalists devise convenient terms to identify groups of animals.[44] But nomenclature is also historical, growing out of specific contexts, conflicts, and circumstances. The historian can fairly ask why a certain term was coined. In creating the
term *Mammalia*, Linnaeus intended to highlight an essential trait of
that class of animals. Etienne Geoffroy Saint-Hilaire and Georges
Cuvier, in their article "Mammalogie" for the *Magazin encyclopé-
dique* of 1795, summed up the practice of eighteenth-century taxonomists, stating that primary organs determine classes, while secondary organs determine orders. In 1827, Cuvier continued to
argue that the mammae distinguished the class bearing their name
better than any other external character.[45]

Is Cuvier's statement, in fact, true? Does the longevity of Linnaeus's term reflect the fact that he was simply right, that the mammae do represent a primary, universal, and unique characteristic of
mammals (as would have been the parlance of the eighteenth century)? Yes and no. Paleontologists today identify the mammary
gland as one of at least six uniquely mammalian characters.[46] Linnaeus himself, though, was perhaps overly exuberant in singling
out the breast or teat itself—a sexually charged part of the female
body—rather than its function. Indeed one could argue that the
term *Lactantia* (the lactating ones, derived from Linnaeus's own description of female mammae) would have better captured the significance of the mammae; certainly Linnaeus was wrong to think
that the number and position of the teats themselves were significant. But *Lactantia* still refers exclusively to females. *Lactentia* or
Sugentia (both meaning "the sucking ones") would have better uni-
versalized the term, since male as well as female young suckle at
their mothers' breasts.

The fact remains that the mammae was only one among several traits that could have been highlighted. Even by eighteenth-
century criteria, there was not one characteristic alone that could
determine class assignment. As Buffon recognized, species—defined for sexually reproducing organisms as members of a group of
individuals that can mate and produce fertile offspring—is the only
taxon that exists in nature.[47] Even today, this does not mean that

higher units (genera, families, orders, classes, and on up) are arbitrary; these must be consistent with evolutionary genealogy.[48] Yet, as we have seen, Linnaeus could have chosen from a number of equally valid terms, such as *Pilosa*, *Aurecaviga*, *Lactentia*, or *Sugentia*. Because Linnaeus had choices, I will argue that his focus on the breast responded to broader cultural and political trends.

Breasts and Mother's Milk: Problematic Icons

Long before Linnaeus, the female breast had been a powerful icon within Western cultures, representing both the sublime and bestial in human nature.[49] The grotesque, withered breasts on witches and devils represented temptations of wanton lust, sins of the flesh, and humanity fallen from paradise. The firm spherical breasts of Aphrodite, the Greek ideal, represented an otherworldly beauty and virginity. In the French Revolution, the bared female breast—embodied in the strident Marianne—became a resilient symbol of freedom.[50] From the multibreasted Diana of Ephesus to the fecund-bosomed Nature, the breast symbolized generation, regeneration, and renewal.

Linnaeus created his term *Mammalia* in response to the question of humans' place in nature. In his quest to find an appropriate term for (what we would call) a taxon uniting humans and beasts, Linnaeus made the breast—and specifically the fully developed female breast—the icon of the highest class of animals. It might be argued that by privileging a uniquely female characteristic in this way, Linnaeus broke with long-established traditions that saw the male as the measure of all things. In the Aristotelian tradition, the female had been seen as a misbegotten male, a monster or error of nature. By honoring the mammae as sign and symbol of the highest class of animals, Linnaeus assigned a new value to the female, especially women's unique role in reproduction.

It is important to note, however, that in the same volume in which Linnaeus introduced the term *Mammalia*, he also introduced the name *Homo sapiens*. This term, man of wisdom, was used to *distinguish* humans from other primates (apes, lemurs, and

54

Page 342.

bats, for example). In the language of taxonomy, *sapiens* is what is known as a "trivial" name (Linnaeus at one point pondered the choice of the name *Homo diurnus*, designed to contrast with *Homo nocturnus*).[51] From a historical point of view, however, the choice of the term *sapiens* is highly significant. "Man" had traditionally been distinguished from animals by his reason; the medieval apposition, *animal rationale*, proclaimed his uniqueness.[52] Thus, within Linnaean terminology, a female characteristic (the lactating mamma) ties humans to brutes, while a traditionally male characteristic (reason) marks our separateness.

The notion that woman—lacking male perfections of mind and body—resides nearer the beast than does man is an ancient one. Among all the organs of a woman's body, her reproductive organs were considered most animallike. For Plato, the uterus was an animal with its own sense of smell, wandering within the female body and leaving disease and destruction in its path.[53] The Greek physician Galen and even the great anatomist Andreas Vesalius (for a time) reported that the uterus had horns. Milk production of the female breast had already been seen as linking humans and animals. Aristotle, in his *Historia animalium*, had recognized that all internally viviparous animals—women, sheep, horses, cows, and whales, for example—nurse their young. Beyond noting how breast size relates to milk production, and noting the number and position of teats in various animals, Aristotle was not much interested in the breast itself. His interest lay more in the utility and variety of milk from different animals—which among these made the tastiest cheese and which kinds of grasses promoted milk production.[54]

In Judaic traditions, too, the discomfort women feel during menstruation and childbirth were considered curses, rendering them unclean, undesirable, and beastlike. The disgust associated with menstruation also sullied lactation; Aristotle's theory that lac-

---

FIG. 2.1. A bear suckling a child, from Bernard Connor, *The History of Poland* (London, 1697), vol. 1, p. 342. By permission of the Houghton Library, Harvard University.

tation was related to menstruation remained current in the West until well into the eighteenth century. For Aristotle, milk was concocted blood, which in males was secreted as semen. In nonpregnant females, it was secreted as menstrual fluid, in pregnant women, as a vital fluid nourishing their embryos, and in postpartum women, as milk for newborns.[55]

Myths and legends also portrayed suckling as a point of intimate connection between humans and beasts, suggesting the interchangeability of human and animal breasts in this respect. A nanny goat, Amaltheia, was said to have nursed the young Zeus.[56] A she-wolf served as the legendary nurse to Romulus and Remus, the founders of Rome. From the Middle Ages to the seventeenth and eighteenth centuries, bears and wolves were reported to have suckled abandoned children (FIG. 2.1). Children were thought to imbibe certain characteristics of the animals that nursed them—the "wild Peter" found in northern Germany in 1724 was thought to have grown thick hair all over his body as a result of his nurturance at the breast of a bear. Linnaeus believed that ancient heroes, put to the breast of lionesses, absorbed their great courage along with their milk.[57]

In rarer instances, humans were reported even to have suckled animals. Veronica Giuliani, beatified by Pius II (1405–1464), took a real lamb to bed with her and suckled it at her breast in memory of the lamb of God. In the eighteenth century, William Godwin recorded that as Mary Wollstonecraft lay dying after childbirth, the doctor forbade the child the breast and "procured puppies to draw off the milk."[58] The practice of animals suckling at human breasts was also reported outside Europe. Voyagers related that native South Americans kept their breasts active by letting animals of all kinds feed from them.[59] In Siam, women were said to have suckled apes.

Linnaeus thus followed well-established Western conceptions when he suggested that women belong to nature in ways that men do not.[60] As Carolyn Merchant has shown, nature itself has long been conceived as female in most Western intellectual traditions.[61] For the seventeenth-century alchemist Michael Maier, the earth was literally a nourishing mother (FIG. 2.2).[62] The identity of woman with

FIG. 2.2. "His nurse is the earth," from Michael Maier, *Atalanta fugiens* (Oppenheim, 1618), p. 17. On the right Romulus and Remus are suckled by a wolf; on the left Jupiter is nursed by a goat. The verse attached asks: "How much greater will be the child whose nursing mother (*Säugmutter*) is the earth?" (Sign.: Nv 7886 R.) By permission of the Staatsbibliothek zu Berlin—Preußischer Kulturbesitz.

the fecund and nurturing qualities of nature was highlighted in the influential eighteenth-century artists and engravers Hubert-François Gravelot and Charles Cochin's personification of Nature as a virgin, her breasts dripping with milk (FIG. 2.3).[63]

It is significant that Linnaeus used the mammiferous Diana of the Ephesians, an ancient symbol of fertility, as the frontispiece to his *Fauna Svecica*, where he first defended his inclusion of humans among quadrupeds (FIG. 2.4).[64] Linnaeus's Diana, half captive in the

NATURE

H. Gravelot inv.

Delongueil sculp.

fecund earth, emerges to display her womb, the center of life, and her nourishing breasts.[65] In this classic image, her curiously immobilized trunk is covered with symbols of both fertility (bees, acorns, bulls, crabs) and chastity (stags, lions, roses). Her pendulous breasts, heavy with milk, represent the life force of nature—mother and nurse of all living things. In ancient statues, Diana's breasts were often carved from a white stone while her head, neck, hands, and feet were made of darker stone.[66]

For Linnaeus to suggest, then, that humans shared with animals the capacity to suckle their young was nothing new. This uniquely female feature had long been considered less than human. But it had also been considered more than human. In the Christian world, milk had been seen as providing sustenance—for both body and spirit. Throughout the Middle Ages, the faithful cherished vials of the Virgin's milk as a healing balm, a symbol of mercy, an eternal mystery. As Marina Warner has pointed out, the Virgin Mary endured none of the bodily pleasures and pains associated with childbearing (menstruation, sexual intercourse, pregnancy, or labor) except for suckling. The tender Madonna suckled the infant Jesus both as his historical mother and as the metaphysical image of the nourishing Mother Church.[67] During the twelfth century, maternal imagery—especially suckling and nurturing—extended also to church fathers. Abbots and prelates were encouraged to "mother" the souls in their charge, to expose their breasts and let their bosoms expand with the milk of consolation.[68] Even the full breasts of God the Father were said to be milked by the Holy Spirit into the cup of the Son of God.[69]

FIG. 2.3. Nature portrayed as a young virgin. Though a virgin, her breasts are shown dripping with mother's milk (the virgin mother is a persistent theme in Christianity, where the ideal female is both chaste and fecund). Her nudity expresses the simplicity of her essence. The lion and stag are symbols of chastity. The multibreasted Diana of the Ephesians in the background represents the Ancients' image of nature, "the Mother of all Being." From Charles Cochin and Hubert-François Gravelot, *Iconologie par figures, ou Traité complet des allégories, emblèmes, &c.* (1791; Geneva: Minkoff Reprint, 1972), s.v. "Nature." Courtesy of the Pennsylvania State University Libraries.

In subcurrents of religious traditions, mother's milk was thought to impart knowledge. Philosophia-Sapientia, the traditional personification of wisdom, suckled philosophers at her breasts moist with the milk of knowledge and moral virtue (FIG. 2.5). Augustine of Hippo, too, imagined himself drinking from the breasts of Sapientia.[70] Centuries later, men of science still sought the secrets of (female) nature within her bosom, though with a rather different purpose. Goethe, probing her innermost recesses, waxed poetic on the point: "Infinite Nature, where are thy breasts, those well-springs of all life on which hang heaven and earth, toward which my withered breast strains?"[71] For Goethe, at least, the scientist's new desire was not to suckle at the breast of nature but to imitate its nourishing power.

Mother's milk was valued for its medicinal as well as its spiritual virtues. As a cure for deafness, Sicilians drank the milk of a woman who had borne a first son. Mother's milk was used as an abortifacient in sixteenth-century Germany. In Alsace, it served as a remedy for consumption. It was also used for treating earaches, fevers, and sores.[72] Linnaeus recommended it to adults as a laxative. Mother's milk was also considered regenerative: legend held that the sixteenth-century priest Bartolomé de Las Casas, defender of Native Americans against the horrors of Spanish conquest, was nursed back to life by a native woman.[73]

In a certain sense, Linnaeus's focus on the milk-bearing breast was at odds with trends that found beauty (though not necessarily salvation) above all in the virginal breast. In both Greek and Christian traditions, the ideal breast was an unused one, small, firm, and spherical; the process of milk swelling the breast was thought to deform it. Mythical female figures—the goddesses Artemis and Aphrodite, the martial Amazons (who supposedly burned away one

---

FIG. 2.4. Frontispiece to Linnaeus's *Fauna Svecica* (1746), featuring a Diana *polymastos*. Linnaeus's Diana is relatively modest with only four breasts; earlier depictions often featured twenty-eight or more breasts, sometimes encircling her entire upper body. Diana's breasts, spouting water, also became a favorite motif for fountains (those at Villa d'Este, Tivoli, for example). (Sign.: Lv 11 575.) By permission of the Staatsbibliothek zu Berlin—Preußischer Kulturbesitz.

breast so that their bows would lie flat against their chests), and the nursing mother of Christ—were all virgins.[74] Of all the female Virtues, only Charity possessed a nonvirginal body: infants drank maternal bounty, love, and humility from her breasts.[75]

The classic aesthetic ideal of the firm, unused breast was indeed realized in the bodies of many medieval and early modern upper- and middle-class European women who avoided the burden of suckling their own children.[76] François Clouet's painting of Henri II's mistress, Diane de Poitiers, naked in her bath, contrasts the smallness of her classic, rosy bosom to the swollen breasts of the wet nurse suckling a child in the background (nurses' nipples were said to "grow black" with overuse and old age).[77] Wealthy women in Europe bore children but most often did not nurse them. For this task, they employed women who were considered closer to nature: peasants and, in overseas colonies, native and Negro women ("often but one remove above a brute," in the words of one observer).[78] Even when, late in the eighteenth century, fashionable women did for a while nurse their infants, the shape and size of the breast was at issue. Moderately sized, nicely oval breasts with small but protuberant nipples were thought to produce better milk than large, pendulous breasts.[79]

Ideals of the breast, however, changed over time. After roughly the 1750s, the maternal breast vied for a while with the virginal for cultural preeminence. Barbara Gelphi has traced the stunning way in which the maternal breast was eroticized in late-eighteenth-century medical literature. Male physicians, including Erasmus Darwin, described in rapturous prose the sensuous pleasures experienced by nursing infants. (Darwin went so far as to attribute to the curvaceous breast filled with milk the origins of the human idea of beauty—an idea impressed on the senses of the infant.) Medical eroticization of the maternal breast paralleled changing fashions in women's clothing, which by the end of the century

---

FIG. 2.5. *Sapientia* (the personification of wisdom) suckling two philosophers. From a fifteenth-century German manuscript, reproduced in Lieselotte Möller, "Nährmutter Weisheit," *Deutsche Vierteljahrsschrift* 24 (1950), fig. 2, facing p. 351.

were designed to expose the full shape of the breast and nipple. Gelphi argues that this new fashion was as much cultivated by women as imposed upon them. While, for legislators, the breast came to guarantee women's disenfranchisement (see below), women, adopting Rousseau's vocabulary of the new domesticity, flaunted their breasts to celebrate their newfound power to nurture the future sons of the state (a power, Gelphi emphasizes, that was restricted to the confines of the home).[80]

Colonial relations also affected perceptions of the breast. Late nineteenth-century anthropologists classified breasts by beauty in the same way that they measured skulls for intelligence (FIG. 2.6). The ideal breast—for all races—was once again young and virginal. Europeans preferred the compact "hemispherical" type, found, it was said, only among whites and Asians. The much-maligned breasts of African (especially Hottentot) women were dismissed as flabby and pendulous, similar to the udders of goats (see chapter 5).[81] When women of African descent were portrayed sympathetically, they were typically shown having firm, spherical breasts, as in John Stedman's illustration of his fifteen-year-old mulatto mistress and later his wife, Joanna.[82] For Charles White, the Manchester physician and notorious racist, the hallmark of European superiority was found on the bosom of European women:

> In what quarter of the globe shall we find the blush that over-spreads the soft features of the beautiful women of Europe, that emblem of modesty, of delicate feelings, and of sense? . . . Where, except on the bosom of the European woman, two such plump and snowy white hemispheres, tipt with vermillion?[83]

Thus Linnaeus's fixation on the female mammae, though new to the zoological tradition, emerged from deep cultural roots. It is hard to say how aware the Protestant Linnaeus was of the extent to which he was drawing from these broader images and cultural practices (many of them Catholic), which we can recognize today in his work. As a university-educated man he was well versed in both the classics and Scripture, and his use of the multibreasted Diana in the frontispiece to his *Fauna Svecica* reveals at least some familiarity

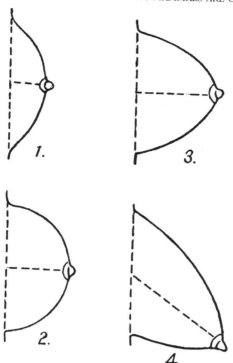

FIG. 2.6. Breast shapes among humans from Hermann Ploss, Max Bartels, and Paul Bartels's *Woman: An Historical Gynecological and Anthropological Compendium*, ed. Eric Dingwell (St. Louis: C. V. Mosby Company, 1936), vol. 1, p. 399. The first is described as "bowl-shaped," the second is "hemispherical" (characteristic of whites and Asians, and identified by the authors as beautiful), the third "conical," and the fourth (found primarily in blacks) "elongated," as in "the udder of the goat," with nipples pointed downward.

with these traditions, which may help to explain, at least in part, the easy acceptance of his innovation both within science and the broader culture.

Gender Politics in Taxonomy

Europeans' fascination with the female breast provided a receptive climate for Linnaeus's innovation. But more immediate political concerns compelled him to focus scientific attention on the mammae. His scientific vision arose alongside and in step with important political trends in the eighteenth century—the restructuring of both child care and women's lives as mothers, wives, and citizens. Despite the Enlightenment credo that all "men" were by nature equal, middle-class women were not to become fully enfranchised citizens or professionals in the state, but newly empowered mothers within the home.

Most directly, Linnaeus joined the ongoing campaign to abolish the ancient custom of wet-nursing.[84] The eighteenth century was the heyday of wet-nursing. More Europeans than ever before—including not just aristocrats and wealthy merchants but farmers, clergy, and artisans—sent their children to the countryside to be nursed. By the 1780s, Paris and Lyon were sending up to 90 percent of their children to wet nurses.[85] Although wet-nursing had provided a solution to the problem of child-rearing for middle- and upper-class mothers and fathers, it also resulted in high infant mortality.[86] Fears began to grow that Europe's population was declining at a time when governments were looking for increased labor power to bolster military and economic expansion. Concern for increasing population was so great in Denmark, for example, that a law was passed in 1707 authorizing young women to bear as many children as possible, even if they were bastards. Joseph Raulin, physician to Louis XV of France, judged children to be "the wealth of nations, the glory of kingdoms, and the nerve and good fortune of empires."[87] The physiocrat marquis de Mirabeau traced depopulation to the neglect of mothers for their children, alongside other factors such as the concentration of property in few hands, luxury, and the decadence of agriculture.

The preservation of family and maternal duties became important matters of state.[88] For state ministers, the simplest way to increase birth rates was to reduce infant mortality by improving the training of obstetricians, midwives, and, most important, mothers. A central element in this campaign was a series of health and conduct manuals written for women by medical doctors.

In this context, Linnaeus—himself a practicing physician—prepared a dissertation against the evils of wet-nursing in 1752, just a few years before coining the term *Mammalia* and while watching his own children suckle (his wife bore seven children between 1741 and 1757). Linnaeus's work entitled "Step Nurse" (translated into French as "La nourrice marâtre, ou Dissertation sur les suites funestes du nourrissage mercénaire") sounded the themes of the Enlightenment attack on wet-nursing.[89] First and foremost, wet-nursing violated the laws of nature. Nature—herself "a tender and provident mother"—had set the course for female reproduction; digression from her laws endangered both mother and child. Linnaeus recognized (as did other physicians and some midwives) that a newborn nursed by another woman was deprived of the mother's first milk, colostrum, crucial for purging the child of meconium. He also warned that, because most nurses came from the poorest classes, they ate fatty foods, drank too much alcohol, were riddled with pox and venereal disease—all of which produced unhealthy, if not lethal, milk. He also emphasized that "forcing the milk" back might prove harmful to the mother. Uterine contractions after birth forced the voluminous humors associated with pregnancy to flow toward the breasts; if these humors did not emerge as milk, the woman might fall ill. For Linnaeus, the laws of nature thus dictated the road to health for both mother and child.

In this 1752 pamphlet, Linnaeus also foreshadowed his subsequent nomenclature by contrasting the barbarity of women who deprived their children of mother's milk with the gentle care of great breasts—the whale, the fearsome lioness, and fierce tigress—who willingly offer their young the breast.[90] The idea that women should follow the example of beasts was a common feature of anti-wet-nursing literature flooding Europe.[91] Charles Whitlaw put the matter succinctly in his *New Medical Discoveries, with a Defence of the Linnaean Doctrines*:

> A great number of children are born of parents who think it below their dignity to take care of them, and trust the important charge to a hireling. If we search nature throughout, we cannot find any equal to this. Were animals to bring up their young by proxy, they would share the same fate as the human species.[92]

Appealing to natural law and order, the French midwife Marie-Angelique Anel le Robours pleaded with women to follow the "animal instinct" that prompts a mother to care for her young immediately after birth. Anel le Robours admonished mothers to disregard the wishes of husbands, who sought to rid the house of troublesome infants and to cultivate instead the "superior attachment that animals have for their young." She also advised women to disregard the advice of midwives who failed to recognize the value of colostrum (it was customary for women to wait twenty-eight hours after childbirth before nursing). Infants, just like other small animals, Anel le Robours explained, will search for the breast immediately after birth.[93]

These and other critiques of baby farming went a long way toward countering the ignorance and abuses surrounding wet-nursing. Babies in this period had a much better chance of surviving when nursed by their mothers. The anonymous author of *The Ladies Dispensatory* may have exaggerated, though, when she charged that sending a child out to a wet nurse was little better than exposing it to die in the street.[94] More plausible were the reports of abuses, especially in France, where nurses desperate for pay often took in more nurslings than they could nourish adequately.[95] At the same time many of the attacks on wet-nursing also reiterated age-old myths and superstitions. Linnaeus, for example, cautioned that the character of the upper-class child could easily be corrupted by the milk of lower-class nurses. Using examples drawn from Erasmus, he blamed the bitter, wicked milk of nurses for Nero's addiction to alcohol and for Caligula's tyranny.[96]

While authors of these pamphlets showed genuine concern for the well-being of mothers and children of their own classes, they seldom considered the evils of baby farming for the "lower classes of mankind" (as one influential voice in the anti-wet-nursing movement called them).[97] Children of wet nurses were often neglected or even "disposed of" (for a small fee, no questions asked).[98]

The attempt to abolish wet-nursing was tied to another aspect of the restructuring of reproduction in the eighteenth century—the takeover by male physicians of traditional female domains. The story of the demise of midwives and rise of gynecologists and obstetricians is well known.[99] The endeavor by university-trained physicians to professionalize women's health care (and in so doing to drive traditional female practitioners from the field) extended also to the management of newborns. The English physician William Cadogan, perhaps the most emphatic on this point, encouraged fathers, who often considered breast-feeding something low and degrading, to have their children nursed under their "own eye." Nursing, in his view, should not be one of "the mysteries of the *Bona Dea*, from which men are excluded." Supervision of the care of children had been "too long fatally left to the management of women, who cannot suppose to have proper knowledge to fit them for such a task, notwithstanding they look upon it to be their own province." The "grandmothers" should be moved aside, along with their herbs, roots, and other traditional practices.[100] The Jamaican judge Edward Long also admonished white ladies in the colonies to give up the barbarous and corrupting custom of handing their children over to "negro or mulatto wet nurses." Mothers of European descent were encouraged to take up the agreeable task of nursing their own infants, "so consonant to the laws of nature."[101]

For the enlightened savant, the laws of nature dictated more than the rules for reproductive regimes: they also dictated social order. Medical authority, the legal system, and popular literature worked together to create new interest in maternal breast-feeding. As prescribed in Jean-Jacques Rousseau's influential *Emile*, breast-feeding became fashionable among French upper-class women for a short period in the late eighteenth century.[102] In France and Germany, leading medical doctors advocated laws that would force healthy women to nurse their own infants. The French National Convention decreed in 1793 that only mothers who nursed their own children would be eligible for state aid (women in poor health were exempted).[103] Similar laws were put into effect in Prussia in 1794, just a few years after Frederick the Great installed a modern version of Diana of the Ephesians in his Potsdam garden.[104]

Authors of anti-wet-nursing literature—including Linnaeus, Cadogan, Rousseau, and Anel le Robours—were highly moralistic about returning women to their rightful place as loving and caring mothers. This, despite the fact that Rousseau placed his own five children in foundling homes, not even bothering to record their sex or dates of birth.[105] Women's attempts to contravene the laws of nature were seen as a matter of vanity. Cadogan prevailed upon every woman to give up "a little of the beauty of her breast" to feed her young. Linnaeus charged that women only pretended to be unable to breast-feed and ridiculed their many "excuses": that they did not have enough milk, or could not be deprived of fluids precious to their own health, or were overloaded with domestic affairs. The real reason for such a reluctance, Linnaeus imagined, was a disinclination to deprive husbands of the pleasures of marriage—a characteristic, he noted, of all quadrupeds (it was thought that nursing mothers should refrain from sexual intercourse). Rousseau, not so sanguine on this point, charged that wet nurses freed upper-class mothers to return to the gay entertainments of the city, not necessarily their husbands' beds.[106]

Returning to nature and its laws was seen as the surest way to end corruption and regenerate the state, morally as well as economically. Rousseau, the era's self-appointed spokesman for nature, saw the refusal of mothers to nurse as the source of national depravity. "Everything follows successively from this first depravity. The whole moral order degenerates; naturalness is extinguished in all hearts." The bond between mother and child created by maternal nursing was idealized as the cement of civil society, fostering love of sons for mothers, returning husbands to wives. The infant was imagined to imbibe with the mother's milk her noble character, her love and virtue. "Let mothers deign to nurse their children," Rousseau preached, "morals will reform themselves, nature's sentiments will be awakened in every heart, the state will be repeopled."[107] For the enlightened of Europe, the breast symbolized the synthesis of nature and society, the bond between the private and public worlds.[108]

It is remarkable that in the heady days of the French Revolution, when revolutionaries marched behind the martial and barebreasted Liberty,[109] the maternal breast became nature's sign that women belonged only in the home. Delegates to the French National Convention used the breast as a natural sign that women should be barred from citizenship and the wielding of public power. In this case, "the breasted ones" were to be confined to the home. In denying women political power, Pierre-Gaspard Chaumette, *procurer* of the Paris Commune, asked indignantly:

> Since when is it permitted to abandon one's sex? Since when is it decent for women to forsake the pious cares of their households and the cribs of their children, coming instead to public places, to hear speeches in the galleries and senate? Is it to men that nature confided domestic cares? Has she given us breasts to feed our children?[110]

This message was embodied in the "Festival of Unity and Indivisibility" of 1793, celebrating the first anniversary of the Republic. Jacques-Louis David's carefully orchestrated festival featured a "Fountain of Regeneration," built on the ruins of the Bastille, the symbol of absolutism (FIG. 2.7). As described in the popular press, eighty-six (male) deputies to the National Convention drank joyfully from the spouting breasts of "Nature" personified as Isis, the Egyptian goddess of fertility.[111] While the male deputies publicly drank the maternal "milk" of national renewal from the breasts of the colossal Isis, exemplary republican mothers quietly reenacted the scene, giving their virtuous milk to future citizens of the state.

The year 1793 marked the fateful repression of women's demands for active citizenship and also, as Lynn Hunt has shown, a turning point in republican images of women. When publicly represented, women were no longer cast as the strident Marianne, the symbol of Liberty, but increasingly in motherly roles. Festivals featured parades of pregnant women; women in ceremonies, such as the Festival of the Supreme Being of 1794, were all wives and mothers, many pressing nurslings to their breasts.[112]

OVERLEAF: FIG. 2.7. The "Fountain of Regeneration" by Jacques-Louis David, the famous eighteenth-century French painter. From Charles Monnet, *Les principales journées de la Révolution* (Paris, 1838). Spencer Collection. By permission of the New York Public Library, Astor, Lenox, and Tilden Foundations.

72

Dessiné par Monnet J.

La Fontaine de

Sur les débris de la

Régénération

...stille, le 10 Aout 1793.

Gravé par Helman

I should perhaps interject here a word about class. Notions of republican motherhood and sexual complementarity—important doctrines of female sexuality developed in this period—became prescriptive and increasingly descriptive of the lives of middle-class women, not the lives of peasant women, domestic servants, female apprentices, or artisans. Nor in the nineteenth century would these ideals apply to the lives of working-class women, though middle-class domesticity was held up to women of all classes as an ideal to emulate.[113]

Linnaeus's term *Mammalia* helped legitimize the restructuring of European society by emphasizing how natural it was for females—both human and nonhuman—to suckle and rear their own children. Linnaean systematics had sought to render nature universally comprehensible, yet the categories he devised infused nature with middle-class European notions of gender. Linnaeus saw females of all species as tender mothers, a vision he (wittingly or unwittingly) projected onto Europeans' understandings of nature.

The story of the origins of the term *Mammalia* provides yet another example of how science is not value neutral but emerges from complex cultural matrices. The term Linnaeus coined in 1758 solved the problem of how to classify the whale with its terrestrial congeners and did away with Aristotle's outmoded term *quadruped*. But, more than that, it provided a solution to the place of humankind within nature and ultimately of womankind within European culture.

3

The Gendered Ape

Of the Orangutan: It is a brute of a kind so singular, that man
cannot behold it without contemplating himself.

Georges-Louis Leclerc, comte de Buffon,
Histoire naturelle, 1749

*E*uropeans were puzzled when they first came face to face with
anthropoid apes in the seventeenth and eighteenth centuries.
The discovery of the great apes of Africa and Asia seemed to confirm
the notion of a great "chain of being," a hierarchy of creation reach-
ing from God and the angels down through man to the lowliest
worm.[1] Apes' shockingly human character emboldened naturalists
to declare them the long-sought "missing link" between humans
and animals. Were these the degenerate sons of Adam and Noah (as
Augustine had taught)? Or were they "natural man," fully human but
devoid of civilization (as Rousseau and Monboddo would conclude
years later)? Could apes through education become sufficiently cultured to take a seat in the British Parliament, as did the amiable (and
fictional) Sir Oran Haut-ton in Thomas Love Peacock's *Melincourt*?
Were they human or beast?

Scholars have long been fascinated with the distinctions between apes and humans. An enormous and popular literature has
explored whether apes have the ability to walk erect, speak, reason,
and create culture.[2] As we shall see, however, these investigations
were also highly gendered. In his intriguing portrayal of the
"Orangutan and his female," Claude-Nicolas Le Cat characterized

gender (and race) dynamics in early modern natural history (FIG. 3.1).[3] One of the few to draw a male and a female ape together, Le Cat portrays his "Ourang-outang" as a vigorous being, whose forthright gaze and open palms confront the observer. His stunningly erect penis, a sign of his virility, embodies Aristotle's belief that the ape, like the dog, has a bone in his penis. The female orang, labeled "his female," is copied from the Dutch anatomist Nicolaas Tulp's 1641 portrayal of *Homo sylvestris*. She is passive, drawn with downcast eyes, an abdomen swollen as though pregnant, with hands and feet quietly folded. The presence of a native in the background alludes to the means by which early modern natural historians gathered their specimens. European naturalists usually hired native guides, exploiting (though often at the same time discounting) their knowledge of local flora and fauna to track down and capture or kill the desired animal for exhibit in Europe. Absent from the picture is the European naturalist himself whose controlling eye binds the native, the apes, and the jungle-classical landscape (note the pedestal) as objects of common natural historic interest.

What few historians have chronicled, and what we shall explore in this chapter, is how early modern naturalists investigated the *unique characteristics of female anatomy* in their attempt to draw a distinct line between humans and apes. Female apes, most everyone agreed, shared with humans that "obscene organ of brute pleasure"—the clitoris. But did they have hymens, those highly prized anatomical guarantees of virginity? Naturalists also wanted to know if female apes menstruated, if their vaginas were angled like women's, and if so, how this affected coitus and male pleasure.

As we shall see, early accounts of anthropoid apes pouring into Europe in this period often told more about European customs than about the natural habits of apes. Rousseau recognized this general problem in his lament that as Europeans fanned out across the globe they saw little more than themselves and their own habits mirrored in nature:

> For the three or four hundred years since the inhabitants of Europe have inundated the other parts of the world and continuously published new collections of voyages and reports, I am

Planche. I.

Ourang-outang   Sa femelle

FIG. 3.1. The gendered apes. From Claude-Nicolas Le Cat, *Traité de l'existance du fluide des nerfs* (Berlin, 1753), plate 1, p. 35. (Sign.: Kz 1270.) By permission of the Staatsbibliothek zu Berlin—Preußischer Kulturbesitz.

convinced that we know no other men except the Europeans . . . ; furthermore, it appears . . . that under the pompous
name of the study of man no one does anything except study
the men of his own country.[4]

The apes stood mutely by as naturalists (in this case European and
male) ascribed to females the modesty they were hoping to find in
their own wives and daughters, and to males the wildest fantasies of
violent interspecies rape.[5]

Distinguishing Humans from Apes

Anthropocentricism continued to dominate natural history long after geocentrism had been displaced in astronomy. Copernicus dethroned humans from the center of the universe, banishing them to
a small planet circling the sun. Humankind nevertheless remained
the chief of creation, "lord of animals" on that planet.[6] Linnaeus captured these presumptions in the term *Primates*—literally, "of the
first rank"—a term he coined in 1758.[7] Though humans might be
primates, they were no longer uniquely situated just below angels:
apes, monkeys, lemurs, and bats were also considered primates.

Naturalists today recognize four distinct types of anthropoid
apes: the *orangutan* (the name first appeared in scientific literature
in 1641, though the animal described was in fact a chimpanzee); the
chimpanzee (the African term first appeared as *quimpezé* in French
texts in 1738; the English chimpanzee appeared the same year); the
gibbon (first described by Buffon); and the *gorilla* (a term introduced by the American missionary Thomas Savage in 1847, though
gorillas had been described earlier under various other names).[8] In
the seventeenth and eighteenth centuries, voyagers and naturalists
indiscriminately used the term *orangutan* (Malayan for "wild man"
or "man of the woods") with reference to the great apes of both Africa and Asia.[9] Petrus Camper in the 1780s was one of the first to distinguish the African "orangutan" (the chimpanzee) from the Asiatic
or true orangutan.[10] Great apes were also called *satyrs* (after the
creature described in ancient mythology), *pygmies* (another term of
ancient coinage, indicating that apes are a variety of the human spe-

cies), *jocko, pongo*, and various other Europeanizations of native terms.

Firsthand knowledge of the great apes was not extensive among Europeans in this period. In many cases, naturalists never set eyes on the animals they described, but drew their ideas about these creatures from the rather fanciful teachings of the ancients combined with the untrained observations of voyagers. Linnaeus, for example, never saw the "troglodytes" by which he set such store as a second species of *Homo*. It was not until the second half of the eighteenth century that a number of live animals became available in Europe. Buffon housed a chimpanzee with a liking for strawberries at the Jardin du Roi, in Paris. Petrus Camper claimed that George Edwards was the first Englishman to have seen a true orangutan, and this in the 1750s. Camper himself was unusual in procuring a large number of orangutans (eight in all, five of which he dissected) through his connection in Batavia with the East India Company, though, like other European naturalists, he knew these animals only in captivity. In the eighteenth century Europeans had not, of course, yet studied simians for long periods of time in their natural surroundings.[11]

What is striking about the apes brought to Europe in this period is that they were very young, usually only a few months old. Travelogues recount how difficult it was to take adult animals alive. Consequently most of the apes transported to Europe were captured only after their mothers had been shot. Stephen Jay Gould has pointed out (as did James Prichard before him) that the fact that so many of the apes studied by Europeans were immature served to heighten their human appearance. Young apes have many humanlike characteristics that adults eventually lose.[12]

Comparative anatomists were struck by similarities in form and figure between apes and humans. Edward Tyson, in his pioneering *Orang-Outang, sive Homo Sylvestris; or, The Anatomy of a Pygmie Compared with that of a Monkey, an Ape, and a Man* (1699), documented forty-eight ways in which his "pygmie" resembled a human, along with thirty-four ways in which it differed.[13] The French naturalist Buffon characteristically remarked in the eigh-

. century that "if figure alone is regarded, we might consider
nimal [the generic orang] as the first among apes, or the last
ng men."[14] Montaigne, by contrast, rejected the human-animal
lism and suggested that there was more difference between any
two given men than between any given man and a beast. Nonetheless the great apes held a very special place in the European imagination. They seemed to confirm the notion of hierarchy and continuity in nature. Humans—part brute, part angel—were thought to
link the mortal world to the divine. Might apes be human or the link
between humans and brutes, just as asbestos linked minerals and
plants; the *Hydra* (water polyp) joined plants and animals; and the
flying squirrel linked birds and quadrupeds?[15]

Carl Linnaeus jolted the scholarly world when, in 1735, he
placed humans in the same order with monkeys and sloths (see
chapter 2). He shook that world further in 1758 when he declared
to have found among the great apes a second human species—
Homo troglodytes—those golden-eyed nocturnal cave dwellers
whom Buffon dismissed as albino Africans. Concerning his radical
reordering of nature, Linnaeus remarked:

> I know full well what great difference exists between man and
> beast when viewed from a moral point of view: man is the only
> creature with a rational and immortal soul. . . . If viewed, how-
> ever, from the point of view of natural history and considering
> only the body, I can discover scarcely any mark by which man
> can be distinguished from the apes. . . . Neither in the face nor
> in the feet, nor in the upright gait, nor in any other aspect of his
> external structure does man differ from the apes.[16]

It is hard for us today to recapture the excitement and confusion of naturalists as they tried to order nature. Linnaeus, for his
part, never flagged in his efforts to confirm the existence of the
Homo troglodytes, whom he imagined to have descended from the
Atlas tribe of cave dwellers described by the Roman naturalist Pliny
the Elder. Linnaeus was heartened by the supposed sightings of this
species reported by several of his countrymen. He also sent one of
his many students to London to investigate the news of a possible
specimen—a female—being exhibited in London in 1758. He

wanted to know: Did she have a clitoris and well-developed "nym-phae" (labia)? Did she have the *membrana nictitans*, that character-istic feature of the troglodyte eyelid? Linnaeus persuaded the queen to commission the Swedish East India Company to search the world over for a specimen of the *Homo troglodytes*.[17]

Few natural historians went as far as Linnaeus, actually ranking one type of ape (his troglodytes) in the same genus as humans, though Rousseau and the eccentric Lord Monboddo also argued that apes were remnants of "natural man." Most naturalists main-tained that while apes might bear human characteristics, they cer-tainly were not human.[18] Naturalists pondered an enormous array of possibilities for the nature and source of human uniqueness (and superiority). Was the human uniquely a political animal, a laughing animal, a tool-making animal, a religious animal, a cooking animal, or an animal capable of possessing private property? All of these were put forward, at one time or another, as the *sine qua non* of hu-man existence. Debates concerning how nearly apes approximated humans were wide ranging, but four questions pervaded discus-sion: Can they think? Can they speak? Can they walk erect? Can they create culture?[19]

The belief that humans exhibit a superior form of reason can be traced to the ancient world. According to Aristotle, the human soul comprised three elements: the nutritive soul, which humans shared with vegetables; the sensitive soul, shared with animals; and the rational soul, peculiar to humankind. In the Middle Ages, schol-ars raised humans to a point midway between angels and beasts. Humans shared reason and intellect with the angels, body and senses with the animals. Augustine of Hippo thus saw reason as a God-given gift setting humans apart from animals.[20]

Apes were rarely seen, however, as completely devoid of moral and intellectual abilities. Albertus Magnus, the thirteenth-century cleric, gave as proof of simian good judgment the fact that when a female ape sees a human baby or the young of some other animal, she will not attempt to nurse it but will lead it to the breast of its proper mother.[21] In the eighteenth century, comparative anatomists such as Tyson believed that the brain of the orang closely resembled that of man.[22] The question then arose: Does mind reduce to matter as René Descartes taught? Do apes have the ability to reason? John Locke, who derived all ideas from sensation, denied that apes can reason like men. Locke similarly denied that they possess the "power of abstraction," of comparing ideas and generalizing from their experience.[23] David Hume granted animals the power of experimental reasoning, but for Hume experimental reasoning was merely a type of instinct, not conscious reflection upon experience.[24]

Most naturalists concluded that, despite certain bodily similarities, apes failed to measure up to humans in terms of mind.[25] Tyson and Buffon were typical in asserting that organized matter could never produce the nobler faculties of the human mind: there must be some higher principle. Buffon called it "divine spirit."[26] Johann Blumenbach, echoing Linnaeus, proclaimed: "All with one voice declare that here is the highest and best prerogative of man, the use of reason"—and it was reason that made him "lord and master of the rest of the animals."[27] Margaret Cavendish, the Duchess of Newcastle, one of the few women in seventeenth-century England to write boldly and prolifically about natural philosophy, followed Montaigne in suggesting that beasts—and even vegetables and minerals—have their own types of reason and language, and that man's presumed sovereignty is only hubris.[28]

Speech was another traditional mark of humanity. The French Cardinal de Polignac reportedly approached an orangutan on display at the Jardin du Roi, saying: "Speak, and I will baptize you."[29] Some animals did, of course, speak. Cardinal Ascanius had a parrot that could recite the entire Christian creed.[30] Some naturalists claimed that apes, too, were capable of speech. The French physician Claude Perrault demonstrated in the second half of the seventeenth century that their speech organs were identical to those of humans.[31] Linnaeus claimed that the *Homo troglodytes* expressed itself by a kind of hissing (FIG. 3.2). In his dissertation on the "Anthropomorpha," Linnaeus affirmed that troglodytes could speak, although he claimed that their language was guttural and difficult even for *Homo sapiens* to learn. In European languages they could master only "yes" and "no."[32] Voyagers commonly reported that na-

Amœn. Acad. vol. VI.

1. TROGLODYTA *Bonti.*   *2.* LUCIFER *Aldrovandi.*   *3.* SATYRUS *Tulpii.*   *4.* PYGMÆUS *Edwardi.*

Joh. Neubauer sculp.

FIG. 3.2. Linnaeus's *Anthropomorpha* (humanlike figures). The female *Homo troglodytes* (caveman or night person) on the left represents Linnaeus's second species of human. This drawing is taken from Bontius's illustration of an orangutan (compare fig. 3.8) but omits "the Hottentot apron" that Linnaeus describes in the text (p. 73). The figure second from the left represents *Homo caudatus* (tailed man), also a creature belonging to the human genus, but cruder than *Homo troglodytes*. The other two figures portray apes. From Carl Linnaeus, "Anthropomorpha," respondent C. E. Hoppius (1760), in *Amoenitates academicae* (Erlangen, 1789), vol. 6, plate 1. By permission of the Wellcome Institute Library, London.

tive peoples believed certain apes were capable of speech but remained forever silent for fear of being forced to work and live in bondage.[33]

Linnaeus, Rousseau, and Monboddo, however, turned the tables, claiming that language was not natural even for humans. Linnaeus gave as evidence the "wild people" (the boy who lived among oxen in Bamberg, the boy who lived with sheep in Ireland, the wild girl of Champagne), none of whom could speak. For Rousseau, language was an invention of human society—one of the things that made humans weak and effeminate.[34] Monboddo noted that some people were mute but for that reason no less human; the orangutan in his view was perfectly rational and human, eloquent in its silence. In Peacock's novel, Sir Oran Haut-ton's lack of speech proved to be an asset as a member of Parliament, giving him the reputation of a profound thinker.

Most naturalists, however, agreed that apes could not speak. Buffon, who sought to drive a wider wedge between humans and animals, denied that there ever was a time in the state of nature when humans did not think or speak. Even if "natural man" were devoid of speech, he argued, mothers would create language in the process of nursing and nurturing their children. Buffon reported that he had seen several orangutans and wondered if these were the animals that Linnaeus had in mind when he described his *Homo troglodytes*, but they neither spoke nor expressed themselves by hissing. "For this reason," he wrote, "I suspect the truth of the description of this *Homo nocturnus*. I even doubt his existence." Buffon suspected that the creature Linnaeus described was an albino African, whom voyagers had superficially examined and falsely described.[35] Blumenbach, too, held that humans alone possess speech. Apes, he acknowledged, possess the language of the affections—often weeping from sadness—but humans alone possess the voice of reason.[36]

Since Plato, erect posture had also been seen as setting humans apart from other animals. In the *Timaeus*, Plato explained that the soul, located in the upper part of the body, drew our bodies upward toward our kindred spirits in heaven, forcing our bodies upright.[37] In the eighteenth century, Rousseau suggested that humans were naturally bipedal because of the placement of the female breast; the breast of woman was placed in such a way that she must hold her child to nurse, leaving her only two legs for walking.[38] Apes, too, seemed to have a claim to erect posture. The overwhelming majority of illustrations of anthropoid apes in the seventeenth and eighteenth centuries showed them either standing erect or seated in a human manner. Tyson apparently believed that his "pygmie" (actually a chimp) walked on its knuckles only because it was sick; in good health, he believed, it would have walked erect and that was how he had it drawn (FIG. 3.3).[39] While it is true that apes can walk on two legs for short periods of time, naturalists in the eighteenth century tended to exaggerate this capacity. Jean Audebert criticized the overly erect posture of the male chimpanzee shown in Buffon's *Histoire naturelle*, saying that the engraver "tried very hard to make him a man."[40] Pictorially, orangutans and chimpanzees were shown clutching walking sticks, ropes, and other devices to suggest the difficulties they had standing erect. Blumenbach, however, proposed that apes should not be seen as either quadrupeds or bipeds but as *Quadrumana* (four-handed), for their hind feet were furnished not with a big toe but with a second thumb. This reflected the fact, he thought, that their natural home was in the trees.[41]

Central in this quest to determine whether apes were human was ascertaining to what extent they were civil and civilizable. In the mid-seventeenth century voyagers began reporting how apes "counterfeit the countenance, the fashions, and the actions of men"—stories that were told and retold throughout the eighteenth century.[42] It seemed significant to Europeans that these beasts had delicate manners. Tulp's *Homo sylvestris* drank from a water glass no less delicately than would have been seen in "the court of princes." Even Buffon, who argued that apes could be tamed but never cultured, offered the following eyewitness report of an orang:

> I have seen this animal present his hand to visitors and walk gravely along with them as if he were a part of the company. I have seen him sit down for dinner, unfold his napkin, wipe his lips, use a spoon and a fork, pour his drink into a glass, and toast his drinking companions. When invited to take tea, he brought a cup and saucer, placed them on the table, put in sugar, poured out the tea, and allowed it to cool before drinking it. All these actions he performed, without any other encouragement than a sign or signal from his master, and often of his own accord.[43]

Though some suspected that these animals had been taught such behavior so that they could be exhibited in shows, M. de la Brosse reported that European table manners were instinctual. These apes, he assured his reader, had not been trained to eat with a knife, fork,

or spoon. It also seemed significant to Europeans that apes occasionally enjoyed a glass of wine. The orang was also said to sleep like a "most gentle man," covering its body with a spread. By another report, apes along with various sorts of monkeys had served the King of Bengala as coachmen, valets-de-chambre, and pages.[44]

Another mark of culture attributed to orangutans by Europeans was their deep affection for one another. Often brought to Europe in pairs, males and females were seen as developing the same affectionate relationships as those newly idealized between husbands and wives. The eighteenth century saw the rise of what Lawrence Stone has described as "affective individualism," a move away from patriarchal rule within the family and toward equality between husbands and wives which encouraged warmer affective relations between spouses.[45] Naturalists were quick to attribute this newfound romance to simian couples. In one report, a female sickened during transport and died; her male companion refused to eat and followed her to a watery grave within two days. Monboddo suggested that such affection engendered in chimpanzees a deep sense of justice, as illustrated by the story of a male chimpanzee whose "wife" was shot by a villager. The chimpanzee pursued the offender into his house, then seized and dragged him to the place where his wife lay dead. The chimp would not let go of the man until shot by the villagers.[46]

Linnaeus, who found so much that was humanlike in apes, remarked that ape parents—both mother and father—loved their children dearly, carrying them tenderly in their arms and pressing them to their bosoms in the same way that humans do. The English writer Priscilla Wakefield claimed that they mourned their dead.

FIG. 3.3. Edward Tyson's *Homo sylvestris* (a chimpanzee, though he called it an orangutan) with walking stick. Apes—usually males—were often drawn carrying sticks, indicating the extra help the animal needed to maintain an upright stance. The stick also represented the humanlike ability of apes to wield weapons. From Edward Tyson, *Orang-Outang, sive Homo Sylvestris; or, The Anatomy of a Pygmie Compared with that of a Monkey, an Ape, and a Man* (London, 1699), fig. 1. By permission of the National Library of Medicine.

The generic orang was commonly said to build huts and villages, to recognize kings as rulers, and to enjoy games and pastimes. Monboddo assigned particular significance to the fact that apes used weapons: in his mind, the ability to strike enemies with sticks made them humanlike.[47] Blumenbach, ever the skeptic, gave no credence to these stories of "cultured" apes and, unlike many of his colleagues, did not include such accounts in his descriptions of apes.

Females of the Species

While female naturalists were a rare breed, female apes were not. Of the four well-known seventeenth-century illustrations of apes, three are of females. Voyagers attempted when possible to supply Europe with both a male and a female of each species. In some cases, naturalists simply chose to illustrate a female. Jacob Bontius, a Dutch physician working in Batavia (now Djakarta), had observed both a male and a female "Orang Outang" and elected to draw the female (we aren't told why). Tyson, by contrast, had available to him both a male and a female chimpanzee but chose to dissect and describe the male. In any case, Europeans had ample females to study.

Debates concerning the consanguinity of anthropoid apes and humans centered on reason, speech, bipedalism, and so forth. These differences were discussed without attention to sex. Naturalists in this period, however, also studied female apes, thinking that something in their physiology might pinpoint that elusive boundary between humans and simians. When naturalists' attention turned to females, only sexual traits were considered. This was characteristic of European scientific studies of females—human or animal. Since Aristotle, the female had been studied only insofar as she deviated from the male. As Rousseau wrote in his influential *Emile*, woman is man in everything except that which is connected with her sex.[48] This way of thinking, where the male constituted the universal subject and the female a sexual subset, pervaded natural history in the eighteenth century. Females across the kingdoms of nature were viewed as primarily sexual beings. As we will see in eighteenth-century studies of race, when females were compared across cultures (which was rarely), invariably at issue was some aspect of their sexuality, the peculiarities of their breasts or genitalia, parturition, or suckling (see chapter 5). Thus it is not surprising that studies of female anatomy designed to reveal the exact boundary between humans and apes interrogated aspects of their sexuality.

Significantly, comparative studies of human and simian males did not focus so decidedly on sexuality. Blumenbach did once suggest that men were the only animals with nocturnal emissions of superfluous semen; Buffon noted at one point that the organs of generation in apes and men are similar except that the ape's prepuce has no frenum.[49] Tyson even compared the sexual organs of men and apes, but (except perhaps for Camper) none of these observers looked primarily to these organs for marks distinguishing humans from apes.[50]

By and large, female sexual organs were studied in order to highlight the animal side of human life. In some instances woman's sexual organs were said to link her directly to apes. Aristotle asserted that the genitals of female apes exactly resembled those of human females. Male apes' genitals, by contrast, he declared were doglike and not at all like men's. These pronouncements remained unquestioned until 1676, when Perrault showed that the ape's penis lacks the bone present in the dog's.[51]

Debates about human uniqueness in the female came to focus on key sexual characters: menstruation, the clitoris, the breasts, and the hymen—that celebrated "veil of modesty."[52] Menstruation had long puzzled male naturalists. Aristotle postulated that catamenia are more abundant in women than in other animals, just as semen ejected by men is more abundant in proportion to their size than in other animals. Aristotle believed that excess bodily fluids were emitted as sperm in men and menstrual blood in women because humans, unlike animals, had no superfluous parts, such as excess hair or outgrowths of bone, horn, or tusks, absorbing those fluids.[53] Pliny held that woman was the only menstruating animal, though this did not necessarily ennoble her. Women alone had "moles" in their wombs regulating the flow. Contact with menstrual blood was said to turn new wine sour, destroy crops, kill bees, and drive dogs mad.[54] Hildegard von Bingen, the twelfth-century abbess, was one of the few in this early period to assert (correctly) that female apes also menstruated—information she had probably gleaned from hermetic writings such as the *Hieroglyphica* of Horapollo.[55]

Eighteenth-century naturalists, more influenced by Pliny than by Hildegard, were inclined to think that apes and monkeys did not menstruate. Linnaeus, who observed his beloved *Simia diana* at the Swedish Royal Palace Zoo, was said to have believed that she menstruated from the tip of her tail.[56] Blumenbach, by contrast, imagined that apes have no menses. After twenty years of close observation, he concluded that a few of them sometimes suffer from uterine hemorrhages but that these occur at no regular interval. By his account, the only reason that people thought these females menstruate was that owners of circuses and coffeehouses, where apes were displayed, advertised their humanness in this regard in order to draw larger crowds. Buffon was one of the few to recognize that female apes do menstruate periodically—a characteristic, he emphasized, common to both women and female apes with naked buttocks.[57]

Blumenbach's errors regarding simian menstruation may have resulted from the fact that females often do not menstruate in captivity or when poorly nourished. (Buffon noted the case, for example, of a female ape who had menstruated regularly until attacked with scurvy.) Blumenbach's errors may also have arisen from his desire to draw a strict distinction between apes and humans in order to head off a growing tendency to pronounce the peoples of Africa, Asia, and the Americas lesser humans. Early reports from America had insisted that native women do not menstruate and for this reason belonged to a lower class of humans (see chapter 4). At the same time, the French revolutionary and abolitionist, Abbé Grégoire, cited Blumenbach's observation that female apes do not menstruate as physiological evidence that Africans are human and not brutes.[58]

These naturalists—Linnaeus, Buffon, and Blumenbach—had sought to answer a simple empirical question regarding simian menstruation. Not so Charles White, the distinguished Manchester physician and notorious racist, who used the quantity of menstrual flow to rank females along a single chain of being. White made two assumptions: that a copious flow is uniquely human, and that females menstruate more heavily in warm climates than in cold (eighteen ounces in Greece, for example, and only two in Lapland). When investigating the menses of African women and apes he found, however, that despite the warmth of their homelands, "Negresses" menstruated very little, apes and baboons even less, monkeys still less, and some types of monkeys not at all.[59] White resolved this seeming contradiction by judging that a more general law held in this case—namely, that the quantity of flow decreased as one descended the scale of being. Thus he concluded that European women, distinguished by copious menses, were more human than African women or female apes. For White, one's rank in this bloody business determined one's moral worth.

A related question was commonly posed in this period: Do female apes have clitorises? Linnaeus remarked in a footnote that apes lacked clitorises, though they were in other regards quite humanlike.[60] Apart from Linnaeus, most everyone agreed that female apes shared with humans this "instrument of venery." Tyson, who never dissected a female ape, reported that clitorises were extremely brutelike in apes, being larger and more visible than in women.[61] Blumenbach, who devoted many years to this question, found that in mammals clitorises were frequently quite large, especially in certain types of lemurs. The most prodigious clitoris sighted—fifty-two feet in length—belonged to a beached baleen whale in Holland, which Blumenbach examined on a cold winter day in 1791.[62]

Male naturalists also investigated female mammae. Aristotle had noted that apes are similar to humans in having pectoral teats (not ventral like other animals).[63] Indeed, Linnaeus used two pectoral mammae as one of the identifying characteristics of primates (and may for this reason have included bats in this order).[64] Though female apes resembled humans in this respect, naturalists considered their breasts undesirably flabby and pendulous, resembling those of Hottentots. One of the earliest drawings of an anthropoid

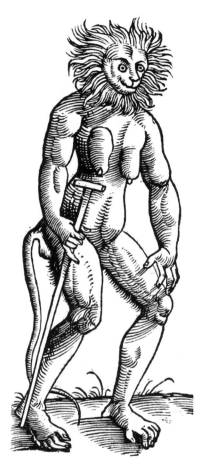

FIG. 3.4. Conrad Gesner's depiction of an ape, said to resemble a human in its face, knees, and certain unspecified "secret parts." Despite its long tail, this animal was taken to be an ape. From Conrad Gesner, *Historiae animalium* (Tiguri, 1551), vol. 1, p. 970. Courtesy of the Clendening History of Medicine Library.

ape depicted her as having prominent, pendulous breasts—this despite the fact that the breasts of these females are quite unremarkable (see FIG. 3.4). Many naturalists simply assumed that the mammae of all animals are udderlike; Tyson, so careful in other matters, mistakenly described the modest mammae of the female orangutans illustrated by Bontius and Tulp as "pendulous."[65]

It was the hymen, though, among all distinctively human characteristics that most intrigued naturalists. This uniquely female
piece of anatomy was named after a male god, Hymen—the Greek
god of marriage.[66] For centuries, the moral worth of unmarried
women was determined by this thin membrane stretching across
the opening of the vagina, sign and symbol of virginal virtue. Its significance was so great that plants, too, were said to have hymen—a
fine delicate skin enclosing the flowers while still buds, then burst-
ing as the flower opened.[67] Despite its cultural significance, men of
science could not even agree about whether the hymen actually existed, in humans or in apes.[68] Buffon believed it to be a figment of
men's imaginations. Preoccupied in being first in so many things,
men (by Buffon's account) had made a physical object of virginity,
which properly speaking was a virtue existing only in a pure heart.
Buffon cited anatomical authorities on both sides but finally concluded that true defloration came when superstition and outmoded
ceremonies submitted young girls to the groping hands of ignorant
matrons or voyeuristic physicians.[69]

Blumenbach, after examining female apes, monkeys, and an
elephant in Germany, concluded that the hymen was something
possessed by the human but by no other animal, even if these animals remained virgins. While both animals and humans had clitorises, only women were blessed with a hymen, "the guardian of
their chastity." In the first edition of his great *De generis humani
varietate nativa* (1755), Blumenbach accepted Haller's judgment
that the hymen had been granted to womankind to serve a moral,
rather than a physical, purpose. By the third edition, written twenty
years later, Blumenbach found this moralistic reasoning weak and
did not attempt to explain the presence of the hymen.[70]

For the conservative French physician Jacques Moreau de la
Sarthe, author of the two-volume *Histoire naturelle de la femme*
(1803), the hymen was very real indeed, but because it is so thin
many anatomists simply had never seen it. Moreau also pointed out
that it could easily be destroyed if a girl wiped herself too vigorously
or if she (intentionally or not) contracted "the habits of Lesbians,"
disrupting her organs in solitary pleasures.[71] Moreau reported that

he had seen hymens in female fetuses and also in two very old nuns, neither of whom had ever suffered the slightest attack on her virginity. Moreau, however, did not believe that the state of the hymen accurately reflected female morals. In some girls the hymen was easily destroyed at an early age through no mischief on their part. Other women could enjoy sexual intercourse with several men and emerge with hymens fully intact, thus appearing to be virgins.

By the end of the eighteenth century, then, male naturalists had identified at least four characteristics unique to human females. One was the presence of the hymen (though Cuvier claimed to have found it in northern manatees, and analogous structures in mares and asses, otters, dogs, cats, ruminants, and hyenas[72]); another was the angle of the vagina. In other animals the axis of the vaginal canal lies parallel to the abdomen; in women this "vestibule of the sanctuary," as Moreau called it, tilts as a result of erect posture.[73] This results in humankind's unique versatility in copulation. Blumenbach, uncharacteristically eloquent on this point, concluded from Leonardo da Vinci's anatomical drawings that humans, though capable of copulating in the manner of beasts, prefer to partake of these "soft delights" face to face. (Blumenbach also commented on how the female vagina uniquely accommodates the male member.) Moreau and Blumenbach pointed to a third characteristic unique to female humans—their great suffering in parturition, another consequence of erect posture. The final characteristic pertaining to women was the position of the opening of the urethra; in beasts it opens backward into the vagina; in women it opens between the lips of the labia.[74] In sum, for eighteenth-century male naturalists, that which distinguished female humans from animals was not reason, speech, or the ability to create culture, but rather distinctive forms of sexual anatomy.

Are Apes Human Hybrids?

Medieval scholastics had seen the ape as *naturae degenerantis homo* (degenerate man). According to biblical and scholastic accounts, the ape—a monstrous offspring of humankind—fell with man from grace with the fateful bite of the apple.[75] The essence of this story was preserved in eighteenth-century accounts of the origin of apes as human hybrids. Even a naturalist of the stature of Stephen de Visme argued late in the century that because the Goloks or "Wild People" (gibbons) had no tails, they must have arisen out of "a mixture with the human kind."[76] Foucher d'Obsonville, claiming the orang to be human (though of the lowest kind), confirmed that it propagated freely and fruitfully with other humans.[77] In the nineteenth century there were rumors that French scientists had set off to Africa to "experiment with breeding a male orangutan and an African woman."[78]

The alleged hypersexuality of male apes provided ample opportunity for such unions, at least in the European mind (FIG. 3.5).[79] Their venery was supposedly so great that male apes were thought to ravish human females in addition to females of their own kind. Buffon wrote that the male baboon proudly presented his nude buttocks and anus especially to women—an extraordinary effrontery that Buffon could attribute to nothing but the most inordinate desire.[80]

Edward Tyson claimed that these animals preferred blondes, and offered the story of an ape that had grown so amorous of a celebrated beauty—a lady-in-waiting—that neither chains, confinement, nor punishment could keep him in check. The lady was eventually forced to have him banished from court.[81] Naturalists more often reported couplings between apes and dark-haired women. Buffon and countless others told stories of East Indian and African women being suddenly attacked and ravished by these shameless animals (FIG. 3.6). Chimpanzees and orangutans were said to carry off girls eight or ten years of age to the tops of trees where rescue was all but impossible.[82]

In these accounts it is invariably the male ape who forced himself on the human female. To my knowledge there was not one account in this period of a female ape taking a man or even of intercourse between a female ape and a male human. Bontius and

FIG. 3.5. A virile male baboon, from Thomas Bartholin's *Acta medica & philosophica Hafniensia* (Copenhagen, 1673), vol. 1, p. 313. By permission of the National Library of Medicine.

The Orang-Outang carrying off a Negro Girl.

Published as the Act directs, May 1st 1795.

FIG. 3.6. The drama of interspecies rape. An orangutan carries off an African woman. From Carl Linnaeus, *A Genuine and Universal System of Natural History*, ed. Ebenezer Sibly (London, 1795), vol. 2, frontispiece. By permission of the Library of the New York Botanical Garden, Bronx, New York.

Blumenbach did suggest, however, that the women involved may have initiated these encounters with apes. Bontius claimed that the orangutan was "born of the lust of the women of the Indies who mate with apes and monkeys to satisfy their detestable desires."[83] Blumenbach intimated that in the "madness of lust" women may have solicited the apes in the same way that the women of Kamchatka were known to have copulated with dogs; others might have prostituted themselves out of religious superstition as the women of Mendes were said to have done with their sacred goats.[84] La Brosse suggested that some women enjoyed their simian paramours; an African woman at Loango was reported to have remained three years with the apes.[85] It is significant in this context that when zoologists wished to emphasize the animality of the "Hottentot Venus," the woman from South Africa exhibited in London and Paris in the early part of the nineteenth century (see chapter 5), they reported that she had a "pronounced venereal appetite" and was known to throw herself "with force" on men whom she desired.[86]

For the most part, however, it was male apes that ravished women in this European fantasy. This is not surprising given that, since Aristotle, males—human or brute—were thought to embody the active sexual principle. Moreover, males were in principle considered more powerful than females—across classes, races, and, in this case, across species. Though a number of naturalists, including Tyson, rejected the notion that apes had issued from such sexual encounters, Blumenbach was one of the very few who found the whole idea dubious, fabulous, and disgusting. He denied that offspring from such a union were even possible, one reason being that women seized and violently raped by baboons perished miserably in these brutal embraces. Nonetheless, many naturalists continued to assert that women of Africa and Asia "mixed" voluntarily or through force with male apes, and that the products of these unions had entered into both species.[87] Rousseau, who remained genuinely puzzled about whether or not apes were human, suggested performing a crossbreeding experiment to find out. A fruitful union would attest to their humanity.[88]

Modesty—A Feminine Universal

By all accounts, male apes and monkeys were rude, lascivious, and given to lewd behavior. Female apes, by contrast, were distinguished by their very great modesty. Early authors—Aristotle, Pliny, Gesner, Battell—had not mentioned the moral disposition of female apes. Neither did Nicolaas Tulp, the Dutch physician, who nonetheless had his chimpanzee drawn in a quietly modest pose (FIG. 3.7). Beginning in the second half of the seventeenth century, modesty became a key attribute of the female ape. In this, naturalists followed newly emerging ideals for middle-class European women.[89] Jacob Bontius was the first to impute great modesty to the female orangutan. In his *Historiae naturalis* (1658), he wrote that the young female inspired admiration by hiding her "secret parts" with great modesty from unknown men (FIG. 3.8). She also hid her face with her hands, wept copiously, uttered groans, and expressed other sentiments so humanlike that Bontius judged nothing human to be lacking in her but speech.

Tyson mistrusted nearly every aspect of Bontius's portrayal: the arms were drawn too short, the hair too long, the feet too anthropic. The one trait he appreciated was her very great modesty. In order to express this pictorially, Tyson covered her privates with fig leaves in his redrawn copy of Bontius's illustration (FIG. 3.9).[90] Foucher d'Obsonville, by contrast, found Bontius's account of the modesty of the female orang much exaggerated: "How can it seriously be presumed that the female Orang exhibits spontaneous acts of instinctive or reflective modesty, when even among the human species, prudence seems chiefly to arise from custom?"[91] Others, however, confirmed Bontius's observations, reporting that the female is indeed bashful, inclined to throw herself into the arms of the male and hide her face in his bosom when stared at.[92] Monboddo repeated reports of female orangutans concealing with their hands the parts that distinguished their sex in the same way that "the ancients thought it was proper the Goddess of love should conceal" her privates.[93]

FIG. 3.7. Nicolaas Tulp's "Orang-outang" from his *Observationum medicarum libri tres* (Amsterdam, 1641), plate 14. By permission of the National Library of Medicine.

Accounts of modesty in females reached their height in descriptions of the celebrated creature—"Madame Chimpanzee"—that arrived in London from Angola in 1738. The *London Magazine* reported that she was shaped "in every Part like a Woman excepting . . . [her] Head, which nearly resembles the Ape" (FIG. 3.10). During the passage she had grown fond of a boy on board, and now she was always sorrowful at his absence. She was clothed with "a thin Silk Vestment" and showed "great Discontent at the opening of the Gown to discover her Sex."[94] Her modesty was complemented by her fine table manners. As Thomas Boreman related:

> The Chimpanzee was very pretty Company at the Tea-table, behav'd with Modesty and good Manners, and gave great Satisfaction to the Ladies who were pleased to honour her with their Visits, . . . it would fetch its Chair, and sit in it naturally, like a Human Creature, whilst it drank Tea: It would take the Dish in its Hand, and if the Liquor was two [sic] hot, wou'd pour the Tea into the Saucer to cool it.[95]

Linnaeus, reporting a similar scene, added that she drank daintily, wiping her mouth with her hand. When retiring, Linnaeus's lady lay on a pillow, covering her shoulders, and slept quietly like "a respectful matron." He noted that her stomach was prominent, unlike those of Europe's "slim maidens," but he also insisted that the reason was not pregnancy, for the animal was still a virgin.[96]

Toward the end of the century, the female apes represented in European natural history became even more demurely feminine. Charles White gave Tulp's well-known female a face-lift in his copy of Tulp's illustration. White removed the wrinkles from her face, slimmed her limbs and belly. Where Tulp had emphasized that "the nostrils are flat and bent inward, as in a wrinkled, toothless old woman," White's ape showed nicely placed teeth beneath a full lip (compare FIGS. 3.7 and 3.11). The rough chest and sagging breasts in Tulp's drawing were lifted and smoothed, the nipples sharply defined, thus achieving more nearly White's ideal—the "plump and snowy white hemispheres, tipt with vermillion"—of the European female (see chapter 2).[97] In addition, White resolved the ambiguities of the hair. In Tulp's drawing the hair looked like whiskers fram-

OVRANG OVTANG.

FIG. 3.8. Jacob Bontius's female "ourang outang" from his *Historiae naturalis & medicae Indiae Orientalis libri sex* (Amsterdam, 1658, p. 84). Buffon a hundred years later looked at this picture and declared it to be merely a hairy woman. Courtesy of the College of Physicians, Philadelphia.

ing the face; in White's it was pushed back (though more delicately drawn whiskers encompass the chin) and lengthened so that the hair of the head and shoulder appeared as one flowing mane.

One of the most highly gendered representations of a female ape appeared in Pierre Latreille's 1801 edition of Buffon's *Histoire naturelle*. Surprisingly, a female was chosen to represent the go-

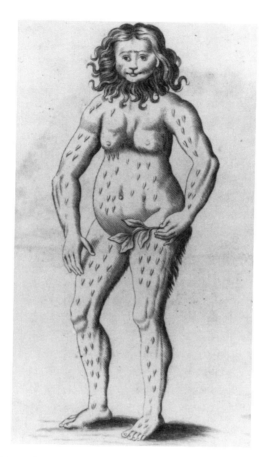

FIG. 3.9. Edward Tyson's redrawn copy of Bontius's orangutan, her privates now covered by a fig leaf. From Tyson, *Orang-Outang, sive Homo Sylvestris*, fig. 16. By permission of the National Library of Medicine.

rilla, the largest and reputedly the most vicious of the great apes (FIG. 3.12). Seated daintily on a branch, this damsel is well proportioned, with comely limbs. The digits of both hands and feet are slender and elegant, matched only by the beauty of her long eyelashes.

Modesty was not exclusively ascribed to primates in this period. William Smellie found this most distinguishing and attractive characteristic of the female sex "even so low [on the chain of being]

CHIMP-   ANZEE
Scotin sculp   A.D. 1738

as the insect tribes."⁹⁸ The French botanist René-Louis Desfontaines found it among the female parts of plants. He reported that while stamens (the male parts) had visible orgasms, pistils (the female parts) experienced little sexual excitement, "as if the law requiring a certain modesty of females were common to all organisms."⁹⁹

Priscilla Wakefield, one of the very few women to write about apes or monkeys in this period, was impressed not by the modesty of female apes (she did not recount any of the standard stories in this regard) but by their maternalism. Embellishing a report from the Scots officer and naturalist John Stedman, Wakefield described how female squirrel monkeys exude great affection for their young. They suckle them (Stedman noted, "like the human species"), preen them, and supervise their play. Invoking images of middle-class English home life, Wakefield drew a picture of the morally in-dignant monkey mother scolding her rambunctious offspring for playing too roughly and, once subdued, whisking them off to their home in the trees.¹⁰⁰

What is surprising in these portrayals is that female apes were *not* depicted as closer to nature than were the males. Even in the state of nature, female apes were chaste, modest, soft, sober, consid-erate, attentive, and tranquil—qualities Linnaeus attributed to civi-lized humans. Portrayals of male apes, by contrast, evoked Lin-naeus's descriptions of uncivilized "man": "foolish, lascivious, imitative."¹⁰¹ In portraying female apes as essentially chaste and modest, male naturalists attributed to nature the modesty—that "fountain head as well as the guardian of . . . chastity and honor"—prescribed for their own wives and daughters.¹⁰² Hume recognized that the need for these prescriptions was purely conventional: mod-

FIG. 3.10. Madame Chimpanzee making her 1738 London debut. She was said to prefer silk dresses; the illustrator nevertheless drew her naked. Here she raises a teacup to her lips. In Linnaeus's copy of this plate (see "Satyrus Tulpii," fig. 3.2, second from right, above), he removed the teacup so that her left hand draws attention to her bare breast (reflecting perhaps Linnaeus's intense interest at this time in female mammae; see chapter 2). From Gerard Scotin, Department of Prints and Drawings, British Museum, C.2* misc. 1882-3-11-1183. By permission of the British Museum.

esty and chastity were required (on the part of wives) to ensure that heirs issued from legal husbands. The foundation for these morals, however, he imagined to be natural.[103] Reports of female apes dressed in silk vestments, showing displeasure when strange men wished to examine them, served to reinforce the notion that females—both human and beast—are by nature modest and demure.

The Enlightened Ape: Sir Oran Haut-ton

A corollary to the question "Are apes human?" arose late in the Enlightenment: Should apes be enfranchised? In this period of democratic expansion the question was first asked of women, then of minorities living in Europe, and finally of brutes. There were some

FIG. 3.11. Charles White's feminization of Tulp's "Orang" (center figure). Compare with Tulp's original reproduced in fig. 3.7 above. From *An Account of the Regular Gradation in Man and in Different Animals and Vegetables* (London, 1796), plate 3. By permission of the National Library of Medicine.

FIG. 3.12. A female pongo or gorilla, described by Buffon as the species most nearly approaching the human. This illustration first appeared in P.-A. Latreille's *Histoire naturelle générale et particulière des singes* (Paris, 1801), vol. 1, plate 2. Courtesy of the Clendening History of Medicine Library.

in this period who claimed human status for the orangutan. Lord Monboddo argued that orangs might be turned into cultivated gentlemen if suitably educated. The conservative Thomas Taylor penned his satirical *Vindication of the Rights of Brutes* (1792), arguing that animals are our equals. Thomas Love Peacock portrayed the fictional Sir Oran Haut-ton as a landowner and member of Parliament.

In the eighteenth century, advocates of animals began to challenge the Cartesian notion that animals are senseless automata. Sarah Trimmer wrote in her 1788 *Fabulous Histories* that a lady of London had been accustomed to considering animals as mere machines, pawns of instinct, until she encountered "the Learned Pig, which has lately been shown in London." The pig could supposedly spell words by picking out the appropriate letter with its snout; it could also tell time.[104]

The question of rights for animals was discussed most baldly by Taylor. Declaring Thomas Paine the father and Mary Wollstonecraft the mother ("though a virgin") of his theory, Taylor argued that brutes possess reason in common with men, though not "in so exquisite a degree." Nonetheless, animals have other assets that overcome any deficiency in reason. "The swiftness of a hare," he argued, "united with hare-like reason, puts the hare upon an equality both with the lion and the man." The strength of the lion, the flight of the bird, the spinning of the spider, the microscopic eye of the fly render them all equal to each other and to man. Given that animals possess both reason and speech (it is our failing that we cannot understand their languages), Taylor, tongue in cheek, considered it unjust to destroy animals, to hunt or eat them. In attempting to render the claims of both Paine and Wollstonecraft absurd, Taylor declared that "what is here asserted of brutes is no less applicable to vegetables, and even minerals themselves" because these things too are endowed with sense. He predicted that Europe would soon be inundated with treatises asserting their rights.[105]

Other satires made extraordinary claims for apes. An essay, jointly authored by Jonathan Swift, Alexander Pope, John Gay,

Thomas Parnell, and John Arbuthnot in the 1730s and heavily in-
debted to Tyson, traced the beginnings of the arts and sciences to
these creatures. "It is universally agreed," wrote the authors, "that
the Arts and Sciences took their rise among the Egyptians and Indians; but from whom they first receiv'd them, is yet a secret." In
Egypt, Swift et al. traced the secret to the satyr, Pan—half man and
half beast; in India they traced the origin of the sciences to the apes.
Transmission of this knowledge to humans was facilitated by the intimate relations these animals had with human females. The progeny of these couplings—Aesop, for example, or Socrates with his
flat nose and prominent eyes—were among the greatest wits of the
ancient world.[106]

While Taylor and Swift used the notion of the learned ape to
ridicule democratic tendencies within Europe, others used apes to
highlight and criticize Europe's vices. The French novelist Nicolas-
Edme Restif de la Bretonne's cultured baboon, César de Malaca (FIG.
3.13), is shown writing a letter of warning to his species: Don't ape
humans! These seeming "kings of the world" (humans) have
wrought destruction and misery with their unchristian wars and in-
humane slavery. Men of reason espouse high ideals of equality and
fraternity, but their practice is otherwise. "Thank God," he con-
cludes, "that I am an ape and not subject to human laws and prejudices." César, the son of a woman of Malacca and a baboon, was
saved by a European from suffocation at birth and transported eventually to France. Under the tutelage of a wealthy woman, who came
to love him dearly, he was given a European education, which he
came to regret. "Ignorance is certainly an imperfection . . . but
knowledge has consequences that frighten me."[107]

Imagination soared with the possibilities of apes becoming
human. For the German writer E. T. A. Hoffmann, as for most advocates of Enlightenment, it was simply a matter of education. The ape
Milo described his upbringing and accomplishments in a letter to
his simian paramour living in Philadelphia. He had been "liberated"
from his brute existence by trappers and brought to Germany.
Schooled by a prominent citizen, he learned to speak, read, write,

III.ᵉ Vol. 18   Lettre d'un Singe.

Cesar de Malaca, écrivant aux Animaux de son espèce.

and play music—in short he became highly cultured. He signed his letter "Milo, formerly an ape, currently private artist and intellectual."[108]

In other stories apes passed happily and, at times, quite successfully as humans in high society. In Wilhelm Hauff's innocently fanciful 1827 "The Ape as Man," a young man was introduced into a small German town by his uncle—himself a recluse so withdrawn from society that the townspeople considered him a madman, a Jew, or a wizard. His nephew, dressed in a fashionable frock coat, wide green trousers, and kid gloves, learned to speak German with a passable accent. The villagers, anxious to cultivate the seemingly well-born gentleman as a future son-in-law, welcomed him into their homes and clubs. During the long winter months, he often won at chess, danced at their balls, and sang "like an angel." His rough manners were regarded as exotic and were imitated by every young man in town. In Hauff's tale, however, nature eventually won out over nurture. One evening at a ball, the mysterious young man reverted to his animal nature, swinging from the chandeliers and leaping wildly from table to table. He revealed himself to be "*Homo troglodytes Linnaei,*" and was sold to a museum owner anxious to have the skin for his collection.[109]

The most elaborate of these stories was Thomas Love Peacock's *Melincourt*. Drawing heavily on Monboddo, Peacock declared the orangutan to be "a specimen of the natural and original man—a genuine facsimile of the philosophical Adam." Still a natural being, the future Sir Oran Haut-ton, Baronet of Redrose Abbey, displayed prodigious physical strength, uninterrupted health, and an amicable simplicity of manners, exactly those qualities Peacock saw lacking in his fellow English. Sir Oran's natural qualities—his

---

FIG. 3.13. The learned baboon, César de Malaca, writing to his brethren. His hand on his forehead shows him reflecting on the ills of human society. The parrot—the other "imitator of man" for its ability to speak—on the windowsill counsels him; the dog and cat are his companions. On the wall are portraits of others of his species. From Nicolas-Edme Restif de la Bretonne, *La découverte australe* (Leipzig, 1781), vol. 3, facing p. 18.

sense of justice, selfless rescue of Anthelia (Lord Melincourt's daughter), fine manners, and flute playing—were more than enough to make up for certain deficiencies, such as his inability to speak, read, or write. Throughout his story, Peacock suggested that his ape was more human than people who judge the value of an individual by the weight of her or his purse. Sir Oran Haut-ton eventually acquired an estate and a seat in Parliament, a move his friends considered necessary to secure for him the respect of people such as Mrs. Pinmoney, who had earlier judged his looks "odd" but now found there to be something "very French in his physiognomy."[110]

Female apes rarely figured in these reveries of simian potential. In one case, however, a female—the London chimp—was featured in a political satire on Queen Caroline who had died in 1738. In the anonymous *Essay Towards the Character of the Late Chimpanzee who died February 23, 1738–9*, Madame Chimpanzee was portrayed as temperate, modest, neat, and quiet, the standard of genteel breeding. Intended to ridicule the German-born Caroline, who served as self-appointed mediator in the famous Leibniz-Clarke debate, the London chimp was cast as a liberal, a deist, a freethinker, and above all an intellectual—choosing to cultivate her mind and not her wardrobe. She eschewed frivolous card-playing women and preferred the company of serious men.[111]

It is significant that, but for this one exception, the protagonists in these stories were predominantly male. Though female apes exhibited human qualities—sipping tea from a cup, or climbing down a ladder to relieve themselves discreetly overboard during transport—no female was portrayed as a heroine in a fictional account of an ape entering into high society. No one *denied* that female apes were capable of such accomplishments; the question did not arise. Europeans simply assumed that active, cultured individuals were male. Though female apes were omitted from the ranks of the civilized, females numbered among the "wild people" whom Europeans imagined to populate their forests. Prominent among wild people in this period was the tree-climbing, carnivorous, club-wielding girl of Champagne who, when "tamed," became a Catholic nun.[112]

The question of the humanity and rights of apes was intimately tied to the question of rights for women. Peacock, who made a parliamentarian of Sir Oran Haut-ton, also spoke out in favor of women's rights. His novel opened with a portrait of Sir Henry Melincourt, Lord of the old Westmoreland manor, who devoted himself to the cultivation of his daughter's intellect. Melincourt upheld the "heresy" that women are, or at least may become, rational beings; the paucity of examples was the unfortunate result of the great pains taken to make them otherwise. Peacock was also an enemy of slavery; his spokesman in the novel, a Mr. Forester, boycotted sugar and other products of slave economies, never allowing an "atom" of West Indian produce to cross his threshold.[113]

Apes, of course, are not human and were not enfranchised in human society (neither were women until more than a century later). Animals, however, did make some gains in this period. Enlightenment debates increased sympathies for the plight of both wild and domestic animals. In the nineteenth century, Roman law, which gave owners *jus utendi* and *jus abutendi* over their animals, was increasingly called into question. By 1804 the French were agitating for laws to prevent cruelty to animals; the *Loi Grammont* was passed in 1850. In England, the Royal Society for the Prevention of Cruelty to Animals was founded in 1824.[114]

This chapter, however, has not been primarily about the welfare of apes. It has been about naturalists and the science they produced. The great apes became unwitting objects in debates the consequences of which went far beyond descriptions of simian habits and character. Naturalists have looked (and sociobiologists still look) to these our closest relatives to resolve questions about the "nature" of humankind. Are humans naturally aggressive or altruistic? Do males invariably dominate females? Are humans genetically predisposed toward crime, rape, or homosexuality? As this study has shown, even careful observation of our simian cousins has often been mediated by highly gendered lenses.

That science still often tells as much about its participants as about the laws of nature is brought into sharp relief in Donna Haraway's *Primate Visions*. Primatology changed dramatically when

114   women entered the field in the twentieth century. Their questions were different, their assumptions were different, and their results were different. Jeanne Altmann, for example, shifted the focus from male to female subjects. Altmann initially shied away from looking at females (for a woman to study females was considered too "natural" a thing and threatened to undermine her authority as a scientist). As she spent more time in the field, however, she recognized that male researchers had a preference for high drama and tended to focus attention on murder, hunting, and sex. Altmann found a deeper evolutionary story in the longer, sustained dramas surrounding females and food. Though Altmann's contributions led to a more balanced picture of gender in primates, as Haraway points out, her studies reflect, to a certain extent, her own class and racial biases. For her 1980 *Baboon Mothers and Infants*, Altmann took the career mother as her organizing metaphor—a move that tended to impose on baboons the problems of white, middle-class professional women.[115] Though the notion of a great chain of being no longer animates exploration of nature, all too often hierarchies of natural worth are established—consciously or unconsciously— that mirror the faces dominating scientific communities. Objectivity in science cannot be proclaimed, it must be built.

4

The Anatomy of Difference

Determining the exact boundaries between the human races,
their origins and natural condition, has recently become more
of a business than most people would find worthwhile. . . .
Opinions among the learned varied considerably. There are
those, for example, who really do not care to see their
esteemed selves as belonging to the same species as the
Hottentot and Carib; others, by contrast, . . . give no thought to
acknowledging orangutans as their legitimate cousins.

Göttinger Taschen Calender, 1776

*I*n the 1780s, Duke Frederick II of Hessen-Kassel settled a colony
of Africans at Wilhelmshöhe, near Frankfurt, with the intention
of studying their customs and anatomy. Originally intended to
house Chinese, the colony was furnished with pagodas and oriental
gardens. Since Chinese were too expensive and often simply not
available, the colony was settled instead with Africans. The medical
doctor in charge, Ernst Baldinger, noted that the Africans did not
flourish there; most died of tuberculosis or committed suicide.[1]
Their bodies were turned over to Germany's leading anatomist,
Samuel Thomas von Soemmerring, for dissection.[2] From his analysis of "several Negro bodies of both sexes" (one woman, one child,
and at least two men), along with his earlier observations of the Wilhelmshöhe colonists at public baths, Soemmerring prepared his
1784 book, *Über die körperliche Verschiedenheit des Mohren vom
Europäer* (Concerning the physical difference between the Moor
and the European), which served as a basic text on the African physique until well into the nineteenth century.[3]

Though people from various parts of Africa had lived in Europe since Roman times, they began arriving in significant numbers
with European colonial expansion in the sixteenth century. For a

time, it was fashionable among the wealthy to collect Africans as *exotica*—along with apes, camels, leopards, and elephants. Dukes paraded them as buglers and drummers in their militia, and noble families exchanged them as gifts, dressing them in gay uniforms to serve as butlers and maids, pages and coachmen. Louis XIV himself was once said to have had a "Moorish" mistress. Africans were brought to Europe as visiting princes, mercenaries, musicians, and slaves (though technically slavery was illegal in most of Europe at this time), and stayed on as artisans, cooks, prostitutes, and scholars. It is estimated that by the late eighteenth century between fifteen and twenty thousand persons of African descent lived in England and between one and five thousand lived in France (numbers for Germany are unavailable). When not among the intransigent poor, they occasionally married Europeans, bought property, and (usually after baptism in a Christian church) became respected members of the community.[4]

For European anatomists, blacks were exotic. But, as we shall see, to men of the academy, European women were in many ways just as exotic. Soemmerring, some years after his book comparing the Negro to the European, turned his attention to female anatomy, seeking to differentiate female from male physique. Indeed, a vast and still largely unexplored literature on the anatomy of both race and sex arose in the eighteenth century.[5]

Twentieth-century historians of science have tended to treat racial and sexual science in separate studies.[6] While eighteenth-century studies of race and sex admittedly formed distinct literatures, they also shared an intimate history having to do with the rise of what Michel Foucault has called "political anatomy."[7] The body—stripped clean of history and culture as it was of clothes and often skin—became the touchstone of political rights and social privileges. It is precisely this interplay between racial and sexual science that we explore in the next several chapters. In this chapter, I analyze how gender influenced the study of race in the eighteenth century; one could also demonstrate how race influenced the study of sex, but not within the confines of a book primarily about gender. It is extraordinary, for example, that male investigators should have thought so highly of a secondary sexual characteristic such as the beard that they made its presence or absence an important marker of race.

Fixing Racial and Sexual Types

The eighteenth century was the great age of classification. The voyages of discovery had flooded Europe with new and strange specimens of plants, animals, and humans. Natural historians attempting to lay the grid of reason over the unwieldy stuff of nature sought new and simple principles that would hold universally.

Eighteenth-century naturalists had at hand several bodies of knowledge about the races and sexes. From the ancients (Aristotle, Galen, and others) they had inherited the theory of humors that attributed distinctive temperaments to the various peoples of the world. From Christianity they had still powerful explanations of the subordination of both Ham, the original African, and Eve. Travelogues offered what claimed to be firsthand descriptions of the habits, language, character, and physique of specific peoples. Naturalists also received reports from surgeons on slave ships that carried seven million Africans to European plantations in the Americas in the course of the eighteenth century. Increasingly, too, comparative anatomists provided detailed measurements and illustrations from the bodies and body parts they amassed in their private museums. Johann Blumenbach, widely recognized as the father of physical anthropology, called his collection of 245 skulls his "Golgotha," after the hill near Jerusalem where Jesus was crucified.[8]

Eighteenth-century naturalists sought to make sense of this mass of often contradictory information by sorting humankind into distinct types. For them the crucial question became: Of the myriad observable differences between people—in skin, hair, or bones—which were significant, actually differentiating one race or sex from another? How was humankind to be divided? In his textbook of anatomy, Samuel Thomas von Soemmerring suggested that skeletons be categorized according to age, sex, nationality, nourishment, susceptibility to illnesses, life-style, and clothing.[9] Of these, age, sex, and nation (the term *race* was not yet in vogue) emerged as central categories of analysis.

Some anthropologists immediately recognized the difficulties in establishing hard and fast categories. Blumenbach, for example, charged his colleagues with exaggerating sexual differences. He ridiculed the idea that the bones of Abelard and Héloise that had lain together for nearly five hundred years could be differentiated by sex and placed in separate graves, as had been ordered by the Abbess of Paraclet in 1630.[10] Joseph Wenzel, one of Soemmerring's students, joined Blumenbach in stressing the ambiguities of sexual difference. "One can find," he wrote, "male bodies with a feminine build, just as one can find female bodies with a masculine build." In fact, he suggested, one could find skulls, brains, and breast bones of the "feminine type" in men. Johann von Döllinger further claimed that certain parts of the male (such as the prostate) are feminine and parts of the female (such as the uterus) are masculine.[11]

Eighteenth-century anatomists faced similar problems regarding differentiation when thinking about race. Blumenbach recognized, for example, that occupation or social class might determine skin color. "The face of the working man or the artisan," he wrote, "exposed to the force of the sun and the weather, differs as much from the cheeks of a delicate [European] female, as the man himself does from the dark American, and he again from the Ethiopian." Blumenbach also pointed to the problem that anatomists procured corpses from what he described as the "lowest sort of men" (the poor). These European men, he remarked, have skin around the nipples and on the testicles that comes nearer to the "blackness of the Ethiopians than to the brilliancy of the higher class of Europeans."[12] Though with these examples Blumenbach revealed his prejudices against dark skin and the lower classes of his own countrymen, he questioned the notion of hard and fast divisions between the races. Blumenbach also emphasized the diversity invariably found *within* races. Of Africans he wrote: "Among Negroes and Negresses (whom I have been able to observe attentively, . . . plus the seven skulls of adult Negroes in my collection) it is with difficulty that *two* can be found who are completely alike."[13]

Blumenbach and Wenzel's efforts to diminish sexual and racial difference ran counter to the larger effort to fix racial and sexual types. It seems quite remarkable to us today that Europeans in this period reduced the vast diversity among peoples of the globe to four or five types. While biologists today recognize that humans are differentiated along geographic lines, most argue that distinct races do *not* exist, that geographical groups exhibit tremendous individual variation and are constantly undergoing modification as they migrate and mingle with people from other areas.[14]

Before the development of the modern theory of evolution, however, naturalists generally assumed that racial distinctions were sharp and static and that well-defined "natural types" could be identified. François Bernier, credited with using the term *race* for the first time in its modern sense in his 1684 "Nouvelle division de la terre," identified four distinct human races.[15] Linnaeus also distinguished four, a number derived—in starkly premodern fashion— from the four elements (air, earth, fire, and water), the corresponding four corners of the world (north, south, east, and west), the four humors (black bile, blood, yellow bile, and phlegm), and the then-known four continents (America, Europe, Asia, and Africa).[16] Blumenbach's great innovation in the 1790s was to distinguish five "principal varieties" (as he called them): Caucasian, Mongolian, Ethiopian, American, and Malay. Blumenbach's became the most widely accepted racial classification in the pre-Darwinian era.[17]

The sciences of race and sex tended to underscore distinctions between groups by downplaying variation within those groups. Soemmerring's book comparing the Negro and the European is typical in this regard. The *Negro* (he sometimes used the term *Moor*) signified a universal black body embracing all peoples of Africa without attention to cultural heritage, region, or even sex. In like manner, *European* referred to a generic white body, including peoples of complexions as different as those living in Greece and Norway, Russia and France. Petrus Camper's categories, "European" and "Negro," were even more wide ranging. In his influential study of skulls, he let the head of a European represent the peoples of "Europe, Turkey, Persia, and the largest part of Arabia, as far as Indostan," while the head of an "Angolese Negro" stood for the peoples of "all Africa; also the Hottentots, . . . the Caffres, and the natives of Madagascar."[18] Buffon, more interested in variety than classification, distinguished two separate Negro races.

Eighteenth-century comparative anatomists sought distinctive morphological characteristics that would capture natural boundaries of race and sex. To do so, they developed new methods and indices for measuring physical differences; in short, they founded new sciences of race and of sex. But how did considerations of sex influence their studies of race?

"That Majestic Beard"

In his lectures given at the University of Uppsala in the 1740s, Carl Linnaeus taught that "God gave men beards for ornaments and to distinguish them from women."[19] Though debates about skin color dominated eighteenth-century anthropology, some naturalists, notably Charles White, felt that hair, its color, texture, and length, had not been given the attention it deserved for differentiating the races.[20] The beard, in particular, took on special significance. The presence or absence of a beard not only drew a sharp line between men and women, it also served to differentiate the varieties of men (FIG. 4.1). Women, black men (to a certain extent), and especially men of the Americas simply lacked that masculine "badge of honor"—the philosopher's beard.[21]

Today the choice of the beard as a trait worthy of scientific investigation might seem whimsical. Beards, however, have been greatly cherished, especially by those who wore them. Among the ancient Egyptians, the beard symbolized virility—the sign of a leader. Even their female monarchs were portrayed wearing beards, among them Hatshepsut, the only woman aside from Cleopatra VII to rule Egypt single-handedly. Since she proved herself capable of ruling as a king, she was given the symbol of kingship. In the first century A.D., the Roman naturalist Pliny the Elder reported *121* that the beard was held in such esteem that agreements concerning "shaving the beard" were among the first conventions made between nations (the other two were uniform use of the Ionian alphabet and ways of reckoning time).[22]

In the seventeenth century, Philip Camerarius, a government official of Nuremberg, reflected upon the significance European males attached to hair. According to Camerarius, the Greeks cherished their beards to such an extent that if a hair was plucked, a man considered himself dishonored. The German Emperor Frederick Barbarossa punished extracting a hair from another man's head or beard with a fine of thirty pounds. Among the Anglo-Saxons the penalty for damage to a beard was twenty shillings, while breaking a thigh bone was only twelve. In France, princes cherished their long "royal" hair, curling, braiding, and perfuming it from earliest childhood. The heads of their vassals, by contrast, were cleanshaven to symbolize their subordination (the heads of slaves were also shorn). Camerarius went on to recount that in many places throughout Europe serious criminals, such as fornicators, were punished by having their beards "chopped off publicly with a keen axe." (Adulteresses often had their heads shaved.) Across Europe, the beard signified lordship and virility. For a man to swear by his beard was regarded as a holy and solemn oath. It was considered a bad omen even to dream that one's beard had been cut.[23] Charles de Rochefort, also writing in the seventeenth century, recognized the cultural relativity of such notions, noting that while the great nobility of France cherished their beards, the ancient Romans considered the beard a mark of infamy suitable only for criminals.[24]

This is not the place to present a full cultural history of the beard. Though significance given to beards has varied greatly across cultures, over time, social stations, and occupations, beards have been commonly associated with masculinity, virility, and strength. With some notable exceptions—angels in the Christian religion had no beards, nor did Adam before the Fall—beards have been considered a mark of both physical and moral strength and energy, respect and honor.[25] Beards even lent dignity to certain animals in the eighteenth century. The Scottish Lord Monboddo reported that the "barris" (probably an orangutan) husbanded a long white beard. Monboddo went so far as to attribute to these apes the wisdom associated with the philosopher's beard, stating that they excelled in judgment and intelligence.[26]

Given the beard's cultural significance, it is not surprising that when François Bernier distinguished his four species of humankind in 1684, he included the lushness of the male beard as a key racial characteristic. He simply took for granted that the chins of his first species (*espèce*), Europeans and north Africans, were blessed with flowing beards. Black Africans, his second species, were distinguished by their thick lips and broad noses, their dark skin, woolly hair, and scant beards of "three or four" hairs. His third species, the peoples of east Asia, he considered white but with "flat faces, small flat noses, little pig's eyes," and, again, with a deficient "three hairs of beard." The Lapps, his fourth species, he viewed as "stunted little creatures," very ugly and animallike in appearance.[27]

The English naturalist Richard Bradley also used the beard to distinguish different "sorts of men." Among the five human types he identified in his 1721 *Philosophical Account of the Works of Nature* were two white races—the Europeans and the Americans—differing from each other only in regard to the beard. He also identified two black races distinguished solely by the texture of their hair:

> We have five sorts of men: the white men, which are Europeans that have beards; and a sort of white men in America (as I am told) that differ from us in having no beards; the third sort are the Malatoes, which have their skins almost of a copper colour, small eyes, and straight black hair; the fourth kind are the Blacks, which have straight black hair; and the fifth are the Blacks of Guiney, whose hair is curled, like the wool of a sheep.

Though Bradley judged non-Europeans to be lacking proper beards, he did not think that this supposed deficiency betrayed a less noble mind. He postulated instead that all peoples had similar intellectual capabilities. "I suppose," he wrote, "there would not be any great difference [between peoples of the world]; if it was possible they could be all born of the same parents, and have the same

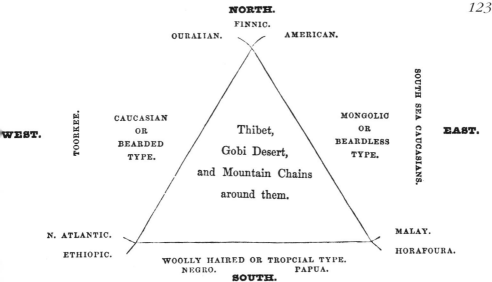

FIG. 4.1. The beard was used to differentiate the races. As late as 1848, Charles Hamilton Smith, friend and disciple of Georges Cuvier, devised this chart delineating the "Caucasian or Bearded Type" from the "Mongolic or Beardless Type." From *The Natural History of the Human Species* (Edinburgh, 1852), p. 187. (Sign.: La 2290.) By permission of the Staatsbibliothek zu Berlin—Preußischer Kulturbesitz.

education, they would vary no more in understanding than children of the same house."[28]

By the middle of the eighteenth century, however, a number of natural historians took the absence of a beard in native American males to be a sign that they belonged to a lower class of humans; some even argued that this absence of hair follicles on the chin proved them a separate species. Richard McCausland, an army surgeon, reported in the *Philosophical Transactions of the Royal Society of London* in 1786: "It has been advanced by several travellers and historians that the Indians of America differed from other males of the human species in the want of one very characteristic mark of the sex, to wit, that of a beard."[29] Montesquieu had reported in *The Spirit of the Laws* that the Spanish justified enslaving native Americans near St. Martha because they ate unpalatable food (crabs, grasshoppers, and locusts), smoked tobacco, and trimmed their scanty beards in an unseemly fashion.[30]

Other naturalists resisted this entire line of investigation, arguing that it was simply wrong to think that Indians were naturally beardless or that the occasional appearance of beards arose from an admixture of European blood. De Rochefort maintained that the Caribs had a "secret" that prevented the hair—once shaven—from reappearing. These men, he remarked, were "astonished" to see Europeans nourishing their beards because they considered having one a great deformity.[31] Colonel Butler, deputy superintendent of Indian Affairs in North America, believed a proper beard to be merely a matter of cultivation. He maintained that if an Indian shaved from the time of his youth, he would develop a lush European beard. Thayendanega (or Tayadaneega), a Mohawk consulted on this matter, confirmed that the men of the Indian nations generally plucked the hairs of their beards by the roots as soon as they began to appear; and since they continued this practice all their lives, they appeared to Europeans as having no beards.[32] Blumenbach pointed out that plucking their beards was but one of the many forms of artifice Indians employed; they also colored their bodies with pigments and paints, pricked their skin with needles, and enlarged their ears so that they could "cover their whole body with them." Though Blumenbach admitted that the beards of Americans were thin and scanty, he suggested that Americans ought no more to be called beardless than men with sparse hair ought to be called bald.[33]

A secondary sexual characteristic, such as the beard, could play such a role in racial evaluation in this period only because anthropological classificatory interests focused almost exclusively on males. Interest in beards did, however, hold consequences for placing women in nature as well. Medical observers, perplexed by the absence of beards in native American males, also reported that native American females did not menstruate. Beards were associated with catamenia in the minds of eighteenth-century natural historians through the outmoded, though still influential, theory of humors which taught that, in men, vital heat processed excess bodily fluids into sweat, semen, and beards (beard growth resulting from reabsorbed semen) and, in women, into catamenia (which explained the hair that sometimes appeared after menopause).[34] Logically, a people whose males were beardless should have females lacking menstrual flux. The charge that native American women did not menstruate was indeed serious, considering that naturalists in this period had sought (in vain) to establish periodic menstruation as a uniquely human characteristic (see chapter 3).

Though physicians and anthropologists did not banish beardless women from the human race, they did see the absence of beards in females as confirming their less noble character. The seventeenth-century English physician, Helkiah Crooke, taught that women needed no "sign of majesty" (no beard) because they were born subject to men. Immanuel Kant launched his diatribe against learned women at the end of the eighteenth century, choosing the symbolic value of the beard as his weapon. Scientific learning in women, he decreed, ran counter to the laws of nature; a learned woman—such as the classicist Madame Dacier or the physicist Emilie du Châtelet—"might just as well have a beard, for that expresses in a more recognizable form the profundity for which she strives."[35]

That the absence of chin hair should have been taken as a sign of imperfection in native American males and in women is curious, given that Blumenbach had listed relative hair*less*ness as one of the traits distinguishing humankind from animals.[36] Other hairy parts of the body—the armpit and groin, for example—carried no particular prestige. That a few hairs on the chin should have become a major subject of debate among European natural philosophers in this period seems extraordinary unless one considers the circumstances. The beard controversy illustrates how research priorities can reflect the patterns of inclusion and exclusion in academic communities. Had women and native Americans held chairs of anatomy in European universities, would the same question have arisen? Or if it had, would it have occupied university-trained anthropologists to such an extent that Blumenbach had to report he was "almost ashamed" of the trouble he had taken to prove that men of the Americas did in fact have beards?

The Caucasian Mystery

Was there a female equivalent of the beard? Did European anthropologists of the eighteenth century divide the varieties of humankind by a uniquely female trait? One might imagine that the hold the female mammae had on naturalists' imaginations in this period might have led them to differentiate peoples according to breast size and shape (see chapter 2). Naturalists and travelers did comment extensively on female beauty and breasts, but degrees of female beauty or breast size were not used to classify peoples (only briefly after 1870 were breasts classified systematically by racial types). Nonetheless, beauty, both male and female, deeply influenced anthropologists' assessment of the world's peoples. Most remarkably, as we will see, notions of female beauty led Blumenbach to what he considered the very cradle of humanity, and to name his premier race *Caucasian*.

Early modern anthropologists were as intrigued by beauty as their nineteenth-century *confrères* were by skulls. Bernier devoted half of his article on race to the matter of physical beauty among the world's women. The Dutch artist and anatomist Petrus Camper devoted much of his *On the Connexion between the Science of Anatomy and the Arts of Drawing, Painting, Statuary, etc.* to defining geometric principles for capturing the beauty unique to each race. This is not to say that beauty was denied men. To the extent, however, that environment was thought to determine comeliness, women—the more delicate and malleable sex—were said to succumb more easily to its influences (handsome women, it was said, could not be found in areas where the water was bad or the soil infertile).[37]

For many Europeans skin color determined beauty (as it did political power and moral worth). Göttingen professor and inveterate racist Christoph Meiners divided humankind into two types—the beautiful and the ugly—primarily by color. For him, a white skin radiated beauty while a dark skin evoked disgust.[38] European voyagers, too, treasured an ivory skin touched with vermillion, and dutifully recorded the degrees of pinkness in the peoples they encountered. By the nineteenth century, this "blush of modesty," said to express the emotions of the soul, took on moralistic innuendo. "How," Alexander von Humboldt asked, "can those be trusted who know not how to blush?"[39] Few Europeans took the view of the peoples of Cape Verde who, Buffon reported, saw beauty only in the deepest shades of black.[40]

Other Europeans, more generous than Meiners or Humboldt, thought of Africans as brothers "though carved from ebony."[41] For them, color was "only accidental" to beauty, which consisted wholly in the proportion and symmetry of facial features.[42] Despite their more liberal attitudes, these friends of blacks also suffered from ethnocentrism. Aphra Behn, in her novella *Oroonoko* (1688), developed the prototype of the royal African—the slave Oroonoko who revealed his princely origins through the classic features of his rising "Roman nose," his Greek body, and long flowing hair.[43] The painters Rubens and Van Dyck also subscribed to a European ideal of beauty, presenting Africans painted from European models whose faces had been blackened for that purpose.[44] Even Blumenbach, the champion of Africans, saw blacks through European eyes. Of a "Negress" living in Switzerland he wrote: "All the features of her face, even the nose and lips (the latter of which were a little thick, though not so as to be disagreeable) had they been covered with a white skin, must have excited universal admiration."[45]

Jakob Le Maire, Buffon, and Blumenbach all agreed that there were Moorish women who, "blackness excepted," were as well made as the ladies of Europe. Even women whose color was "exceptionally black" could have features exactly the same as those of whites—fine eyes, a small mouth and nose, thin lips, and thick but smooth hair.[46] The sentiment that the physiognomy of beauty was the same the world over animated Bryan Edwards's "Ode to the Sable Venus"—a Venus (FIG. 4.2) whom he considered as lovely as her Florentine sister: "Both just alike, except the white,/no difference, no—none at night."[47] Few eighteenth-century naturalists could imagine the relativism of Joshua Reynolds who wrote in a London newspaper in 1759 that "I suppose nobody will doubt, if one of their [the Africans'] Painters was to paint the Goddess of

128

Z. Stothard pinx.   W. Grainger sca.

The VOYAGE of the SABLE VENUS, from ANGOLA to the WEST INDIES.

Beauty, but that he would represent her black, with thick lips, flat nose, and woolly hair; and, it seems to me, he would act very unnaturally if he did not."[48]

An extraordinary example of the sway that notions of beauty, and female beauty in particular, held over science can be seen in Blumenbach's coining of the term *Caucasian,* an epithet still used today to describe what Webster tells us are "peoples indigenous to Europe, northern Africa, southwestern Asia, and the Indian subcontinent."[49] In one stroke Blumenbach assigned the greatest beauty to a particular people, gave them the honor of being the original humans, and bequeathed a name to his premier race that stands even today as a potent marker of privilege.

According to his own account, Blumenbach took the name from the Caucasus mountain range (seated between the Black and Caspian seas) because this region, especially its southern slope, produced what he considered the most beautiful of all humans— the Georgians. He chose the Caucasus for this honor because "all physiological evidence converged on this region" as the birthplace of humankind. As proof, he pointed to the unsullied whiteness of its inhabitants. "It is very easy," Blumenbach reasoned, "for white skin to degenerate into brown, but very much more difficult for a darker skin already impregnated with carbonaceous pigments to become white, when the secretion and precipitation of . . . carbonaceous pigment has once deeply struck root."[50] (This opinion was not shared by all in this period; John Hunter and James Prichard maintained that humans were originally black, arguing that black animals bred white ones [albinos] accidentally, but no white ones bred black ones. In this instance, however, their blackness marked primitive-

FIG. 4.2. "The Voyage of the Sable Venus, from Angola to the West Indies." In reality, Edwards's Venus would have been carried on a slave ship, not a half shell pulled by fanciful sea serpents. Nor would she have been holding the reins of her own destiny. From Byran Edwards, *The History, Civil and Commercial, of the British Colonies in the West Indies* (London, 1794), vol. 2, facing, p. 27. By permission of the Rare Books and Manuscripts Division, New York Public Library, Astor, Lenox, and Tilden Foundations.

ness.)[51] Even more important than skin color for Blumenbach was the pleasing symmetry of the Georgian skull. For him, the Caucasians' great beauty simply revealed them as the original humans—the archetype from which all other races had degenerated.

How did this odd myth of origin, dubbed by Thomas Huxley as the "Caucasian mystery," arise? The question is complex and merits further study. Biblical traditions surely played a role, as we shall see in a moment. But the aesthetic dimension should also not be ignored. In crowning the Georgians with this honor, Blumenbach followed the opinion of renowned world travelers (notably, Guillaume Delisle and Jean Chardin) and experts in aesthetics (Petrus Camper and Johann Winckelmann).[52] Blumenbach cited the French traveler Jean Chardin, who described the women of Georgia as the most beautiful in all the world:

> The blood of Georgia is the best of the Orient, and perhaps in all the world. In that country I have not observed a single ugly face in either sex, but I have seen angelical ones. Nature has lavished charms upon the women there not to be encountered elsewhere. I consider it impossible to see them without loving them.[53]

Writing in the late seventeenth century, Chardin found no need to justify his opinion; by his day the great beauty of Georgian women was taken for granted.

Why was this? For one thing, Georgia lay in the "temperate zone," which, according to the ancient theory of humors, formed the most perfect humans. This region, defined quite precisely by Buffon in the eighteenth century, encompassed those areas lying between the fortieth and fiftieth degrees of latitude, including Spain, Italy, Greece, France, southern Germany, Georgia, and the Caucasus mountains (but not England, France's long-standing rival).[54] To Blumenbach's credit he did not place the cradle of humanity in his native Germany, though parts of it conveniently lay in the temperate zone. Nor did he present as the archetype of his premier "Caucasian" race a face particularly familiar to his European audience as one might have expected in this age of ethnocentrism. Instead, he bestowed that honor on one Jusuf Aguiah Efendi, an ambassador to London whom Blumenbach identified as coming from the Caucasus (FIG. 4.3). In so doing, Blumenbach followed the European tendency in this period to place the origins of humankind in the highlands of central Asia, not in the river valleys of the Nile or Euphrates, as the ancients had done.[55]

Deeper reasons than ancient theory, however, lay behind the assessment of the beauty of Georgian women that so influenced Blumenbach. The value ascribed to these women apparently emerged from the slave markets of the Levant that flourished from the thirteenth to the late fifteenth centuries.[56] Bernier reported in his 1684 article on race that great numbers of slaves came into Greece and Turkey from Georgia and Circassia along the northeastern coast of the Black Sea. Many were women, who were traded along with wax and furs for spices and silks from the Orient. White slaves, especially females, fetched a high price; those who could sing brought an even higher bid. The Turks apparently so valued the women from the Caucasus that they reserved them exclusively for Turkish harems; Christians and Jews were not allowed to buy them.[57]

Other factors may also have led Blumenbach to choose the Caucasus as the cradle of humanity (though yet other accounts held that God had created the first man on a small column of earth— about four feet high—near Damascus).[58] Noah's ark had come to rest on Mount Ararat in the southern Caucasus, and Blumenbach may simply have taken this biblical account as his starting point.[59] The Caucasus were also the traditional site of the imprisonment of Prometheus, commonly portrayed as an ancestor of the Europeans.[60] But these were not the reasons Blumenbach gave; for him beauty alone was the key unlocking the secret of human origins.

Blumenbach's reverence for beauty may also explain why he singled out a female skull to represent the Caucasian race. Departing from medical traditions that for centuries had established the male as the paragon of human excellence, Blumenbach chose from his vast anthropological collection the skull of a young Georgian woman to represent "the Caucasian."[61] Blumenbach's normative illustration of the young Georgian woman's skull quickly became a

Jusuf Aguiah Efendi.

FIG. 4.3. Blumenbach chose the portrait of Jusuf Aguiah Efendi to represent the Caucasian race—the most perfect human type according to European anatomists. Blumenbach wrote that he could have chosen a Milton or Raphael for this portrait, but he chose this man because his home lay near the Caucasus from which the entire race took its name. From Johann Blumenbach, *Abbildungen naturhistorischer Gegenstände* (Göttingen, 1810), no. 3. By permission of the General Research Division, New York Public Library, Astor, Lenox, and Tilden Foundations.

standard, printed and reprinted in anthropological texts throughout Europe as the quintessential image of the Caucasian. Samuel
Thomas von Soemmerring, for example, borrowed it for his depiction of the (European) female skeleton, checking to see that his
model's head recapitulated its virtues.[62] The English surgeon William Lawrence praised Blumenbach's Georgian skull for combining
physical and moral virtues in equal portion. By contrast, he complained that the head of the Medician Venus—the traditional standard of feminine beauty—was so small that the goddess of love was
surely "an idiot."[63]

Aesthetics continued to influence racial science in the nineteenth century. James Prichard and William Lawrence held that
men's perceptions of physical beauty shaped racial characters.
Beauty, they argued, was the chief principle throughout the world
directing men in marriage (which they considered a form of selec-
tive breeding). Each nation had its own sense of beauty—Africans
preferred flat noses and thick lips, Asians favored angular eyes, and
Europeans appreciated high foreheads—and men selected these
qualities in their brides. In this way, diverse notions of beauty came
to shape the distinctive features of each nation.[64] Prichard and Lawrence offered the Persians as a historical example of this process.
Drawing from Chardin, Prichard reported that the noble families of
modern Persia were originally a tribe of "ugly and bald-headed
Mongols" but because they constantly selected the most beautiful
females of Circassia for their harems, they gradually developed fine
features. Charles Darwin, agreeing with Prichard, wrote some years
later that there was hardly a man of rank in Persia not born of a
Georgian or Circassian mother.[65]

Prichard and Lawrence argued further that aesthetics influenced physical differentiation between England's social classes.
Prichard attributed the handsome physique of the English upper
classes to the men of those classes having long selected beautiful
women for their wives. While the physiognomy and physique of the
higher social ranks gradually improved through this form of selec-
tive breeding, those of "inferior people" deteriorated. The lower
classes, Prichard reported, had little freedom to choose mates, since

for them marriage was often driven by economic necessity and the caprice of their superiors.[66]

Beauty also played a powerful role in Charles Darwin's theory of sexual selection—a theory used to explain racial diversity. According to Darwin, human and animal senses are so constituted that certain colors, shapes, and sounds give pleasure; these are called beautiful. Animals acquire secondary sexual characteristics, such as beards in mammals (one of Darwin's prime examples) or brilliant plumage in birds, as ornaments "to excite and charm the opposite sex." Darwin also included racial characteristics—skin color, the shape of noses and skulls—among secondary sexual characteristics influencing mating patterns. Racial variation thus arises from the fact that notions of beauty are not universal. Each race accentuates the characteristics it prizes through sexual selection. While Prichard and Lawrence had placed sexual selection firmly in men's hands, Darwin refused to say whether he thought racial characteristics were acted upon chiefly by the male or the female.[67]

Do Women Shape the Race?

One of the most remarkable ways in which race intersected with sex in the eighteenth century was that women—regardless of race— were commonly thought to help shape racial characteristics. This age-old notion that women manually mold a number of racial traits, dating back at least to Hippocrates, was embedded in *environmentalism*—one of the two leading theories of racial diversity in the eighteenth century (the other was an early form of what we now call *biological determinism*). For Buffon, Blumenbach, John Hunter, and other environmentalists, racial characteristics—the shape of noses and lips, the color of skin and texture of hair, and the shape of the skull—were fluid, formed over a number of years by external forces working on the body. These forces included climate, diet, and customs; the vagaries of epidemics or disease; the crossing of different races; and, last but not least, the manipulative hands of women.[68] In the idiom of Buffon, mothers and midwives took the homogeneous stuff of humanity and carved from it the peculiarities of national types.

Noses in particular were thought to be shaped by the rhythms of mothers' lives. Blumenbach characteristically wrote that "the thick nose and swelling lips of Ethiopians are always attributed to the way in which, while in their infancy, they are generally carried on the backs of their mothers, who give them suck while they pound millet, or during their hard and heavy tasks."[69] The pounding of the baby's head against its mother during such activities flattened their facial features. Blumenbach conceded that racial contours of the nose could be recognized even in aborted fetuses (that is, before being shaped by maternal habits), but he took Hippocrates' view that after bodily features had been artificially shaped for a very long time a kind of "natural degeneration" takes place, so that eventually no more manual pressure is required to produce a flat nose. In the subsequent formulation of Lamarck, acquired characteristics could be inherited.

If the noses of these children somehow escaped unintentional transformations, mothers were thought apt to seek the same effect as a matter of aesthetics, depressing the nose and squeezing the lips to make them thick. Peter Kolb, the German astronomer who compiled a comprehensive ethnography of the "Hottentots" (the Khoi-khoi of southwestern Africa) in the early eighteenth century, reported that they considered a prominent nose very ugly. No sooner had a woman delivered her infant, reported Kolb, than she broke the bridge of its nose with her thumb. Kolb related that he had once seen a child grow up with its nose unbroken, but that this horridly pointy nose was to serve as a reminder of its mother's infamy (her husband suspected her of having conceived by a European).[70]

More significant than their supposed agency in shaping noses was women's role in shaping skulls. Skull shape and size became by the late eighteenth century the measure *sine qua non* of intelligence. It seems most remarkable, then, that mothers and midwives should have been seen as a crucial force molding this particular characteristic. But again environmentalists emphasized the manipulative hands of mothers. If Germans had especially broad heads, it was because German mothers always slept their babies on their backs. Belgians had oblong heads because Belgian mothers wrapped their infants in swaddling clothes and slept them as much as possible on their sides and temples. Greeks and Turks had nearly spherical heads through the special care of midwives.[71] American Indians had flat heads because their mothers cradled them in such a way that the weight of their bodies bore down on the crowns of their heads, making their faces appear remarkably broad. Caribs had flat foreheads, peaked crowns, and convex parietal bones because mothers and midwives banded their heads (FIG. 4.4). As Rousseau remarked, if we are not satisfied with the way God has shaped our heads, we have them modeled from without by midwives and formed from within by philosophers.[72]

In this period, too, mothers' imaginations were judged potent enough to alter skin color. Black babies might have been born to white families as a result of maternal impressions during conception or pregnancy. It was said that Lot's daughters saw smoke as they fled burning Sodom and that their imaginations fixed that color upon their children.[73] At the same time, an African queen who dreamed of snow was said to have borne a white child.

The role ascribed mothers in fashioning bodies took on truly remarkable proportions. Voyagers regularly noted the Hottentot practice of removing the left testicle of young boys. This ceremonial castration, which some traced to Hottentots' supposed Jewish descent (likening castration to circumcision), was explained as a way to make males fast runners and keen hunters. Europeans further supposed that Hottentots removed one testicle as a means to avoid conceiving twins or to promote conceiving males (this latter being a projection of the European notion that females had their origins in the inferior left side of the body). According to some rather fanciful accounts, "villainous" mothers dominated these castration ceremonies, tearing out with their teeth and eating the left testicle of their newborn males.[74]

The notion that external forces (the heat of the climate or mothers' hands) molded racial features figured in debates about

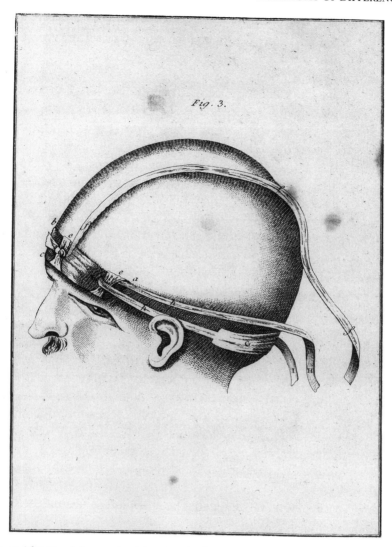

FIG. 4.4. The Guadeloupe physician Amic's plates showing banding practices among the Caribs of St. Vincent's island. Disinclined to believe that mothers were responsible for the peculiar shape of Caribs' heads, Amic studied the matter for himself in 1791 when a number of Caribs arrived in Guadeloupe in dugout canoes. "Lettre de M. Amic à M. De La Métherie sur les têtes des Caraïbes," *Journal de physique, de chimie, de histoire naturelle, et des arts* (August 1791): 132–138, plate 2. By permission of the Science and Technology Research Center, New York Public Library, Astor, Lenox, and Tilden Foundations.

slavery and the moral worth of non-Europeans. As played out in the eighteenth century, environmentalism tended to foster liberal attitudes. Continental environmentalists were by and large opposed to slavery and its attendant racism.[75] Most environmentalists were monogenists who believed that all humanity shared a common ancestry with Adam and Eve. They opposed the polygenists, the worst of the racists who taught that human races were immutable physical entities created separately at the beginning of time. Environmentalists, such as Buffon and Blumenbach, saw all humans as potentially equal. For them, physical differences resulted from the effects of diverse environments acting on an otherwise uniform human nature. If bodies differed simply in response to the environment, then all peoples were made of the same raw material and had the same potential for intellectual and moral achievement. Racial traits were not fixed but impressed into heredity by climate or food, and could easily be modified by new conditions. According to this theory, racial characteristics marked "accidental"—not essential—differences between peoples. A flat nose, for example, revealed human manipulation, not innate inferiority.[76]

As one might imagine, eighteenth-century Africans writing against slavery favored the environmentalist argument that all men were by nature equal. Ottobah Cugoano, kidnapped and sold into slavery by fellow Africans, is a case in point. Transported from the Guinea Gold Coast to Grenada in the English Antilles, he was eventually purchased by an English lord and taken to England. There he published his elegant plea against slavery in 1787. Like the majority of abolitionists, Cugoano favored Christian and humanitarian arguments. To the extent, however, that he appealed to science, he used environmentalism to argue that differences in complexion resulted from the effects of climate. Denying that there was such a thing as a chain of being where blacks were merely a "link . . . fitted only to be slaves," Cugoano urged that the light of nature and dictates of reason taught that no man ought to enslave another. "Africans, though not learned, are just as wise as the Europeans."[77] Olaudah Equiano, a freed Ibo slave who fought for abolition, also found environmentalism the best scientific argument for equality. In his 1789 autobiography, he noted that a person's complexion modulated with the climate. Spaniards, it was commonly said, turned dark in hot climates. This fact, Equiano declared, should have removed all prejudice against Africans. "Surely the minds of the Spaniards did not change with their complexions!"[78]

Though environmentalism was better than the alternative, it nonetheless harbored a strident ethnocentrism. Lurking in the background of the notion that mothers shaped facial features was the assumption that the raw material (from which the varieties of humankind were formed) was European. Environmentalists presumed that all children—African, Chinese, Tahitian—were born with fine Indo-European features until some outside force intervened to deform them. According to Blumenbach (who had it on the testimony of "the most credible eyewitnesses"), it took considerable force to depress the noses of African babies. Blumenbach also identified upper-class Ethiopian noses with those of Europeans: the noses of upper-class Ethiopians were not wide and flaring because their mothers did not engage in the hard labor characteristic of lower-class women.[79] One observer argued that any child who happened to escape these pressures would have had an elevated nose, thin lips, and features as fine as those of Europeans.[80] Some men of African descent seemed to accept this aspect of environmentalism. Francis Williams, a free black from Jamaica who studied at Cambridge University in the eighteenth century, identified himself as "a white man acting under a black skin."[81]

The notion that women, as agents of custom, shaped human bodies continued to hold sway in the eighteenth century. As late as 1795, Blumenbach culled from medical texts and travelogues a comprehensive bibliography of cultures said still to be forming physical features by artificial means. But things were to change. Beginning in the middle of the eighteenth century a number of medical men began to deny women this power over nature. William Lawrence belittled such stories as "old-wives tales" that no "physiologist" would believe.[82] At stake in these debates concerning female agency was the origin and significance of racial characteristics. Essentially the question was whether racial characteristics were merely accidental, as environmentalists maintained, or inborn as biological determinists taught—sign and symptom of mental and moral deficiencies.

Petrus Camper was among the first to launch a major assault on the notion that women shaped the race. He devoted two chapters of his book on facial angles to refuting the "ridiculous" notion that "midwives, mothers, or nurses" flattened or lengthened noses by perpetually compressing or pulling them.[83] Though an environmentalist in many matters, he broke with his male counterparts in denying that human intervention, particularly the manipulations of midwives or mothers, shaped racial characters. Variety in human noses he considered natural; and skulls, if modified at all, were molded by mothers' pelvises during the throes of labor and delivery. The German Soemmerring, a leading biological determinist, paid close attention to the question of how noses became flat while studying blacks at the Wilhelmshöhe colony. "The Moors are said to flatten the noses of their children," he wrote in his *Vom Baue des menschlichen Körpers*, "but this characteristic is certainly innate. All of the Moorish children born at Kassel had flat features, though their noses were not pressed in."[84] Camper and Soemmerring opposed the view that noses were pressed flat at birth, maintaining instead that racial features could be distinguished in the fetus. The nose question was of particular interest to Soemmerring because, though personally opposed to slavery, he thought that blacks were naturally inferior to Europeans: the "cold facts" of anatomy showed them to be "nearer the ape." Soemmerring, like Buffon and Blumenbach, was a monogenist, yet he also believed that the peoples of the earth differed in morally and intellectually significant ways.[85]

Soemmerring's purpose was to show that racial characteristics ran deeper than generally thought. Responding to the notion of the "royal slave," he wrote: "If skin were the only difference, then the Negro might be considered a black European," but this was not the case. Soemmerring was instrumental in shifting attention from the study of skin color to bones—skeletons and skulls—because, he argued, these were the parts of the body least affected by climate. More permanent than skin color, they seemed a more reliable measure of true racial character. If racial differences could be found in the bones of the body, biological determinists felt they could show that differences between the races penetrated the entire body of the organism.[86]

Soemmerring did not entirely deny that custom molded biology. He railed against elite European women who deformed their daughters' bodies through the unnatural use of the corset. He complained that trusses caused pubic bones to protrude, that too much horseback riding deformed legs, that too much kneeling widened kneecaps, that shoes ruined feet. But these, he argued, were relatively superficial transformations affecting only one generation. They were not, in other words, transformations that were heritable.

Environmentalists and biological determinists faced off over the origin and significance of racial characteristics, yet their debates centered around the question of women's agency. Why should this be so? Though not mentioned in these debates, this was a period when women's agency in health matters was being challenged more generally. For hundreds of years, midwives had held a monopoly on the entire field of women's health care. Beginning in the seventeenth and increasingly in the eighteenth century, the new "man-midwives" (of whom Camper was one) began encroaching on this ancient monopoly and, by the nineteenth century, as is now notorious, university-trained obstetricians had taken over the more scientific (and lucrative) parts of birthing.[87] Midwives were run out of business by the attempt to make birthing more dependent on university training in anatomy, from which women were excluded. Camper, who argued strenuously that women do not shape racial characteristics, had spent several years in London training with William Smellie, the inventor of the obstetric forceps and a key player in the movement to displace the traditional midwife.

This is not to say that women's role (partly real, partly mythical) in accentuating racial characteristics was necessarily admirable. In addition to their relatively benign shaping of heads, elite women of Europe deformed their daughter's rib cages with whalebone corsets; women of China maimed their daughters' feet by binding them to conform to aesthetic ideals; women in various parts of Africa mu-

142   tilated young girls, circumcising them in highly ritualized ceremonies. Nonetheless it is significant that the issue of women's intervention in the human body emerged along with larger transformations
in science and politics. As I have shown elsewhere, the consolida-
tion of the (predominantly male) medical profession coincided
with a scientific revolution in definitions of sex and the development of a new image of women as essentially nonscientific.[88] It also
coincided with the revolution in definitions of race and the attempt
to ground scientifically the exclusion of men of color from science.
In France, the traditional exclusion of people of color from European professions was codified in 1763 by a royal ordinance that
among other things forbade any man of African origins, whether
slave or free, to practice medicine or surgery.[89] Thus women stood
at the center of a debate concerning race at a time when the exclusion of both women and peoples of color from science was being
formalized. European men, dominating academic science, increasingly tightened the reins on what was recognized as legitimate
knowledge and who could produce that knowledge.

5

Theories of Gender and Race

The volcanic eruption of freedom in France will soon bring on
a larger explosion, one that will transform the destiny of
humankind in both hemispheres.

Henri Grégoire, *De la littérature des nègres*, 1808

The expansive mood of the Enlightenment—the feeling that all
men are by nature equal—gave middle- and lower-class men,
women, Jews, Africans, and West Indians living in Europe reason to
believe that they, too, might begin to share the privileges heretofore
reserved for elite European men. Optimism rested in part on the
ambiguities inherent in the word "man" as used in revolutionary
documents of the period. The 1789 *Declaration of the Rights of Man
and Citizen* said nothing about race or sex, leading many to assume
that the liberties it proclaimed would hold universally. The future
president of the French National Assembly, Honoré-Gabriel Ri-
queti, comte de Mirabeau, declared that no one could claim that
"white men are born and remain free, black men are born and remain slaves."[1] Nor did the universal and celebrated "man" seem to
exclude women. Addressing the convention in 1793, an anonymous
woman declared: "Citizen legislators, you have given men a constitution . . . as the constitution is based on the rights of man, we now
demand the full exercise of these rights for ourselves."[2]

Within this revolutionary republican framework, an appeal to
natural rights could be countered only by proof of natural inequalities. The marquis de Condorcet wrote, for instance, that if women

were to be excluded from the *polis*, one must demonstrate a "natural difference" between men and women to legitimate that exclusion.[3] In other words, if social inequalities were to be justified within the framework of Enlightenment thought, scientific evidence would have to show that human nature is not uniform, but differs according to age, race, and sex.

Scientific communities responded to this challenge with intense scrutiny of human bodies, generating countless examples of radical misreadings of the human body that scholars have described as scientific racism and scientific sexism.[4] These two movements shared many key features. Both regarded women and non-European men as deviations from the European male norm. Both deployed new methods to measure and discuss difference. Both sought natural foundations to justify social inequalities between the sexes and races. Eighteenth-century anthropologists, though, did not always perceive that what they said about sex had a bearing on race and vice versa. Leading theories underlying scientific racism (the doctrine of a great chain of being, for example) did not incorporate new views on sexual difference, while leading theories explaining sexual divergence (the doctrine of sexual complementarity being a prime example) applied only to Europeans.

In the preceding chapter we saw how gender conventions molded certain aspects of racial studies. Here we explore the paradoxes and incompatibilities plaguing eighteenth-century theories of sexual and racial difference. Where did naturalists place women along the great chain of being? To what extent did the theory of sexual complementarity reach beyond Europe? How, in other words, did notions of gender influence the study of race, and how did notions of European superiority influence studies of sex? The anatomy of sex and race was caught up, as we shall see, in eighteenth-century politics of participation—struggles over who should do science and who should be actively involved in affairs of the state. Eighteenth-century male anatomists in Europe were obsessed with black men (the dominant sex of an inferior race) and white women (the inferior sex of the dominant race). It was these two groups, and not primarily women of African descent, who challenged European male elites in their calls for equal rights and political participation.

Were Women on the Chain?

One of the most powerful doctrines governing theories of race in the eighteenth century was the great chain of being. This doctrine postulated that species were immutable entities arrayed along a fixed and vertical hierarchy stretching from God above down to the lowliest sentient being. The historian Winthrop Jordan has shown that the notion of a chain of being became the darling of eighteenth-century conservatives in their attempts to stem the leveling tide of democracy and abolitionism.[5] The conservative British naturalist William Smellie, for example, taught that social hierarchies issued from natural hierarchies. "Independently of all political institutions," Smellie wrote in his 1790 *Philosophy of Natural History*, "Nature herself has formed the human species into castes and ranks."[6]

Europe's anatomists dissected and analyzed the skeletons of animals and humans from every corner of the world in their attempts to substantiate the notion that nature shades continuously from one form to another. Of special interest were the transitional forms bridging the gap between animals and humans. Although different animals vied for a time as the "missing link" (elephants, for their intelligence, and parrots, for their ability to talk), by the eighteenth century naturalists had settled on the ape, and especially the orangutan (still commonly used as a generic name for both chimpanzees and orangutans), as the animal most resembling humankind. What, though, was the "lowest" sort of human? Voyagers, coming into contact with Africans in the course of colonial expansion and the slave trade, had already suggested that the people of this continent resembled the apes who inhabited this same region.[7] (Some went so far as to suggest that the black race originated from whites copulating with apes.)[8] Within this context arose a project central to eighteenth-century anatomy: investigation into the exact relationship among apes, Africans, and Europeans.

Much has been written about the racist implications of the chain of being.[9] What has not been investigated, however, is the place of females in that hierarchy. The notion of a single chain of being stretching throughout nature (and society) created a problem of where to fit women. Scientific racism and scientific sexism both taught that proper social relations between the races and the sexes existed in nature. Many theorists failed to see, however, that their notions of racial and sexual relations rested on contradictory visions of nature. Scientific racism depended on a chain of being or hierarchy of species in nature that was inherently unilinear and absolute. Scientific sexism, by contrast, depended on radical biological divergence. The theory of sexual complementarity attempted to extract males and females from competition with or hierarchy over each other by defining them as opposites, each perfect though radically different and for that reason suited to separate social spheres.[10] Thus the notion of a single chain of being worked at odds with the revolutionary view of sexual difference which postulated a radical incommensurability between the sexes (of European descent).

Before investigating further women's place on the chain, we must turn to the glaring asymmetries in studies of race and sex in this period. Most strikingly, racial science interrogated males and male physiology, while sexual science scrutinized European subjects. As one might imagine, eighteenth-century comparative anatomists and anthropologists were overwhelmingly male. What is especially revealing, however, is that they developed their theories about race by examining male bodies. Females were studied, but only as a sexual subset of any particular race. Consider the work of the German anatomist Samuel Thomas von Soemmerring in this regard. His 1785 book on race, *Über die körperliche Verschiedenheit des Negers vom Europäer*, compared the bodies of Africans and Europeans, most of which were male.[11] His preference for male bodies was not simply an artifact of availability. He had dissected at least one female African in Kassel, observed "dozens" of blacks (including females) at the public baths,[12] and had at least part of a female African skeleton (probably from the dissected female) in his anthropological collection.[13] Soemmerring also knew black women personally, having arranged transportation to Amsterdam for one of "his Mohrin" (he commonly referred to Africans as Moors).[14] It is not clear, though, what was meant by calling her "his" Mohrin—she may have been his servant or perhaps simply one of his objects of study.

At the same time, when anatomists turned their attention to sexual difference, they tended to confine their studies to middle-class Europeans. While Soemmerring's study of race focused on males, his study of sex, epitomized in his classic illustration of the female skeleton undertaken eleven years after his anatomy of race, treated only Europeans.[15] Indeed, anatomists' portrayals of distinctively female skeletons, ushering in the eighteenth-century revolution in views of sexual difference, were all of Europeans. The canonical texts of that revolution—by Rousseau, Roussel, Ackermann, and Moreau de la Sarthe—similarly compared males and females of undifferentiated European origin.[16] Females were rarely compared across racial lines in the eighteenth century; or, if they were, it was commonly in relation to their sexual parts. Only in the nineteenth century did Virey's *De la femme*, written to complement his work on race published some twenty years earlier, explore the "natural history of woman" with some attention to race.[17]

This assumption that the racial subject was male and that sexual differentiation was primarily about Europeans had deep roots. At least since Aristotle natural historians had given preference to the study of male bodies, or more precisely, the bodies of male citizens. Woman, considered a monstrous error of nature, was studied for her deviation from this male norm. The philosopher Elizabeth Spelman has recently shown that when Aristotle spoke about "women," he referred, in fact, only to free women (the wives of citizens). She goes on to show that when Aristotle spoke about slaves, he assumed a male subject, even though he recognized that there were significant numbers of women among slave populations. Aristotle's political philosophy drew no distinction between male and female slaves; it was also neutral with respect to the relation between slaves and free women because both women and slaves found their place in the polis through the services they rendered to male citizens.[18]

Physical anthropologists in the eighteenth century did not consciously center their studies of race on the male body. For them, the "European," "African," and "American" were assumed to be generic, sexless universal types. While men of science argued over whether a skull, arriving from overseas stripped of skin and hair, was genuinely that of an African, Carib, or Brazilian (suppliers were often unreliable concerning the provenance of their specimens), they rarely queried the sex of the specimen. Inventories of their collections of hair, skulls, skin, genitalia, and other soft tissues reveal that, where the sex of the specimen was known and recorded, it was most often male.[19] Even Buffon, who drew his information from travelogues (not dissection tables) and had quite a lot to say about women, assumed that the person described was male unless specifically labeled female.[20]

One might suppose that anatomists lavished attention on males in this period because there were simply more men among foreign populations living in Europe, and their bodies were more readily available for study. Three quarters of the 765 *gens de couleur* living in Paris between the years 1777 and 1790, for instance, were male.[21] Men (both European and non-European) traveled more freely and were active in foreign armies. But the attention given to males in this period also reveals a recalcitrant preference for them. Charles White collected data primarily from men (at a ratio of about six to one) in settings where women were equally available. When measuring the upper arms and forearms of living subjects in Manchester, he used his butler, gardener, coachman, and footman, not his maid or (female) cook. He also sought out measurements from a male apothecary at the local lying-in hospital—an environment abounding with potential female subjects whom he investigated only when studying distinctively female features, such as changes in pigmentation during pregnancy.[22]

That males were taken as universal racial subjects can best be seen in anthropological studies of skulls. In the eighteenth century, skulls were used to forge a new, racial chain of being. Interest in the faculty of reason, considered by many the generic characteristic responsible for humankind's vast superiority over all other animals, and increasingly important for citizenship in European society, brought to the fore the study of skulls as measures of intelligence. Reason had long been considered a masculine trait in Western cultures, and the skulls used in these studies were overwhelmingly male.[23]

Petrus Camper was one of the first to suggest that skull measurements could illuminate the natural relationship among apes, Negroes, and Europeans. Significantly, he was one of those who opposed the idea that skulls were shaped by women's hands (see chapter 4); for him, skulls revealed *natural* relations between humans, not cultural artifice. Regarding his collection of skulls, he wrote:

> It is amusing to contemplate an arrangement of these [skulls], placed in a regular succession: apes, orangs, negroes, the skull of an Hottentot, Madagascar, Celebese, Chinese, Moguller, Calmuck, and divers Europeans. It was in this manner that I arranged them upon a shelf in my cabinet.[24]

Camper sorted apes and humans by his newly devised *linea facialis* ("facial line"). Having invented an elaborate instrument for this purpose, he took numerous measurements of skulls in order to determine the angle of "prognathism," or forward jutting of the jaw. He set as the ideal an angle of one hundred degrees, a facial angle acknowledged not to exist in reality but often used to portray gods and goddesses in Greek statuary. Measured with this ideal in mind, apes were said to have a facial angle of forty-two to fifty degrees, African Negroes and Kalmuks (the Mongolian peoples of northwestern China) a facial angle of seventy degrees, and Europeans a more noble angle of eighty degrees.[25] Even animals were judged by their facial angle. As William Lawrence explained, the owl's perfectly vertical facial line lent it an "air of intelligence" such that it had been selected as the emblem of Athena, the goddess of wisdom.[26]

With his facial angle Camper developed the central visual icon of all subsequent racism: a hierarchy of skulls passing progressively from lowliest ape and Negro to loftiest Greek (FIG. 5.1). As the primary instrument of racism in the nineteenth century, the facial line became the most frequent means of explaining the gradation of species. Despite his role as the founder of craniology, recent scholars have argued that Camper was, in fact, not a racist—that the whole reason for his constructing the facial angle was to provide a more realistic standard for depicting racial physique. Troubled by Western portraits of Africans as black-faced whites, Camper set out to devise simple guidelines to define the chief characteristics of each human group. In this sense, he tried to do for non-European bodies what Leonardo da Vinci had done for Europeans. His point was not, in other words, to value the European race over all others. Disputing the commonly held opinion that humans created in the image of God were originally white, Camper boldly wrote that Adam might have been created "black, brown, tanned, or white."[27] Perhaps even more telling, Camper, using the approach of the new empiricism, claimed that "objects have no color in themselves; and that the idea of color is excited in us according to the manner in which the rays of light are refracted."[28] Stephen Jay Gould and others have used this and Camper's other heterodox statements to argue that the man celebrated as the father of craniometry did not in fact believe that one race was superior to another.[29]

It is not clear that Camper is so easily exonerated from charges of racism. Others in this period made a point of avoiding unfavorable racial comparisons. Johann Blumenbach, the German father of physical anthropology, was famous for having amassed one of the largest skull collections in Europe (he claimed it was *the* largest). Though Blumenbach was keenly interested in identifying racial

---

FIG. 5.1. Camper's study of racial types classified by facial angle from the orangutan (fifty-eight degrees) to the majestic Pythian Apollo (a perfect one hundred existing only in Greek sculpture). Only the orang is female. From Petrus Camper, *Über den natürlichen Unterschied der Gesichtszüge in Menschen*, trans. Samuel Thomas von Soemmerring (Berlin, 1792), plate 3. (Sign.: Nn 11 760.) By permission of the Staatsbibliothek zu Berlin—Preußischer Kulturbesitz.

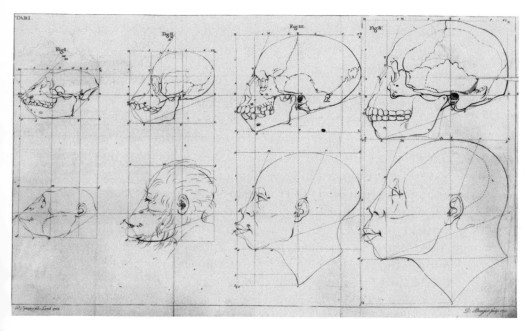

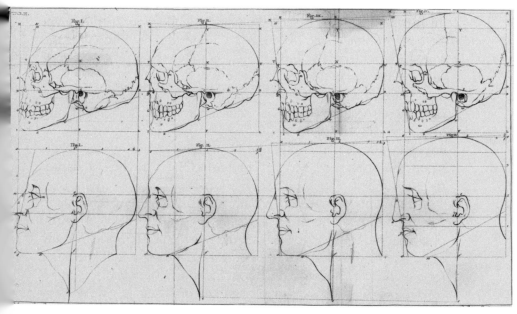

variation, he vigorously resisted ranking humans along a single scale of being. "I am indeed very much opposed to the opinions of those [physico-theologians, as Blumenbach called them], who, especially of late, have amused their ingenuity so much with what they call the continuity or gradation of nature."[30] When Blumenbach compared the skull of an ape and a human, he made a point to organize his materials differently. Quite aware of the implications of his work, Blumenbach excised Africans from the comparison, specifically choosing *not* to compare the skull of an ape to that of a Negro as was customary. Indeed, Blumenbach likened the skull of an orangutan to the skull of a Caucasian—his beloved Georgian. Writing some years after Camper and in the thick of debates about slavery and the slave trade, Blumenbach remarked that he might have chosen the skull of a Negro for this purpose, but he deliberately did not. He did not, like Camper, present images that could easily be used to produce unfavorable comparisons.[31]

What is telling, in relation to our theme, is that the skulls highlighted in these studies were predominantly male. The only female skull Camper used was that of an orangutan (see again FIG. 5.1), though he had other female skulls in his collection that he might have incorporated into his image.[32] Camper did not often note the sex of his subjects (he himself may not always have known their sex), yet the sex of this series of skulls is suggested by the head of the great Pythian Apollo crowning this progression of the human races. Again, Camper might have chosen as the capstone of the human race the Venus de Medici, whom anatomists commonly invoked in this period as a universal standard of beauty (especially when their purpose was to emphasize the brutality of darker races).[33]

Blumenbach was, indeed, unusual in using female skulls to represent three of his five major races (Caucasian, Malay, and Ethiopian) in his classic *On the Natural Varieties of Mankind*.[34] At the same time, he labeled as female only the Caucasian skull; the other four skulls were presented without mention of sex (FIG. 5.2). In regard to his choice of skulls, he remarked only that they were "very select" specimens.[35] Blumenbach followed more general patterns

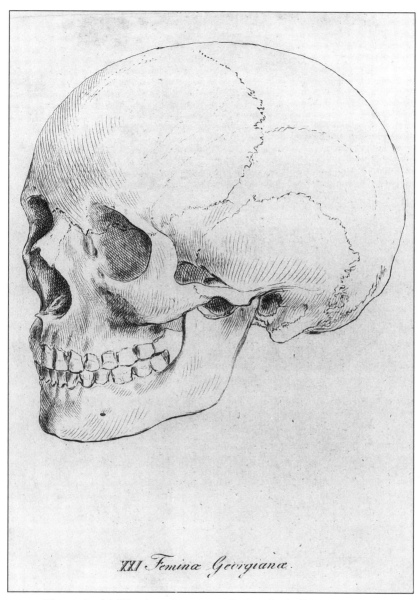

XXI Feminæ Georgianæ.

FIG. 5.2. Blumenbach's "Feminae Georgianae," a female skull from the Caucasus. Blumenbach considered the Caucasian skull the most beautiful in all the world. From Blumenbach, *On the Natural Varieties of Mankind*, plate 4.

Feodor Iwanowitsch.

FIG. 5.3. Blumenbach's five model heads were all male. From Johann Blumenbach, *Abbildungen naturhistorischer Gegenstände* (Göttingen, 1810), nos. 1–5. By permission of the General Research Division, New York Public Library, Astor, Lenox, and Tilden Foundations.

in racial science, however, when he presented five fully fleshed portraits, one for each of his major races of humankind. These five "model heads" were all male (FIG. 5.3).

Blumenbach seemed unconcerned that female skulls underlay the flesh of three of his male model heads. (The model heads were drawn to accompany the five skulls presented in his *On the Natural Varieties of Mankind*; Blumenbach invited his readers to compare the skulls from this earlier work with these portraits.) This is all the more surprising given that Blumenbach set such store by the correspondence between skull and portrait that he devised a gadget for comparing the two. Using a glass plate, he drew the outline of a skull onto one piece of paper and the outline of the portrait onto another. He then overlaid the two pieces of paper, holding

Tayadaneega.

Jusuf Aguiah Efendi.

Omai.

Jac. Jo. Eliza Capitein.

them up to a light to see if the fundamental shape of the two coincided.[36]

When anthropologists did compare women across cultures, their interest centered on sexual traits—feminine beauty, redness of lips, length and style of hair, size and shape of breasts or clitorises, degree of sexual desire, fertility, and above all the size, shape, and position of the pelvis. For the anatomists among them, it was the pelvis (and its procreative virtues) that ultimately emerged as the universal measure of womanliness.[37] The female pelvis, however, never achieved the symbolic standing of the male skull. No chart of pelvises took on the mythic proportions of Camper's skulls and their successors. Skulls, and indeed male skulls, remained the central icon of racial difference until craniometry was replaced by intelligence testing in the late-nineteenth and early-twentieth centuries.[38]

Initially, anatomists steered away from the pelvis when ordering the races because it posed problems for their supposed chain of racial being. While their rankings of skulls were devised to show the proximity of apes and Negroes, pelvises threatened to tell a different story. African women's alleged extraordinary ease in parturition seemed to indicate pelvises more capacious than European women's—bigger in this case being better. Voyagers and ships' surgeons had long reported that women of African descent gave birth easily (this was also assumed to be true of apes and other quadrupeds). Buffon assured his eighteenth-century readers that African women "bring forth their children with great ease, and require no assistance. Their labors are followed by no troublesome consequences; for their strength is fully restored by a day or, at most, two days' repose."[39] The historian Barbara Bush has pointed out that this myth justified working slave women throughout their pregnancies and returning them to the fields shortly after parturition.[40]

Camper made sporadic attempts to measure female pelvises beginning in the 1750s. His initial results seemed to confirm the "well-known fact" that women of warm climates gave birth easily. Devising a pelvic angle from various measurements of the pelvic aperture, he set the optimum for the well-built (European) woman at one hundred degrees. He then procured "not without much trouble and great cost" pelvic bones from a female African, Asian, and American. In each of these subjects he discovered the pelvic opening to be "wider and noticeably rounder" so that the child's head could easily "shoot through."[41] Elsewhere, however, Camper drew the conclusion that Africans had *narrower* pelvises than Europeans from his comparison of the ratio of the length to the breadth of the pelvis in seven humans (one European female and probably two others, three European males, and one male Negro) and from his examination of pelvic measurements from three statues (the Farnese Hercules, Pythian Apollo, and Venus de Medici).[42] His explanation in this text was that Africans' pelvises were narrowed during childhood by virtue of the fact that the back part of their skulls were proportionally heavier than whites'. In order to keep their balance, Africans tended to throw their heads back and jut their necks forward in such a manner that their pelvises gradually bent inward.[43] Soemmerring confirmed Camper's conclusion that Africans had narrower pelvises than Europeans after measuring four male subjects (but not the African female he had dissected).[44] Prichard and White suggested that Camper and Soemmerring's conclusions were flawed because too many of their subjects were male.[45]

While the study of skulls emerged prominently in the late eighteenth century, systematic study of the racial pelvis did not begin until the 1820s. Moritz Weber, a pioneer in this respect, proclaimed in his 1830 *Theory of Fundamental and Racial Forms of the Skull and Pelvis in Humankind*: "That racial skulls exist is now a matter of fact; that racial pelvises also exist . . . has only very recently been proven."[46] When pelvises were studied systematically, they were ranked superior or inferior, lower or higher in accord with the principles of the supposed chain of being. Studies of the "racial pelvis" brought the female pelvis into line with the chain. Differences in sex, which had long been discussed, were subordinated to racial types which, in turn, were arrayed along the chain. In Africans, the female pelvis, by contrast with the male, was said to be light and delicate; the male pelvis was said to be so dense that it resembled the pelvis of a wild beast. When compared to the pelvis of the European female, however, the African woman's was described as entirely destitute of the transparent delicacy characteristic of the female European. The Dutch anatomist Willem Vrolik made a point of saying that no matter how light or fine the pelvis of African females, they were of the same race as African males. Their pelvises shared with the males the *Urform* of that race: an elongated form said to recall the shape of the pelvis in apes.[47]

In the 1830s, Weber sorted pelvises into distinct racial types. The oval pelvis was found most commonly in Europeans; the round pelvis in Americans; the square in Mongolians; and the oblong (the most narrow, bestial type) in Africans. The seeming contradiction of the African pelvis had been resolved. Ease of parturition no longer suggested a larger African pelvis, but a smaller African skull (there was assumed to be a natural complementarity between head and pelvis). Effortless birthing was also assumed to result from their primitive way of life (simple diets and constant labor).[48] The notion that Africans had crudely narrow pelvises spawned the absurd notion current in the late nineteenth century that steatopygia (the enlarged buttocks characteristic of Hottentot females) was a natural adaptation mimicking the large pelvis of the "higher races." Their large buttocks were seen, in other words, as nature's way of compensating for racial deficiencies.[49]

This brings us back to the question: Where were women on the postulated chain of being? Recent scholars, discussing nineteenth-century racial science, have argued that scientists of that period saw sex and race as two aspects of the same problem. Women and Africans were seen as sharing similar deficiencies when measured against a constant norm—the elite European man. Women and black males had narrow, childlike skulls; both were innately impulsive, emotional, and imitative. European women shared the apelike jutting jaw of the lower races, while males of the lower races had prominent bellies similar to those of Caucasian women who had borne many children.[50]

This assessment, however, does not take into account the contrasting ways in which European naturalists described women of different ethnic and cultural backgrounds. The eighteenth-century revolution in views of sexual difference applied only to Europeans.

The theory of sexual complementarity born of that revolution offered a new picture of the middle-class European female. Fragments of the old picture of woman as man *manqué* did persist: she did not measure up to the male in terms of physical and intellectual strength, for example. But her portrait was no longer entirely negative. In this era of the polarization of public and private spheres, the ideal of republican motherhood saw woman as delicate, pure, and passionless, a bastion of moral and spiritual virtue—"the better half" of her robust, solid, and assertive companion.

The black female (and by various degrees of skin hue, other non-European women) did not fit this vision of womanhood. African women were seen as wanton perversions of sexuality, not paragons of piety and purity. They served as foils to the Victorian ideal of the passionless woman, becoming, as Sander Gilman has written, the central icon for sexuality in the nineteenth century.[51] Women of African descent were not idealized as angels of the household, but forced to labor in the fields like beasts whom they were said to resemble. Elite European naturalists who set such store by complementarity when describing their own mothers, wives, and sisters refused to include African women in their new definitions of femininity.

Blumenbach, who ridiculed attempts to identify a natural scale of being as "metaphorical and allegorical amusements," discussed the impossibility of building a single sexual and racial hierarchy. In animals such as silkworms, he suggested, there was so great a difference in the appearance of either sex, that if you wanted to refer them to a scale of that kind, "it would be necessary to separate the males as far as possible from their females, and to place the different sexes of the same species in the most different places."[52] Such a separation would have been, in his view, absurd.

To the extent, then, that comparative anatomists in this period devised a scale of being, it emerged from the comparison of male virtues across races, especially the virtues of male skulls. In most instances, sexual differences were considered secondary to racial differences. As Camper wrote, "men, women, and children bear the characteristic marks of their race from their births," for, as Virey explained a half century later, the two sexes are submitted to the same general laws of nature.[53] Europeans were not particularly interested in whether African females were physically and morally superior or inferior to African males, rather both sexes were compared to Europeans. Females in general were considered a sexual subset of their race; unique female traits only served to confirm their racial standing. In eighteenth-century Europe, the male body remained the touchstone of human anatomy.

The Hottentot Venus

The fact that the male body dominated studies of race and the European body dominated studies of sex does not mean that women of color escaped the prurient eye of European anatomists. What is significant, however, is that neither the dominant theory of race nor of sex in this period applied to women of non-European descent, particularly black women. Like other females, they did not fit comfortably in the great chain of being. Like other Africans, they did not fit European gender ideals. As a recent book on contemporary black women's studies put it, all the blacks were men and all the women were white.[54]

The revolution in views of sexuality, as I have suggested above, applied only to Europeans. Certainly African males did not share the traits of heroic manhood presumed inherent in (European) males. African males were thought to be childish, primitive, and sensuous—the obverse of their colonizers. Neither did the gender ideals prescribed for European women extend to African women. Whereas in Europe, middle-class women increasingly became emblems of chaste modesty, black women, by contrast, were thought to embody sexual promiscuity.[55] This European fantasy of the sexual and fecund African woman was reinforced by colonial relations, where European male planters commonly took black and mulatto women as concubines or sold them as prostitutes.

It was therefore doubly determined that the study of black

women, as Africans and as women, would focus on their sexuality.
Europeans had long been obsessed with the sexuality of Africans—
both male and female.[56] Seventeenth-century voyagers accused
male Hottentots of dancing wantonly like baboons about the Hol-
landers, shaking "their Privy Parts, with an offer . . . that they should
lye with their wives for a bit of rolled Tobacco." Female Hottentots
were said to prostitute themselves to European men "for the least
recompense imaginable" and to live promiscuously with their own
men like troglodytes, whom they were said to resemble.[57] Condorcet, in his 1781 "Reflections on Slavery," equated black women's
sexuality with strong liquor—both of which drained white male
planters of any productive energy.[58]

African women shared with European women and female
apes the incommodious condition of being female in a male world,
and thus the scientific gaze fell upon their private parts—breasts
and genitalia. As we have seen in chapter 2, the fresh virginal breast
was greatly cherished in European culture. When portrayed sympathetically, women of African descent were drawn with breasts fitting the European ideal—firm and spherical. When portrayed un-
sympathetically, their breasts were shown to be pendulous and
sagging. Within Europe, sagging breasts signified witchcraft, old
age, and females fallen from grace; outside Europe, they signified
savagery and cannibalism.[59] (One should also recall that the earliest
illustrations of female apes showed them with pendulous breasts, a
mark of their bestial nature, even though apes have small, unremarkable mammae.) European naturalists commonly exaggerated
the length of African women's breasts—so long and limp, it was reported, that these women flung them over their shoulder to nurse
the infants they carried on their backs (FIG. 5.4).[60] European voyagers
compared the breasts of Africans to calabashes (a kind of gourd)
and to the udders of goats or cows.[61] The breasts of African women
took on truly mythic proportions in the male European mind. Some
voyagers reported that they hung like "great sacks to the waist," others that they dragged the ground. "Observers" in the colonies reported that some slave women would lay their long breasts upon

breast

162

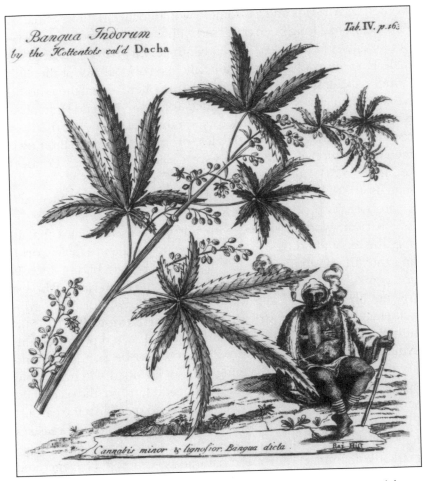

FIG. 5.4. Hottentot woman suckling a child on her back. Peter Kolb reported that the Hottentot woman's breasts are "so long that she can toss the nipple to the child over her shoulder." According to Kolb, mothers usually smoked *dacha* (marijuana) while nursing. From Peter Kolb, *The Present State of the Cape of Good Hope*, trans. Guido Medley (London 1731), vol. 1., p. 163, plate 4.

the ground before lying down beside them to rest. Others imagined that when slave women stooped to work the fields, their breasts made them appear to have "six legs." The most outrageous story passing among European naturalists in the late eighteenth century was that the breasts of Hottentot women were so large that tobacco pouches were made from them and sold in great quantity on the Cape of Good Hope.[62]

Voyagers reported what they considered the raw facts about Hottentot breasts, while naturalists tried to explain their unusual size and shape. As in the case of noses, African breasts were also considered a perversion of the European prototype. When young, African women's breasts were thought to be "as finely formed as any [European] woman's." They became loose and flaccid only through the influence of custom and climate.[63] C. P. Thunberg, Linnaeus's student and professor of botany at Uppsala, traced the distention of Hottentots' mammae to the intense heat of their climate and the fact that they frequently smeared themselves with grease, thus softening and elongating the tissues. Richard Ligon attributed the length of their breasts to the Hottentot custom of binding their mammae tightly when carrying infants on their backs. In his list of racial characteristics, Linnaeus noted that African mammae were "especially productive of milk"; he did not comment on the disposition of breasts in other races.[64]

Blumenbach was one of the few who attempted to shift the tenor of debate. He dismissed the purported proportions of African women's breasts as exaggerated and argued further that breast size is not a uniform racial characteristic. Not all African women have large breasts (witness the beautiful breasts of Ethiopian women found in European markets), nor do all Europeans have small, comely breasts (he mentioned the large breasts of Irish women). Blumenbach also observed that many peoples of the globe consider large breasts beautiful and often enlarge them by artifice. At the same time, Blumenbach equated large breasts with licentiousness. He suggested that early venereal excitement swelled the breasts, evidenced (so he thought) by the heavy mammae displayed by London's hordes of immature prostitutes.[65]

In the nineteenth century, the pendulous breast, identified with primitives abroad, was discussed increasingly in terms of class, becoming a staple characterization of the laboring poor at home. Princeton University president Samuel Stanhope Smith traced the origin of what he considered unsightly breasts to the poverty, hardship, and exhausting toil of the lowest classes. Flaccidity increased with age, he noted, because the poor nursed their many children for prolonged periods of time.[66]

Though naturalists had a good deal to say about breasts when considering racial characteristics among females, nothing excited these men more than the elongation of the labia minora, or inner vaginal lips, among the Hottentot. This "Hottentot apron" became the subject of countless books and articles, and much prurient popular and scientific speculation. Linnaeus was so taken with this supposed aspect of Hottentot anatomy that he (quite mistakenly) made it a characteristic of the entire "African" race. As late as 1936, the German anthropologists Hermann Ploss, Max Bartels, and Paul Bartels devoted a separate section of their massive anthropology entitled simply *Woman* to the Hottentot apron, in which they reported that there was still no consensus among medical men on whether this elongation of the labia was congenital or artificially produced. Ploss was inclined to believe, however, that it resulted from masturbation, and because methods of masturbation differed, the length and shape of labia differed accordingly.[67]

Originally called simply a "flap of skin," this supposed aspect of Hottentot genitalia, known for a time by the Latin *sinus pudoris* (translated variously as "loincloth," "veil of shame," or "drape of decency"), was finally domesticated as an "apron" (*tablier* in French; *Schürze* in German). Naturalists hailed the "apron" as a primitive vestige of Hottentots' animal origin. Linnaeus reported finding it also in the female *Homo troglodytes*, his second and lowest species of human. Indeed Linnaeus searched for a similar genital (de)formation in apes, but found none.[68]

From its first sightings in the seventeenth century, the so-called Hottentot apron was pronounced a deformity—a departure from the European norm. John Ovington wrote in his *Voyage to Suratt in the Year 1689* that women sporting these pieces of skin must be hermaphrodites.[69] Voltaire, in the eighteenth century, found the apron so unusual that he argued that these women must belong to a separate species of humans.[70] Even the celebrated

French voyager François Le Vaillant, who had a certain affection for the women of this region, having fallen madly in love with a young Gonaqua girl, could barely suppress his laughter on first sight of an "apron." He called it ridiculous, a product of "depraved" taste.[71] Peter Kolb, who provided one of the earliest and more sensitive ethnographies of the Hottentots, swam against the current by suggesting that this flap of skin revealed a certain modesty among these people, serving as a natural fig leaf to conceal a woman's private parts.[72] The British admiral and voyager Sir John Barrow, writing at the end of the eighteenth century, added that it had the advantage of guarding women against male violence, insofar as it appeared impossible for a man to have sexual relations with an "aproned" woman without her consent.[73]

European naturalists argued amongst themselves about whether the so-called apron actually existed, much as they argued about the existence of the hymen (see chapter 3). Few had actually seen African genitalia; much of the information filtering into European universities and academies was second- or third-hand—if not totally fabricated. Blumenbach placed "aproned" women in the same category with beardless Americans, tailed people, centaurs, and sirens—all of which he regarded as figments of travelers' rich imaginations.[74] Other naturalists argued that these bits of flesh existed but that their proportions had been vastly exaggerated. A physician residing on the Cape of Good Hope reported that each one of the many hundreds of Hottentot women he had treated for various gynecological complaints had hypertrophied labia but of lengths varying from about one-half to four inches. These fleshy appendages he imagined to be what some writers had described as a flap, or apron.[75]

While most anthropologists eventually agreed that some sort of flap of skin did exist, they were not sure if it was an elongation of the skin of the stomach, of the labia majora, or of the labia minora, hanging down (as some said) so as to resemble flat teats of cows or the wattle of turkeys.[76] They also wanted to know if these aprons were natural or, once again, the product of female artifice. Many naturalists, including Le Vaillant, suggested that women created these flaps of skin by pulling, pinching, twisting, and wrapping normal labia around little sticks and twigs (for the same inexplicable reasons that Hottentot men cut off their left testicles).[77] Far from natural, Le Vaillant judged these elongated labia a "caprice of fashion, . . . a refinement of coquetry," practiced only by a few women still adhering to ancient custom.[78] Others, critical of Le Vaillant, considered this aspect of Hottentot anatomy natural, caused either by their hot climate or lethargic way of life. The Good Hope physician, who had reported that all Hottentot women had elongated labia, argued that even young girls displaced in the colonies with no sense of cultural origin or contact with other Hottentot women had them.[79]

Le Vaillant's testimony, however, carried some weight because he produced an illustration of this appendage said to be drawn from life (FIG. 5.5). After his Hottentot scouts (all male) located a woman with an apron, the French naturalist pleaded with her to let him examine it. "Confused, abashed, and trembling," the woman finally succumbed and, "covering her face with both her hands," allowed him to untie her apron and contemplate it at his leisure. Le Vaillant, sensitive to the delicacy of his investigation, assured the "honest and provident mothers" among his European readers that he had been reluctant to compromise this woman. In the end, however, he opted for truth, as he put it, over decency: "I cannot think of omitting in my work these circumstances of my travels; and since my female Hottentot consented to improve my knowledge at the expense of her modesty, too much reserve on my part might be considered childish bashfulness."[80]

Elizabeth Helme, one of several English translators of Le Vaillant's work, was of a different mind about the matter. She deleted the eight-page discussion and the illustration of the nude Hottentot

FIG. 5.5. A Hottentot woman with an "apron." Eighteenth-century illustrators favored frontal views of Hottentot women to focus attention on their "aprons"; nineteenth-century illustrators portrayed these women in profile to highlight their buttocks. From François Le Vaillant, *Voyage de François Le Vaillant dans l'intérieur de l'Afrique* (Paris, 1798), vol. 2, facing p. 349. Courtesy of the Pennsylvania State University Libraries.

HOTTENTOTE A TABLIER. *Tom. 2, Pag. 349.*

woman, explaining in the preface: "I have softened (if I may be allowed the expression) a few passages that possibly might be accounted mere effusions of fancy and vivacity in a French author, but which would ill accord with the delicacy of a female translator, or indeed with the temper and genius of English readers."[81] John Barrow, her compatriot, also criticized Le Vaillant's illustration as more a product of his imagination than a true image of nature.[82]

Le Vaillant perhaps rightly judged that "scrupulous nicety is improper concerning a subject to which nature has attached no shame."[83] Subsequent history, however, was not tempered by such "niceties." By the early nineteenth century European interest in this aspect of Hottentot genitalia had grown into a grotesque voyeurism to which naturalists were not immune.[84] In 1815, Georges Cuvier, France's premier comparative anatomist, performed his now infamous dissection of the South African woman known as the "Hottentot Venus" to solve once and for all the mysteries of the renowned apron. "There is," he wrote in his report, "nothing more celebrated in natural history."[85] The very name given this woman—Cuvier always referred to her as *Vénus Hottentotte*—emphasized her sexuality. (Passionate tendencies found in warm climates were often attributed to the planetary influence of Venus. Europeans also often gave Africans and slaves classical names. In the 1860s, prehistoric fertility symbols found in Europe at Lespugue and Willendorf were also christened Venus. These fleshy "Venuses" were mistakenly assumed to be steatopygous.)

The story of this woman, whose given Dutch name was Saartjie Baartman (her original name has gone unrecorded), has been recounted many times, most recently by Percival Kirby, Stephen Jay Gould, Sander Gilman, and Anne Fausto-Sterling.[86] Baartman was in her twenties when she was transported from the British colony on the Cape of Good Hope to London in 1810 by a ship's surgeon, Alexander Dunlop, who supplemented his income by exporting museum specimens from South Africa. He apparently told her she could make a "grand fortune" by exhibiting herself to the curious in the capital cities of Europe. Upon her arrival in England she became one of the most successful shows of London, displayed (not unlike

Madame Chimpanzee) "on a stage two feet high, along which she was led by her keeper, and exhibited like a wild beast; being obliged to walk, stand, or sit as he ordered her."[87] Spectators could catch a glimpse of her "brutal figure" for a mere two shillings. At this time attention focused not on her apron (she was clothed in a costume resembling her skin as nearly as possible) but on her protruding buttocks which, for an extra charge, viewers could poke and prod.

Almost immediately, antislavery forces initiated court pro-ceedings to stop these offensive displays, charging that Baartman was "little other than a slave or chattel." The government felt obliged to protect this foreigner, taken illegally from South Africa. (The slave trade had been abolished in Britain three years before her alleged abduction.) Indeed, as the court record stated paterna-listically, the British Governor of the Cape of Good Hope acted as guardian for the whole Hottentot nation "by reason of their general imbecile state."

The court eventually dismissed the case when Baartman's keepers produced a contract (drawn up, it has been suggested, only in face of the court proceedings) showing that she had come from the Cape of her own free will and that she was to receive a certain percentage of the profits for exhibiting herself in England and Ire-land. According to the contract, she was also to serve her keepers as a domestic for a wage of twelve guineas per year. Though the case was dismissed, the adverse publicity undermined her popularity and she was taken to Paris to be shown in an animal show in the Rue Neuve des Petits-Champs. While still in England, Baartman was bap-tized and given the English name Sarah Bartmann.

It was in Paris that Sarah Bartmann became the object of in-tense scientific investigation. In the spring of 1815 she was sum-moned to the Jardin du Roi by a commission of zoologists and phys-iologists, where she was examined for three days. Henri de Blainville, professor at the Muséum d'Histoire Naturelle in the Jar-din du Roi, set out his purposes in observing her: (1) to provide a detailed comparison of this woman with the lowliest race of hu-mans (the Negro) and the highest type of apes (the orangutan);

(2) to provide the most complete possible description of the anomalies of her genitalia.[88]

This investigation required that Bartmann strip naked in the austere rooms of the museum in front of at least three formally dressed men. Georges Cuvier simply noted that she was kind enough to undress and sit nude for two portraits (these were destined to represent the only human contained among five volumes of mammals in Cuvier's brother's and Geoffroy Saint-Hilaire's *Histoire naturelle des mammifères*).[89] De Blainville's account, however, tells a different story and is unique in revealing something of what happened in the museum during the three days of investigation. According to de Blainville, the men (apart from de Blainville, Cuvier, and Geoffroy Saint-Hilaire, there is no record of who else was present) had great difficulty convincing Sarah (de Blainville adopted this familiar address) to let herself be seen nude. It was only with "great sorrow" that she let drop for a moment the handkerchief with which she had been covering her genitals. She took a particular dislike to de Blainville because, he supposed, he came too near her, "tormenting" her to get material for his description. At one point, he offered her money, knowing how much she liked it, hoping in this way to render her more docile, but she refused to take it. In the end, despite their efforts, no man of science managed to get a good look at Bartmann's genitalia. De Blainville thought he caught a glimpse of them, but only when she bent over or was observed walking from behind.[90] For the moment Bartmann had preserved her dignity, but hardly with the panache of her proud countrywomen back at the Cape who, according to the voyager François Leguat, stood, hands on hips, regarding the European intruders "up and down" with great disdain.[91]

Bartmann's victory was short-lived. Upon her death from "inflammation" some nine months later at the age of about twenty-six, her body was brought to the museum for further examination. Dissection of her apron—"that extraordinary appendage which nature made a special attribute of her race"—was the first order of business. Cuvier relished this opportunity to resolve the mysteries of her apron, which during her lifetime had been "carefully hidden either between her thighs or more deeply." In language reminiscent of Linnaeus's sexual system and Darwin's *Loves of the Plants*, he described the apron as a four-inch development of the inner vaginal lips divided "like two wrinkled fleshy petals." If one raises these two appendages, he continued, they form "the figure of a heart," at whose center lies the opening of the vulva.[92] His countryman Julien-Joseph Virey reminded his readers in his *De la femme* that Linnaeus had been the first to compare the labia to flower petals. African labia and breasts, Virey reiterated, became enlarged and elongated in the same way that the flora of that continent grew large and fleshy in its extreme heat.[93] Upon completing his dissection, Cuvier had the honor, as he put it, of presenting the men of the Academy with Sarah Bartmann's genitalia, prepared in a manner that "left no doubt about the nature of her apron."[94]

Cuvier's now notorious memoir described the Hottentot Venus in remarkably unflattering terms. At every turn he found her physique and manner bestial. He compared her protruding buttocks, an "elastic and shivering mass," to the buttocks of mandrills and of other monkeys that, during certain periods of their life, swell to "truly monstrous" proportions. He found her movements brusque and capricious like those of apes.[95] She had great pendular breasts and the unsightly habit of making her lips protrude like an orangutan. Her thigh bones were heavy and short like an animal's; her humeri (upper arm bones) were spindly and delicate like those of apes, dogs, and other carnivores. She danced in the manner of her country, and played with a fairly good ear upon a Jew's harp. She liked necklaces, belts of glass beads, and other "savage finery." She drank too much. Though by his own report she was gay, had a good memory, and spoke three languages, Cuvier also remarked that while her hands were charming and feet pretty, her ears were small like those of apes. Significantly, her pelvis—the eighteenth-century measure of womanliness—resembled the female ape's. So, too, did her heart.

Like the many apes whose skeletons and skin were sold or donated to natural history museums, Bartmann's body was disassembled and, until quite recently, parts of it—her genitalia preserved in formalin in a bell jar, her skeleton, and a cast of her body—were on display in case number thirty-three in the Musée de l'Homme in Paris (they are now in the museum's storerooms). Her skin was apparently sent back to England, stuffed, and put on display.[96] In 1949, a stereoscopic photograph of her body cast was still available for purchase as a souvenir.

Cuvier's memoir of Sarah Bartmann reveals race and gender dynamics in science at the turn of the nineteenth century. His interest in the body of this South African woman focused on her sexuality; nine of his sixteen pages are devoted to Bartmann's genitalia, breasts, buttocks, and pelvis.[97] Only one short paragraph evaluated her brain. On both accounts—of her sex and her race—Bartmann was relegated to the world of brute flesh.

The New Body Politic

Why, then, did anatomists and anthropologists privilege *male* bodies when investigating race and *European* bodies when examining sex? Looking at the politics of scientific communities, as I have done above, provides only partial explanations of these trends. There were still other, deeper, factors predisposing scientists in this matter. In the eighteenth century, the question of equality was primarily one concerning males and the wielding of public power. In the great public drama of the French Revolution, males struggled with males of different classes for political representation. First and foremost, bourgeois French men fought for political rights equal to their economic strength. The abstract promises of freedom and equality accompanying that revolution also provoked challenge from European women, free peoples of color (both of mixed race and Africans) living in France and its colonies, and slaves. As the "body politic" of the Ancien Régime (the ideal authority of the state embodied in the person of the king) was symbolically destroyed with the beheading of Louis XVI in a cold winter morning in 1793, a new body politic took its place.[98] Increasingly, questions of ethics (particularly those concerning equality) were taken to stand or fall on the findings of anatomists. An individual's place in the *polis* de-

pended on his or her property holdings, and also on sexual and racial characteristics. Scientists, mediating between the laws of nature
and legislatures, often declared themselves impartial in these matters (*unparteyisch*, as Soemmerring and his colleagues put it).
Soemmerring expressed his belief that anatomists did not have to
take a moral or political stand because the body spoke for itself.[99]

The question of political representation for one of the stron-
gest groups of minority males—free and propertied men of mixed
race living in France's colonies—came to the fore in 1789. When the
king called elections for the Estates General, the colonies were excluded from representation, despite their wealth and importance to
the French economy. Saint Domingue (now Haiti) was France's
wealthiest colony, producing over two-fifths of the world's sugar
and more than half its coffee. In 1790, Saint Domingue had a population of approximately 31,000 whites, 24,000 free blacks and mulattoes, and 450,000 slaves (the native population already had been
exterminated by the end of the sixteenth century).[100]

Though not invited to the Estates General, the white French
colonists in Saint Domingue sent a delegation that was eventually
seated. Their right to represent the colony, however, was vigorously
challenged by free men of mixed race (*gens de couleur libres*, as
they called themselves) who sent their own delegation to Versailles
demanding representation. Many of these men, said collectively to
own one quarter of the property in the colony, had European educations, and, like their leader, Julien Raymond, owned large numbers of slaves. Eventually, the National Assembly also seated representatives of these men of color who met established property
requirements.[101]

Electoral laws in France both before and after the Revolution
made fine distinctions among males much in the same way that
anatomists strove to refine racial distinctions. According to Edward
Long, the Spanish had made a "kind of science" of the different
classes and castes of peoples living in the West Indies (see FIG. 5.6).
This system of racial discrimination existed throughout Europe and
its colonies with the Dutch (according to Long) being the most ex-
acting in what constituted whiteness. The hierarchy of color in pol-

174 itics followed link for link the hierarchy of being that was said to exist in nature (both also coincided with differences in wealth and literacy). The Dutch and the French refused political rights to any person with the slightest trace of black blood. In Long's Jamaica, however, a male quinteron (a male three generations removed from black ancestry) was considered physically indistinguishable

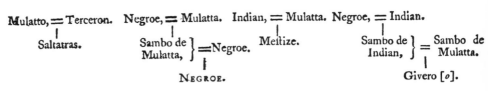

DIRECT lineal Afcent from the Negroe Venter.

White Man, = Negroe Woman.
|
White Man, = Mulatta.
|
White Man, = Terceron.
|
White Man, = Quateron.
|
White Man, = Quinteron.
|
WHITE.

MEDIATE or STATIONARY, neither advancing nor receding.

Quateron, = Terceron.
|
Tente-enel-ayre.

RETROGRADE.

Mulatto, = Terceron. Negroe, = Mulatta. Indian, = Mulatta. Negroe, = Indian.
| | | |
Saltatras.   Sambo de } = Negroe. Meltize.   Sambo de } = Sambo de
                      Mulatta, }   Indian, }   Mulatta.
                         | |
                      NEGROE.   Givero [o].

FIG. 5.6. Edward Long's table of the outcomes of racial crossings. The top half of the chart emphasizes the sexual dynamic in these racial unions. The man was commonly European (a colonist) and the woman of African descent (a servant or slave). The bottom half of the chart shows what Long called "retrograde" unions, that is, unions yielding increasingly darker offspring. According to his scheme, a mulatto crossing with a "terceron" produces a "saltatras," and so forth. From Edward Long, *The History of Jamaica* (London, 1774), vol. 2, pp. 260–261.

from a white person and thus legally white (provided he was also baptized in the Christian faith).[102]

In France, property-owning, tax-paying males of various ethnic origins (including Jews) succeeded in their quest for political representation when in 1791 all men residing in France received the rights of active citizens: "Every man, of whatever color, whatever origin, of whatever country he be, will be free and will enjoy the rights of an active citizen in France, if he meets in other respects the conditions required by the Constitution."[103] Armed revolt in Saint Domingue leaving 2,000 whites and over 10,000 slaves dead brought full equality to mulattoes and free blacks on that island in 1792. Finally, the National Convention, pushed forward by the war with Spain and the threat of an English invasion, abolished slavery in all French colonies in a slow and painful process. On June 21, 1793, male slaves who agreed to be inducted into the army were freed. Their wives and children were freed some weeks later. On February 4, 1794, slavery at last was abolished in all French colonies. Nearly a million slaves suddenly became citizens (and many of them soldiers) of France.[104] That same year three delegates from Saint Domingue (a Negro, a mulatto, and a white—all male) were seated by the National Convention in Paris.[105] Momentarily, men of color entered the public realm of heroic manhood.[106]

As subsequent history has shown, these victories were Pyrrhic. Slavery and the color line were reinstated in French colonies in 1802 (with the exception of Saint Domingue, which declared its independence from France in 1804), and even when rights were restored in 1848, they did not ensure social equality.[107] Nonetheless, in the same way that scientific debates about race centered on males, it was *fraternité*, not *humanité*, that was celebrated alongside *egalité* and *liberté* in the great bourgeois revolution of this era.[108] This is nowhere more evident than in the iconography surrounding racial consanguinity. Though feminine icons of liberty loomed large in this period, male figures, either innocent babes or grown men, dominated portrayals of the "fraternity of colors" (FIGS. 5.7 and 5.8). Guillaume-Thomas Raynal featured male infants—one black, one white—suckling at the many breasts of Nature in his (1774) *Histoire*

Fraternité.

A Paris, chez Basset, rue Jacques, au coin de celle des Mathurins

philosophique et politique . . . dans les deux Indies (FIG. 5.9). Hugh
Honour has pointed out that the racial diversity of these infants was
unprecedented.[109] Colonial relationships, by contrast, were often
portrayed using female figures as in William Blake's depiction of Europe supported by Africa and America (FIG. 5.10).[110]

Barriers to women's political rights were not lifted during the
Revolution, though women were also contenders for political
power. In 1793, two years after the National Convention broadened
male suffrage, women—even women of property—were officially
excluded from citizenship. It was decided that women could not
"exercise political rights" or take an "active part in affairs of government." At the same time, women's political clubs were out-
lawed.[111] Women were now to be silent and modest, waiting in
their homes to receive news of public events "from the mouths of
their fathers or their children or from their brothers or husbands."[112] In May 1795, the Convention voted to exclude women
from its meetings; in the future they would be allowed into the hall
as spectators only if accompanied by a man carrying a citizen's
card. Later that same week the Convention placed Parisian women
under a kind of house arrest. All women were to return to their
domiciles. Those found on the streets in groups of more than five
were dispersed by force.[113]

Women of color also sought political rights both in France and
in its colonies, though because their numbers were small, they
never posed as great a threat as white French women. The most
celebrated moment for a "mulatress" came in June 1793. Jeanne
Odo, *une petite fille* of mixed race reportedly 114 years old, joined
a delegation to the National Convention of blacks of both sexes
demonstrating for the abolition of slavery. The president gave her
the fraternal kiss and seated her in an armchair at his side. That day
Georges-Jacques Danton spoke of "universal liberty." It should be

---

FIG. 5.7. "Fraternity." An African boy (with French curls) and a European boy
embrace beneath the neoclassical mother of humanity shown baring her
maternal breast. It was popularly said: "France, the mother of liberty, does not
permit slavery." By permission of the Musée Carnavalet, Paris.

La raison Gouvernée par un femme Égaré Sur Labbe Le feu Sert
De Guidage Derretter Sur la ure Eiere Jegrenthenrure gaubeleu
Ô Des Compagnon trible le l'Appuie Sur des Droit De L'homme et
les Le D'Allion Mon el la Durin Dans Ren Dirorieler les effa
La Loure Si raite Le penyer par la Retin que el Contelle

Les Morts Sout Égaux Ce N'est pas La Naissance
C'est La Seule Vertu qui fait La Différence

De Fruite mont de Homonelle De la Montée fut en Ordre De ren Du
que fortin Le Nome De Lerxlenne Jugante qui ter Ile Demore
fut tout Amet L'Equente et Ardolen De tante la fait
L'emeurable pret a traureur La Mit ale fut De Iuler

FIG. 5.8. "All men are equal." Reason, portrayed as a woman crowned with the
sacred fire of patriotism, places a level over a white man and a man of color. The
man of color leans on the "Declaration of the Rights of Man" and holds in his
hand the "Decree of 15 May 1791." Reason is supported by a multibreasted
Nature. By permission of the Bibliothèque Nationale, Paris.

noted, however, that the much celebrated Odo received a kiss, not a
voice in the government.[114]

French women taken collectively emerged from the Revolution with fewer rights and privileges than they had had under the
Ancien Régime. Before the convening of the Estates General in
1789, a few privileged women, notably heads of religious orders,
some noblewomen and widows, could vote.[115] In the words of
Olympe de Gouges: "Since the Revolution this sex [woman], once
despicable but respected, has become respectable but despised."[116]

In denying the women of France rights, the Convention advocated republican motherhood as its ideal. In addressing the Convention, Fabre d'Eglantine compared "good mothers and daughters" of the Republic to undesirable *filles émancipées* and *grenadiers femelles* of the Revolution.[117] Nature, it was said, assigned to woman "the tender cares owing to infancy, household details, the sweet anxieties of maternity." Women who transgressed the natural order ran the risk of losing their heads. The "imprudent" Olympe de Gouges, whose political visibility, more perhaps than her royalism or opposition to Robespierre, cost her her life, was accused of abandoning the cares of her household "to get mixed up in the republic." On November 3, 1793, at the young age of forty-five, her head fell beneath "the avenging knife of the laws."[118] Five days later, Madame Roland, also an improperly public figure who "forgot the virtues of her sex," was guillotined.

The fall of women from public grace was replayed in republican iconography. The year of de Gouges's execution, 1793, also saw the fall of the mythic Marianne as the militant and female embodiment of the republic and the ascent of a masculine Hercules on the state seal.[119] This was also the year that male deputies celebrated the first anniversary of the republic by publicly drinking the symbolic milk of regeneration from Isis's maternal breasts (see chapter 2).

When women lost their tenuous foothold in the public realm, reproductive, not electoral, politics came to govern their lives, and here European women and women of African descent had something in common. European legislators had similar aspirations for them all. At home the women of Europe were to breed manpower to fuel military strength and industrial growth; abroad, black women were to breed hands to harvest sugarcane and coffee beans.[120] In the colonies, female slaves who had earlier been regarded as "work units" or sold as prostitutes were by the 1780s more often treated as breeders by planters who rightly feared the demise of the slave trade.[121] The desire by governments to conserve potential manpower for the state brought another policy common to women in both Europe and the colonies: a pregnant woman—regardless of race—was granted a stay of execution until after the birth of her child.[122]

It is significant that in the colonies women of African descent engaged in reproductive resistance (birth control, abortion, and infanticide) in addition to armed revolt.[123] Maria Merian, the German entomologist who worked in the Dutch colony of Surinam, told how native and slave women used the plant *Flos pavonis* to induce abortion:

> The seeds of this plant are used by women who have labor pains, and who must continue to work, despite their pain. The Indians, who are not treated well by the Dutch, use the seeds to abort their children, so that their children will not become slaves like they are. The black slaves from Guinea and Angola have demanded to be treated well, threatening to refuse to have children. In fact, they commit suicide because they are treated so badly, and because they believe that they will be born again, free and living in their own land. They told me this themselves.[124]

Less sympathetic European ladies (and there were many) suggested that women of African descent aborted their children because children interrupted their seductions of the white population.[125]

By the nineteenth century, medical men had convinced themselves of the reality of a universal woman. The French physician Julien-Joseph Virey went so far as to suggest that the word *femme* derived from *fetus* because woman's natural destination was to generate new life.[126] But "woman" was postulated as a universal only when referring, in fact, to middle-class European women. In much the same way that a hierarchy of color governed men's standing in politics, a hierarchy of color regulated women—not in relation to political rights but sexual desirability. In colonial prostitution markets whiteness of skin determined demand and hence price. A popular adage taught that "white women are for marriage, mulattos for

FIG. 5.9. Nature, a universal and multibreasted mother, nurses a black and a white infant, thus suggesting their equality and common origin. From Guillaume-Thomas Raynal, *Histoire philosophique et politique . . . dans les deux Indies* (1770; The Hague, 1774), vol. 4, frontispiece. Courtesy of the Princeton University Library.

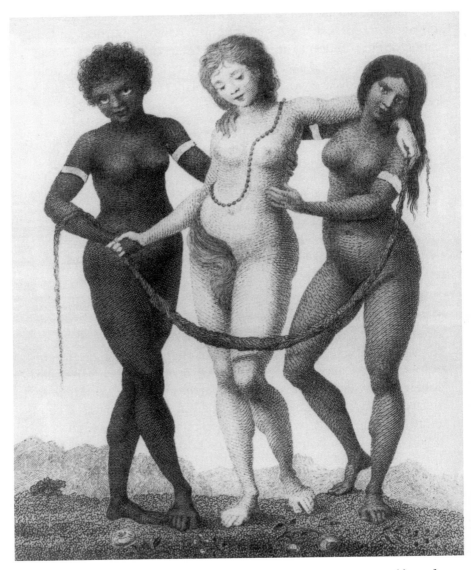

FIG. 5.10. "Europe Supported by Africa and America." Europe wears a necklace of blue beads, while her props—an African woman and a Native American—wear golden bracelets. This is an allegory of colonial relations, not sisterhood. In the text, John Stedman urged that all people are "created by the same hand and after the same mold" but that not all are equal in authority. By William Blake, from Stedman's *Narrative of a Five Years' Expedition against the Revolted Negroes of Surinam* (1796; Baltimore: Johns Hopkins University Press, 1988), plate 80.

fornication, and Negresses for work."[127] Ease in childbirth was also thought to follow a hierarchy of color. White women were considered the most delicate and subject to loss of life; mulatto women were subject to discomfort and suffered "a thousand little complaints"; and black women, who labored in the fields, were thought to breed at an astonishing rate and with remarkable ease.[128]

The purpose of this excursion into political history has been to sketch how the contours of racial and sexual science in the eighteenth century followed broader political struggles. European medical men centered their studies of race on males because of well-entrenched scientific traditions, to be sure, but also because, in this era of Enlightenment, new justifications were required for slavery and for the continued disenfranchisement of males of different skin color but often of equal property holdings. In like manner, medical men focused their scrutiny of sexual difference on Europeans because the greatest political challenge came from their own countrywomen. Questions of political power may also have induced anatomists to draw unfavorable analogies between men of the lower classes of their own countries and blacks, the darkness characteristic of each distinguishing them from their white and upper-class superiors. In this instance, as in others, naturalists did not draw their research priorities and conclusions from a quiet contemplation of nature, but from political currents of their times.

6

Who Should Do Science?

Ethiopians, Egyptians, Africans, Jews, Phoenicians, Persians,
Assyrians, and Indians have invented many curious sciences,
revealed the mysteries and secrets of Nature, put order into
mathematics, observed the motions of the heavens, and
introduced the worship of gods.

Ambroise Paré, *Les oeuvres*, 1575

*I*n his controversial *Black Athena*, Martin Bernal argues that the
celebration of Greece as the cradle of Western civilization began in the eighteenth century as an attempt to erase from historical
consciousness Afroasiatic contributions to Western arts and sciences. Until that time, he argues, Greece had been seen merely as
an outpost of Egyptian and Phoenician culture, a land civilized by
colonizing Africans and Semites.[1] According to Bernal, the myth of
a white dawn of Western civilization resulted from the upsurge in
anti-Semitism and racism at the end of the eighteenth century.

Critics have charged (among other things) that Bernal's project to locate the origins of Western science in Africa is Eurocentric
insofar as its primary goal is to claim for blacks a place in European
science—charges we will investigate below.[2] Bernal has, however,
identified a broad shift in historical consciousness that was important for the definition of European science. In the seventeenth and
eighteenth centuries, men of Western science had commonly celebrated ancient Egypt along with Mesopotamia, Persia, and India as
birthplaces of Europe's classical arts and sciences.[3] Galileo, coin-
ventor of the telescope, believed that ancient peoples had employed similar devices to map the heavens; Newton, too, at least in

his early years, had a rather romantic and far-fetched admiration of
the ancient Egyptians for their science and their philosophy.[4]

By the late eighteenth century, however, the notion of an Egyptian origin of science ran headlong into the growing consensus that people with black skin and sloping foreheads were incapable of abstract thought. William Lawrence framed the issue in stark terms in his lectures before the Royal College of Surgeons in 1819:

> Egypt was venerated, even by antiquity, as the birth-place of the
> arts. . . . With our present experience of the capacity of Negroes, and our knowledge of the state in which the whole race
> has remained for twenty centuries, can we deem it possible
> that they should have achieved such prodigies? that Homer, Lycurgus, Solon, Pythagoras, and Plato should have resorted to
> Egypt to study the sciences, religion, and laws, discovered and
> framed by men with black skin, woolly hair, and slanting
> forehead?[5]

Lawrence refused to believe that the Egyptians "now so devoted to slavery" could have created such grandeur in antiquity.

As the natural sciences gained power and prestige, the question of who was capable of engaging in science took on a new urgency. European men of science debated the intellectual abilities of men of various races and of women. Were women and blacks capable of abstract thought? And just who was black?

Inquiry into these questions took several forms in the eighteenth century, and in this chapter I look rather briefly at two aspects of this larger history. First was the question of the race of those who invented the sciences. If Egyptians had, indeed, been among those who made important contributions to science, what did they look like? Were the ancient Egyptians, whose mummified remains had just been unwrapped as a consequence of Napoleon's invasion, black or white? Second was the question of whether women and black men could be educated. This era saw a number of "experiments" in education. A few European women and African men were admitted to universities in Germany in attempts to see if, "by proper cultivation," they could learn to excel in philosophy, poetry, medicine, and the natural sciences. And could a Madame du Châtelet, an

Anton Amo, or a Phillis Wheatley enter the hallowed halls of Europe's academies of arts and sciences?

The Origins of Science: Black or White?

The notion that Western science had its origins in Egypt, Mesopotamia, India, and Persia had foundations in the ancient theory of humors, according to which dry heat fostered wit and science, while damp cold cultivated bodily strength and a bellicose spirit. At the heart of the humoral tradition lay the teaching that terrestrial elements stood in a hierarchical relationship to one another: things hot and dry were superior to things cold and moist. Predictably this accounted for the dominance of the hotter male over the colder woman. For thousands of years, men's superior heat had explained their social superiority. Less predictably, this theory seemed to hold dramatic implications for the ordering of the races. The intense heat of southern regions would seem to have proclaimed the victory of black over white. For this reason, Ambroise Paré, surgeon to the king of France, went so far as to suggest that peoples inhabiting the middle regions of the globe (that is, Greece and Rome) lacked the natural endowments required for the more "abstruse sciences."[6]

The theory of humors, however, was designed to explain the nature of provident government (and, for Galen, ultimately the success of the Roman empire), not the origin of science—which was not at issue in Europe before intellect and technical innovation became measures of personal worth and national strength.[7] In the case of race, *excess* heat was seen as a liability. Aristotle, in an effort to give pride of place to his own civilization, taught that those burned with immoderate heat (in Africa) or oppressed with excessive cold (in northern Europe) were intemperate, barbarous, and cruel. For him, superiority lay with the people of temperate regions who blended the wisdom of the south with the fortitude of the north.[8] As we have seen, it was within this region that Blumenbach located the origin of humankind.[9]

In the late eighteenth century, men of science, interested in uncovering a genealogy of science, set out to debunk what they considered to be the myth of a black origin of Western science. Physical anthropologists reduced the question of Egypt's contributions to the arts and sciences to the question of whether Egyptians were black or white. The answer seemed to them to lie beneath the cotton wrappings of mummies. Napoleon's foray into Egypt in the 1790s yielded a vast store of scientific spoils, including a large number of mummies which naturalists immediately transported to Paris, London, Göttingen, Leipzig, Kassel, and Gotha.[10] Blumenbach alone unwrapped six mummies and examined many others.[11] Sir Joseph Banks, Christoph Meiners, Samuel Thomas von Soemmerring, and Georges Cuvier studied mummy skulls along with paintings and carvings on sarcophagi, pottery, and murals, all in an attempt to determine whether these ancient people had the upturned noses and high foreheads of Caucasians, or the broad, flat noses and jutting chins of modern Africans.

Constantin-François Volney, in his influential *Voyage en Syrie et en Egypte*, was one of the few to say that the progenitors of modern science had been black. He identified the ancient Egyptians as the true physical (and therefore intellectual) ancestors of modern Africans, sharing with them a smoky yellow hue, flat noses, and large lips. He based his conclusion on his studies of the Sphinx, whose features he found distinctly negroid, and on Herodotus's depiction of the Egyptians as a people with black skin and curly hair. Despite the fact that he saw the ancient Egyptians as "true"—that is, black—Africans, Volney continued to attribute to them the origin of Europe's classical arts and science.

> How astonishing it is to see the barbarism and ignorance of the present day Copts, descendants of the profound genius of the Egyptians and the brilliant spirit of Greece. [It is astonishing] to think that that race of black men, today our slaves and the objects of our contempt, is the same from which we received our arts, our sciences, and our very use of language.[12]

At the other extreme were the influential German classicists Johann Winckelmann and Christoph Meiners, along with the French naturalist Georges Cuvier, who denied that *any* Egyptians had ever been black. Winckelmann considered ancient Egyptians to be essentially of the same racial type as the Chinese (a view that Blumenbach took seriously enough to oppose vehemently), while Meiners considered them to be of the same stock as Hindus.[13] In his memoir on the Hottentot Venus, Cuvier emphatically declared that "no race of Negro produced that celebrated people who gave birth to the civilization of ancient Egypt, and from whom the whole world has inherited the principles of its laws, sciences, and perhaps also religion." Cuvier compared over fifty mummy skulls to the skulls of Europeans, Negroes, and Hottentots, and concluded that, whatever the hue of their skin, the ancient Egyptians belonged to "the same race of men as us, sharing with us a voluminous cranium and brain." Without exception, the "cruel law" of nature had "condemned to eternal inferiority those races with a depressed and compressed cranium."[14]

The British surgeon William Lawrence also argued that if the arts and sciences indeed had emanated from ancient Egypt, it was from those among them who were "Caucasian" (adopting Blumenbach's term). The few true Negroes were, then as now, their slaves. "To give the few Negroes the glory of all the discoveries and achievements of this first-civilized race, and overlook the more numerous individuals of different character would be in opposition to the invariable tenor of our experience respecting human nature."[15] For Lawrence, the vaulted Caucasian skull housed an expansive intellect dominating the instruments of sense and animal needs. It was fitting, he proclaimed, that this race should rule the world, holding in permanent subjection all other races. Edward Long, who believed that blacks constituted a separate and inferior species closely related to simians, simply remarked that Africans—both ancient and modern—were incapable of genius, and that those mechanical arts they might have produced they did in a "bungling and slovenly manner, perhaps not better than an orangutang."[16]

Most European naturalists took a more moderate view, suggesting that ancient Egypt had been a crossroads of commerce and cultural exchange, and that, as a result, its population had been mixed. Blumenbach, from his extensive investigations of mummies, distinguished among them three racial types: (1) the Ethiopian, with its prominent maxillae, turgid lips, broad, flat noses, and protruding eyeballs; (2) the Hindu, with its long, slender nose, long and thin eyelids, ears placed high on the head, and short and thin bodies (similar features, he argued, could also be seen painted on the sarcophagus of Captain Lethieullier's mummy in the British Museum); (3) a mixed type with features somewhere between the Caucasian and Ethiopian.[17]

While Blumenbach participated in debates over the racial features of the ancient Egyptians, he remained silent on the larger issue of whether Africans had contributed to the development of the world's arts and sciences. Unlike many of his colleagues, he did not consider the Africans of his day incapable of scientific pursuit. In his article "Concerning the Negro," he argued vigorously against those who believed that Africans stood far behind others in mental abilities. He argued further that if blacks were to be judged by their *nature*, they should be judged in their natural condition, not after having been brutalized by "white executioners" in a state of slavery.[18] James Prichard made a similar point, arguing that Europeans commonly drew conclusions about African intellectual capacities from skulls of enslaved populations which did not provide the most favorable specimens.

In the eighteenth century, as Europeans began colonizing and plundering Africa, they also attempted to claim part of its cultural heritage as their own. As noted above, questions about the origins of Western science have been revived in recent years by Bernal's *Black Athena*. The main contribution of Bernal's book has been to question why Europeans were so unwilling to grant an African ancestry to European science. Critics have pointed to problems with Bernal's formulations. Bernal tends toward Afrocentrism perhaps in claiming too much for Egypt in his attempt to refute histories claiming that science is an exclusively Greek invention owing little or nothing to earlier civilizations. More seriously, Bernal's project is Eurocentric in attempting to place Egypt within a Western genealogy. In this, Bernal leaves Western science as the culmination of intellectual and cultural achievement and perpetuates the project of valuing one kind of knowledge over all others.[19]

In the eighteenth century, attempts were also made to deny that women had ever contributed to the development of the arts and sciences.[20] As the prestige of science began to grow, history was rallied to lend legitimacy to European males' claims as sole heirs to its fortunes. (Indeed, some of the women stripped of cultural achievement—Isis, the mythical inventor of medicine, for example—were Egyptian.) In the middle of the eighteenth century, Voltaire baldly pronounced that "all the arts have been invented by man, not by woman." He did this by subscribing to a very narrow sense of what is art, namely, "things mechanical, gunpowder, printing, and the clock."[21] If we broaden Voltaire's list to include innovation in other areas he considered the principal occupations of the human species—"lodging, nourishment, and clothing"—he might have been led to evaluate women's contributions differently.

Eighteenth-Century Experiments in Education

As increasingly impressive collections of skulls were gathered to show that women and blacks lacked native intelligence, proponents of equality began collecting examples of learned women and Africans. In both instances the task was the same: to find the exceptional woman or black who had excelled in science or scholarship in order to prove that they were capable of abstract thought. Environmentalists, denying that there was any fixed and obvious relationship between the mind and bodily structure, brought forth examples of learned women and blacks to prove their case.[22]

European literature on learned women is older than that on learned blacks. Giovanni Boccaccio's fourteenth-century *Claris mulieribus*, for example, presents short biographies of one hundred and four queens, some real, some mythical, of the ancient world. Encyclopedias such as these—the most common type of women's history in this period—documented the triumphs of the learned lady.[23] A similar literature, perhaps modeled on the lexicons of learned ladies, was developed for blacks. Blumenbach, who had a library entirely composed of books written by European-educated Africans, published a lexicon of learned black men and women in order to show that "in regard to their mental faculties and capacity, they are not inferior to the rest of the human race."[24] There was the African Freidig, well known in Vienna as a master of the viola and violin. Anton Wilhelm Amo, a native of Guinea (Ghana), received a doctorate from the University of Wittenberg in 1734, the first African to obtain that degree at any European university.[25] Jacobus Elisa Capitein, also from Guinea, studied theology at the University of Leyden, graduating in 1742. Phillis Wheatley, a servant to Mr. John Wheatley of Boston, was listed as the first African to publish neoclassical poetry in English.[26] There was also the unnamed "Negress of Yverdun," celebrated as the best midwife in the Italian part of Switzerland.[27] Blumenbach's essay demonstrating the intellectual capacities of Africans circulated widely among abolitionists for the next half century.[28]

In order to be recognized as equals, learned women or blacks generally had to excel in those arts and sciences recognized by the white male academy—fields such as classical music, astronomy, Latin, or mathematics. The experiments in education carried out in the eighteenth century required that women and blacks assimilate to European university culture.[29] Germany was, perhaps surprisingly, a pioneer among European countries in accepting the occasional European woman or African man for admission to university study. (There were, to my knowledge, no examples of university-educated African women. Phyllis Hazeley was an African woman educated in England in the mid-eighteenth century, but not at a university. Upon her return to her native Sierra Leone, she opened a school to teach reading, writing, arithmetic, and needlework.)[30] German universities were being revived at this time and new universities, including Halle (where Anton Amo matriculated in 1727 and Dorothea Erxleben received her M.D. in 1754) and Göttingen (where Dorothea Schlözer took her Ph.D. in 1787), were founded to foster the growth of Enlightenment ideas.[31] The circumstances surrounding these experiments were similar in several respects. In each case, the student was shepherded by an enlightened patriarch:

Amo was sponsored by the Duke of Brunswick-Wolfenbüttel; Erxleben studied with her father and won special dispensation from Frederick the Great to study at Halle; Schlözer took her degree in the faculty where her father served as a professor. Despite the success of these individuals, European universities generally remained closed to both European women and Africans of either sex until late in the nineteenth and sometimes even into the twentieth centuries.

There were also interesting differences in how European women and black men fared in academic life. The African man, Anton Amo, was publicly feted during his university years. He was chosen to lead the entire student body in a parade celebrating the visit of local royalty to the University of Wittenberg in 1733, where Amo was then studying.[32] Dorothea Schlözer, by contrast, was not allowed to attend her commencement exercises because her father thought it improper for her to take part in the public celebration. "Since I could not go into the church [where the degrees were awarded]," she wrote a friend, "I went to the library, where I could see and hear everything through a broken pane of glass."[33]

Despite their university educations, European women remained barred from the public realm of science and scholarship, while black men were, in rare instances, able to go on to limited professional work. Schlözer never intended for her Ph.D. to lead to any career but marriage; her doctorate served merely as another badge of honor for an already illustrious academic family. Erxleben's degree served to legitimate her medical practice (and shield her from prosecution by jealous local doctors). It should be pointed out, however, that her admission to the university rested on the legal decision that medicine was not a public office and that women should therefore not be barred from its practice.[34] The case of Amo was quite different. Having completed his doctoral degree at Wittenberg, he lectured at Halle for about eight years (from 1739 to 1747) and was then appointed a counsellor at the court of Frederick the Great in Berlin—public positions that never would have been accorded a woman. His education was similar to that of Schlözer; they were both well trained in languages, mathematics, philosophy, and the classics. Yet Amo's degree carried him into a kind of public employment not open to women.

Amo was not the only university-educated male of African descent to go on to public service. Edward Long reported the case of Francis Williams, a Jamaican boy, whom the Duke of Montagu educated in order to discover whether "by proper cultivation" a Negro might become as capable as a white person.[35] The Duke sent Williams first to grammar school in England and then to the University of Cambridge where he excelled in mathematics, poetry, and the classics (FIG. 6.1). The Duke intended to continue his experiment by appointing Williams to a seat in the government of Jamaica, but he never managed to override the objections of the local English governor. Consequently, Williams went on to head a school for black boys. Long, who reported the story, belittled Williams's achievement, saying that the experiment might have been more significant had it been made using a native African. Long implied that Williams succeeded because he was not truly black. He also reported the failure of Williams's protégé (a young boy trained to be his successor at the school) who went mad, it was said, from too much learning. Long took this to prove that the "African head is not adapted by nature to such profound contemplations"; he also quoted with approval David Hume's judgment that Williams himself was like "a parrot who speaks a few words plainly."[36]

The most striking difference, however, between educated minority men and majority women in this period was their eligibility for membership in scientific academies. Europe's major scientific academies were founded in the seventeenth century—the Royal Society of London in 1660, the Parisian Académie Royale des Sciences (the most prestigious European academy of science) in 1666, the Akademie der Wissenschaften in Berlin in 1700. Despite the fact that women, such as the German astronomer Maria Winkelmann or the French physicist Emilie du Châtelet, were trained and ready to take their places among the men of science, they were excluded from these academies for over two hundred years (women were first admitted to the Royal Society in 1945, to the Berlin Academy of Sciences in 1949, and to the Académie des Sciences in 1979).[37] One

FIG. 6.1. Francis Williams at the University of Cambridge. Europeans celebrated blacks who received European educations and assimilated into the white world. Courtesy of the National Library of Jamaica.

might imagine that racial prejudice would have proven as insurmountable a barrier to black men. And in many cases, it did. Francis Williams, for instance, was refused membership in the Royal Society because of "his complexion," even though, as newspapers reported, he was "dressed like other gentlemen in a tye-wig [and] sword."[38] The expansive mood of the Enlightenment did make room for a few minority men. Moses da Costa became the first Jewish fellow of the Royal Society in 1736 (another Jewish fellow, Emanuel Mendes da Costa, was elected in 1747).[39]

The more remarkable case of a man of color elected to an eminent scientific body was that of Jean-Baptiste Lislet-Geoffroy, who became the first black member (albeit a corresponding member) of the Académie Royale des Sciences in Paris in 1786. Lislet was the son of Jean-Baptiste Geoffroy, a French engineer working on the Ile de France (Mauritius), and a black slave from the coast of Guinea whom his father freed in order to take her as his mistress (as allowed for in the *Code noir*). Because he was illegitimate, Lislet took the name of his place of birth, as was customary; his father did not lend him his name (Geoffroy) until Lislet was thirty-eight years old, seven years after he had been elected to the academy. Lislet-Geoffroy worked for the French government for most of his life, as head of the army corps of engineers, as a cartographer (he mapped the Ile de France, Réunion, and Madagascar), as a meteorologist, botanist, geologist, and astronomer.[40]

Lislet-Geoffroy's term as an academician was not without its troubles. Like other members of the Academy, he lost his title during the reorganization of 1793. But unlike most other members, he was not reinstated when the academy reopened. Several explanations have been given. Some said it was the difficulty of communications between France and its colonies that held up his reappointment until 1821; others said he was simply overlooked. Still others said that it was because of racial prejudice. Unable to travel to France because he had been denied a pension, Lislet-Geoffroy founded the *Société des Sciences et Arts de l'Ile de France* (today the *Société Royale des Arts et Sciences de Maurice*). It was reported that whites refused to join this academy because it was founded by a black.[41] Lislet's attempt to mix with the learned men of Europe did not open the doors of the Parisian academy to blacks. As of 1934, he was the only man of color ever to have been a member of the academy in Paris.[42]

This discussion is not intended to suggest that the advantage of being male outweighed the overwhelming disadvantages of being black in European society, but to show the deep confusion about gender and race among Europe's elites in this period. In some cases, being male did open the doors of public institutions to black men. But, in the eighteenth century, these men, like the learned European women, were curiosities educated at the pleasure of patrons. These exceptional individuals lived under constant scrutiny, always representatives of their race or sex, their positions tenuous and easily revoked. Anton Amo, for example, was publicly forced out of Germany after the death of his benefactor, the Duke of Brunswick. He returned to his homeland on the Gold Coast (then under Dutch rule), and nothing more was ever heard of him. Some say he died there in a slaver's prison.[43]

While black males seemed to fare modestly better than females in the newly established institutions of science, one should remember that propertied European women often ruled over men, especially men of African descent. In the frontispiece to his *Traité de la couleur de la peau humaine*, Claude-Nicolas Le Cat featured an upper-class European woman as the principal figure receiving an Ethiopian and American male (see FIG. 6.2).[44] This scene, though presented in a scientific treatise, could have been taken from any number of New World plantations where elite European women ruled over black men. But the power these women held came to them via birth and inheritance—principles governing the Ancien Régime. To the extent that science, supposedly representing a new

---

FIG. 6.2. The three species of mankind, according to Claude-Nicolas Le Cat. The accompanying texts explains that this meeting takes place in America, as one can see by the exotic parrot, monkey, and pineapples. A French woman, the mistress of the house, dominates the scene; she is being served lemonade by her maid. These two women of diverse classes represent "the white or European nation." The black man standing behind her represents the Ethiopian nation. An American, dressed and armed, represents the whole of his nation. He has come to trade with the European woman and regards himself with astonishment in the mirror presented to him by the Negro. The purpose of Le Cat's illustration was to show that the physiognomy and color of faces are different in all parts of the world. Claude-Nicolas Le Cat, *Traité de la couleur de la peau humaine* (Amsterdam, 1765), frontispiece. (Sign.: Kx 10 850 R.) By permission of the Staatsbibliothek zu Berlin—Preußischer Kulturbesitz.

democracy of talent, required certificates such as university degrees for passage into the public realm, women were excluded.

As mentioned above, no woman of African descent ever attended a European university in the eighteenth century. In the late-eighteenth century, however, we have a fictional account (supposedly based on a true story) of a young woman educated in the Parisian salons, an intellectual setting that rivaled universities and academies in this era.[45] The account of Ourika, a young girl from Senegal, reveals the differing experiences of African men and women brought into Europe by enlightened elites. It also throws into sharp relief the fact that the experiences of women imported from Africa into Europe could be very different. Duchesse de Duras's *Ourika* (1824) created a stir—Parisians adopted Ourika's fashions and envied her color—at the same time that, in another part of Paris, spectators ogled Sarah Bartmann's "grotesque figure."

As the tale recounts, Ourika was rescued from a slave ship off the coast of Senegal by Le Chevalier de Beauvau, governor of that settlement, and brought to Paris at the age of two where she was cherished as a daughter by Madame de Beauvau, the governor's aunt. Ourika was given all the advantages of girls of her benefactress's rank and raised amidst the conversation of the most distinguished philosophers of the time in Madame de Beauvau's salon. There she learned music, art, English, Italian, and the elements of good taste. In this rarified atmosphere, she was completely unaware of what it meant to be a black woman in France.

The privileges of her acquired rank, however, could not save her from racial prejudice. One day, Ourika overheard her benefactress lamenting the fact that her charge had no prospects for marriage and was destined to be forever alone. When Ourika became aware of her color, she was struck with horror and disgusted with herself: "When my eyes fell upon my black hands I thought they were like those of an ape."[46] She wept to discover that she belonged to a proscribed race.

According to Duras's story, the French Revolution renewed Ourika's hope that, with the collapse of the Ancien Régime of rank, her personal merits would place her well in society. She did not aspire to become a public figure, as did some of the educated men of African descent living in Europe. Her aspirations were consonant with the new ideals of French womanhood: to find a place in the bosom of a family as a cherished wife and loving mother. But she was to be disappointed. In Europe, black men tended to marry white women. Certainly no French man of significant rank would marry a black woman, even one of high social standing or with a large dowry (after the 1760s the slightest trace of black blood barred one from the nobility). After 1778, it became illegal for a person of color to marry a native Frenchman or woman.[47] At the same time, she was too highly educated to marry according to the dictates of her racial rank, to wed a person of "inferior condition." In despair, Ourika longed to be sent to the colonies as a slave so that she would have a place to call home. She was, as Duras wrote, "a person without a nation, a stranger to the whole human race." During the Restoration, Ourika found salvation not in "equality, liberty, and fraternity," but in religion. God, she was assured, knew no distinction of color or race. Like the wild girl of Champagne who had no place in society or hope for marriage (see chapter 3), Ourika became a nun. As a Sister of Charity she became a mother to orphans, a child to the poor and aged, a sister to all in adversity.

Despite the brilliance of the individuals involved in these eighteenth-century experiments in education, both women and Africans were excluded (but for exceptional cases) from the power and prestige of public life. They were and remained unwelcome outsiders. The traditional exclusion of European women from centers of learning was reaffirmed in the eighteenth century while the exclusion of minority men from European universities and professions was formalized. In France a 1763 royal ordinance forbade any black or man of color, whether slave or free, to practice medicine or surgery in the colonies.[48] Before this time men of color had trained in surgery at Paris and elsewhere. Colonial universities were also closed to people of color. John Baptiste Philip, a man of African descent who earned a medical degree from the University of Edinburgh in 1815, complained of the racial prejudice of the medical board in his native Trinidad. White candidates were admitted after perfunctory examinations, Philip charged, while many well-qualified men of African descent were denied a license merely because of the color of their skin.[49]

The failure of academies and universities to open their doors to blacks and women on a regular basis is especially poignant, considering that they were the objects of intense study by anatomists and medical men in this period. Excluded from centers of learning, women and Africans could say little about their own nature, at least not in the idiom of modern science. What they did write on their own behalf was often lost. It is significant that Amo's dissertation, *De jure Maurorum in Europa*, on the rights of Africans in Europe (one of his earliest works) has been lost, while his writings on traditional philosophical questions—the art of philosophizing and the mind-body distinction, for example—have been preserved in university libraries and archives.[50]

Nature's Body Wronged

A prominent Englishman used to say he acquiesced in Ecclesiastical History, Doubted the Civil, and believed the Natural.

Sir Hans Sloane, President of the Royal Society
of London, *A Voyage*, 1707

*I*n the seventeenth and eighteenth centuries, Europeans created for themselves peculiar visions of nature. Plant taxonomies placed flower parts defined as male above those defined as female; the lactating mamma was chosen as the quintessential characteristic linking humankind to animals. Secondary sexual characteristics, such as beards, were seen as differentiating naturally bounded races of humans; women were studied as a sexual subset of the universal "man." These visions were created almost exclusively by males. It would be fascinating, of course, to know what women had to say about body politics. How did they describe their own bodies, and the bodies of the men pronouncing on their minds and manners? How did they see plant sexuality, and what name might they have given to animals with hollow ears, squamosal jaws, hair, and lactating breasts? These are questions that cannot be answered. In the seventeenth and eighteenth centuries only a few women engaged in anatomical studies of sexual differences.[1] None was a physical anthropologist, studying skeletons and skulls. In eighteenth-century Europe, there was not a single female or black taxonomist of repute.

Few women produced mainstream natural history in this period, but they were not completely absent from its margins. Leisured women were ready consumers of natural history. Lady Margaret Cavendish Bentinck, Duchess of Portland, amassed one of the largest natural history collections in all of Europe; its sale at auction upon her death took thirty-eight days. She was also an influential patron, whose great house at Bulstrode surpassed the British Museum as a center for natural history during the first half of the eighteenth century.[2] Women were also prominent in audiences that flocked to see Madame Chimpanzee and Sarah Bartmann. And botany was even for a time considered a science especially suited to women. But women were for the most part amateurs following, not creating, the latest fashions in science.

As naturalists fanned out across the globe, only a few exceptional women undertook voyages in pursuit of nature's bounty. Jeanne Baret sailed with Bougainville on his voyage around the world disguised as the male valet of Philibert Commerson, the ship's botanist and her fiancé. A Tahitian recognized what had eluded the European sailors—that the comely valet was a woman.[3] Richard Ligon also reported a woman aboard his ship. "A little virgin" saved his ship and crew by spinning thread from a cargo of cotton to mend the sail.[4] But women traveling with merchants, explorers, or missionaries were few and far between; none served as the ship's naturalist. Eliza Haywood, whose *Female Spectator* included much natural history, indeed recommended that women "travel the world over"—but only in their imaginations.[5]

Nor did women often travel as naturalists to Europe's colonies, whose rough climates and disagreeable conditions made them less than inviting places. Travel diaries were replete with accounts of the sexual danger of travel abroad. The Portuguese, for example, kept a close eye on Jemima Kindersley during her sojourn in Brazil to prevent her (they said) from being sexually assaulted.[6] Women were also warned on medical grounds against travel to the tropics. Blumenbach taught that European women taken directly from their own country to very warm climates succumbed to "very copious menstruation, which almost always in a short space of time ends in fatal hemorrhages of the uterus."[7]

There were, of course, some notable exceptions. Maria Sibylla Merian set sail in 1699 for the Dutch colony of Surinam to collect and cultivate specimens of exotic flora and fauna.[8] She may well have been the only European woman in this period to have traveled independently in the service of science. Most women who did natural historical work in this period did so while accompanying their fathers or husbands to colonial posts (as did Lady Mary Wortley Montagu and Jemima Kindersley).

Maria Merian set sail for Surinam just a decade after political upheaval in that colony left the governor dead, shot by his own soldiers. She was not trained, as were Linnaeus's students, to be sent into the field, nor was she commissioned to go to Surinam by a scientific academy or trading company (though the mayor of Amsterdam offset some of her costs). Her interest was self-generated, part of her lifelong quest to find another variety of caterpillar as economically profitable as the silkworm.

Uncertain what to expect, Merian deposited her will before embarking on the perilous voyage. This was, incidentally, a voyage Linnaeus refused to undertake when offered the post as doctor for the Dutch East Indies Trading Company in Surinam in 1737.[9] Despite the warnings of the mayor of Amsterdam who had lost four daughters in Surinam, Merian set sail at the age of fifty-two accompanied only by her daughter, Dorothea. For two years she collected, studied, and drew the insects and plants of the region, anticipating her classic *Metamorphosis insectorum Surinamensium* published in 1705. The climate was oppressive and planters uninviting. Her daughter, whom she had trained in observation and illustration, served as her assistant; her slaves hacked paths for her through dense "thorns and thistles" which later in the century would harbor large numbers of runaway slaves.[10]

Maria Merian's work is still today recognized for having broadened the empirical base of European entomology. Yet even the bold Merian felt certain constraints not noted by other naturalists. In the preface to her *Metamorphosis* she wrote, "I could have given a much fuller text, but because the world today is very sensitive, and because the views of the learned differ so greatly, I present only my observations."[11] In her *Metamorphosis*, where she detailed the life cycle of various caterpillars, worms, maggots, moths, butterflies, beetles, bees, and flies, she presented only her observations, leaving classification to her male colleagues. Taxonomy was a university-driven enterprise, and though Merian knew Latin, she may have felt that she lacked the book learning—knowledge of Aristotle, Gesner, and Ray—critical to this enterprise. As I have argued elsewhere, she participated more in the artisanal side of science in this period, making her reputation primarily as an observer and illustrator.[12] Merian was an independent woman directing her own business interests, training young women in her trade, and following her own scientific interests. She worked at the beginning of the eighteenth century when women could still insinuate themselves into science via noble networks and craft guilds.[13]

Maria Merian's experience contrasts sharply with that of Maria Riddell, who wrote a natural history of Antigua for the entertainment and edification of friends. By the end of the eighteenth century, women had been moved to the peripheries of science by the twin developments of professionalization in the sciences and privatization of the family. Riddell, better known for her poetry, collected information for her 1792 *Voyages to the Madeira, and Leeward Caribbean Isles with Sketches of the Natural History of these Islands* while traveling with her father, William Woodley, the British governor of St. Kitts and the Leeward Islands. She wrote much of the book while in the West Indies, where she lived in "almost total seclusion from society and dissipation." Her marriage, which took place soon after her arrival, interrupted her work, burdening her with domestic duties that, she complained, "prevented me from finishing, with any degree of accuracy, an undertaking that required more time and labour than I had then leisure to bestow on it." She identified animals using Thomas Pennant's system of classification which she judged "more elegant and perspicuous and better adapted to the simplicity of my plan than the grand scale upon which the immortal Linnaeus has erected his *Systema naturae*."[14]

Her descriptions were not, however, primarily abstractly taxonomic. She was interested in how plants were used in foods, cos-

metics, and medicines. She described, for example, how women of
this region used the oil of the cashew shell to whiten their skin and
remove freckles: "They spread it all over their hands, neck, and face,
in a few days the skin peels off in great flakes after which the complexion appears for sometime exquisitely fair, but is more liable
to sunburn than ever; besides the pain of this operation is
excruciating."[15]

It was not, however, a foregone conclusion that women would
be excluded from science. In concrete instances one can see how
women might have figured more prominently in the making of
modern science. Maria Winkelmann, the prominent eighteenth-
century astronomer, was denied a position at the Berlin Academy of
Sciences in 1710. Had she succeeded in her bid for this post, it is
possible that she, rather than Peter Kolb, subsequently well known
for his account of the Hottentots, might have traveled to the Cape of
Good Hope on Academy business. Kolb, trained as an astronomer,
was sent to the Cape to measure the lunar parallax—a project conceived by Gottfried Kirch, Winkelmann's husband and chief astronomer at the Berlin Academy. According to Kolb's account, he traveled to Amsterdam and from there took passage on a ship of the East
India Company, becoming sick and lonely during the long voyage.
When he arrived at the Cape, Kolb neglected his mission, setting to
work observing the Hottentots instead, and the project failed. Gottfried Leibniz, president of the Berlin Academy, bemoaning the failure of the expedition, suggested that had Maria Winkelmann been
sent instead of Kolb, the Academy would have received more reliable astronomical observations.[16]

In this period European women discussed natural history primarily in romances and plays. Like Buffon, whose forty-four-volume
Histoire naturelle has been described as a "cosmological novel,"
women such as Marie Anne de Roumier Robert, Françoise de Graffigny, and Olympe de Gouges wove information from travelogues
into their own accounts of foreign peoples.[17] The fact that women
did not collect the stuff of nature firsthand did not necessarily ban
them from writing natural history. Many of Europe's leading naturalists (Linnaeus, Buffon, and Blumenbach) never left Europe. And

206   while the line between science and literature was not always strictly
drawn in this period, there were significant differences between
women using anthropological observations in their fiction and
male naturalists who, like Carl Linnaeus, sat at the center of vast scientific empires. After Linnaeus became professor of botany at Uppsala University, he was inundated with specimens from his students
who, like ambassadors, fanned out around the globe to acquire information for their master.

Male naturalists also developed far-reaching networks for exchanging information and scientific cargo brought to them by Europe's trading companies. Blumenbach, for instance, made a special
trip to London to study mummies under the auspices of Sir Joseph
Banks, president of the Royal Society. Soemmerring borrowed Blumenbach's cherished Georgian skull for his studies. Women working in natural history, such as Priscilla Wakefield or Maria Riddell,
were not part of those networks. Their work, even when providing
new interpretations, rarely influenced male naturalists.

Women's voices, of course, were not the only ones excluded
from Europe's fantasia of nature. Africans or Native Americans
might have combined a knowledge of their flora and fauna with the
European urge to order nature. How different our knowledge of the
earth's plants and medicines might have been had men and women
from around the globe begun sharing their knowledge in the eighteenth century as equals, not colonizers and colonized. Some naturalists of the period recognized the value of such perspectives.
Charles-Marie de La Condamine, for example, appreciated the
enormity of the task he undertook when he set out to classify in European style the plants and trees of the Amazon basin in the 1740s.
How much greater would be the accomplishment, he suggested, "if
we were to comprehend herewith, an examination into the virtues
ascribed to them by the natives of the country."[18]

As it was, Enlightenment enthusiasms for comprehensive
knowledge of nature were sobered by the difficulties they encountered in dealing with foreign cultures. Indigenous peoples responded to Europeans' scientific curiosity in different ways. Some
were eager to please; others were astute enough to seek a profit.

Foucher d'Obsonville remarked, "Because of our European air of eager admiration, they [the Asians] make serious and important objects which otherwise would have drawn no particular attention, and demand an exorbitant price."[19] There was also the problem that objects of study were altered significantly by the presence of observers. Early in the eighteenth century when Hans Sloane, a future president of the Royal Society, sought to record the appearance, history, and uses of plants of Jamaica, "by the best information [he] could get from books and the inhabitants, either Europeans, Indians or Blacks," much of the flora and fauna, and local knowledge of it, had been disrupted or destroyed. As Sloane noted, all the indigenous peoples of the island had been killed in the preceding century by the Spanish. The Indians he consulted about the use of native plants had come as slaves from Florida and surrounding areas. Jamaica had been further transformed by the Spanish who had brought many fruit trees from the American continent and along with them, no doubt, insects and disease until then unknown on that island.[20]

European naturalists did often hire native guides in order to profit from their knowledge of local flora and fauna. Foucher d'Obsonville, for example, believed his Malaysian guide when he said that "the orangutan is a wild man of the same genus as humans, though constituting a very distinct species" (d'Obsonville obviously imputed to his guide the classificatory apparatus of European taxonomy).[21] At other times, Europeans used indigenous knowledge of herbs and medicines to ensure their own survival in foreign environments. The Dutch traveler Paul Isert observed that European (male) travelers often bought local women to serve as concubines and domestic servants because these women knew how to prepare local food and medicines, and could care for the Europeans when they were sick—which was often.[22]

Europeans more often discounted or ignored local knowledge. Naturalists' tendency to favor European learning over native reports is highlighted in Thomas Boreman's 1739 discussion of the size of adult chimpanzees. The Angolan who procured "Madame Chimpanzee" in the 1730s did so by shooting her mother—an animal, he claimed, to be five-foot tall (which is about right when the animal is standing erect as it was commonly depicted in the eighteenth century; see chapter 3).[23] Boreman contrasted this with the English anatomist Edward Tyson's report that these animals—literally "pygmies" as described by the ancients—measured a little over two feet (Tyson had falsely regarded the young chimp he dissected in his London home to be nearly full grown).[24] Boreman, discussing this clash between the reports of the eyewitness and the learned European, remarked that "if what the Negro related, who shot the Mother of this Chimp [Madame Chimpanzee] be true, viz. that she was upward of five Foot high, it will quite overthrow the Ingenious conjecture of Dr. Tyson." Boreman went on to announce, "For my own part I am inclined to believe Tyson . . . who has with much labor, learning, and good reasoning upon the subject made it so evident that I think everyone who reads him impartially, will acquiesce with him in that opinion." Boreman, unsure how to judge the "misinformation" provided by the African, wondered "whether the Negro-man, who reports this, understood our measure, or was faithful in his account? Or whether to get a better price for the young, he did not paint the old one to be such a huge fierce beast? Or to imagine his own courage and skill in killing the one and taking the other?"[25] Even in an age of empiricism, Boreman accepted Tyson's estimate based on the writings of the ancients over reports by native peoples who had actually seen these animals alive.

The European disregard for local knowledge of indigenous plants and animals went beyond discounting particular facts or observations. European naturalists collected specimens, sometimes specific facts about that specimen, but not world views, cosmologies, or alternative ways of ordering and understanding the world. They stockpiled specimens in cabinets, put them behind glass in museums, accumulated them in botanical gardens and princely menageries. They collected the bounty of the natural world, but a bounty divested of traditional names, cultural meanings (symbolic and allegorical), and increasingly of medicinal and culinary uses. By the time of Linnaeus, what counted as knowledge of a plant was its name, kind, species, attributes, uses, and *literaria*; the cultural significance of the organism was reduced to one final category.[26] Botanists increasingly engaged in the distinctively European project of classifying plants and animals based on their particular understanding of anatomy and physiology.[27]

In the eighteenth century, Europeans collected plants as though these plants were being seen by humans for the very first time (when they may, in fact, have been used for centuries by other peoples). Following Linnaeus, they considered barbaric any generic name not derived from Greek or Latin: the new names they bestowed often commemorated a king or a patron who may have advanced the cause of botany or otherwise attracted the praise of naturalists.[28] The French botanist Michel Adanson, bemoaning this practice, pointed to the absurdity of Linnaeus's naming a colonial plant *Dillenia* after the renowned Oxford botanist Johann Dillenius rather than retaining its indigenous name.[29] In the early twentieth century Linnaean practices were ratified when international congresses (dominated by Europeans) declared European taxonomy universal, with Linnaean nomenclature forming the starting point for both botany and zoology.

It may well be that the explosion in knowledge associated with the rise of modern science resulted in a loss of knowledge in the long run. Today Western anthropologists and archeologists scramble to preserve remnants of dying cultures, treasure troves of knowledge held by the healers, midwives, and farmers in those cultures. Westerners may now be interested in natural abortifacients and pain remedies, raised-field agriculture, anticancer drugs, and so forth, but much of this is too little too late. Cultural extinction is at an all-time high. Three thousand of the world's six thousand languages and the stores of knowledge embedded in them are today in danger of extinction.

Would the vision of nature Europeans created have been different had a Maria Merian engaged in taxonomy or had La Condamine's project to collect local knowledge of flora and fauna prevailed? A lady writing in the preface of Lady Montagu's *Letters* recounting her travels in Europe, Asia, and Africa asserted that ladies see the world quite differently, and that when a lady travels she strikes out a new path.[30] There are many historical examples one can mention. Maria Merian discussed the uses of *Flos pavonis* as an abortifacient, while her nineteenth-century critic, the Reverend Lansdown Guilding, remarked only that this plant formed a "pretty hedge."[31] Even Hans Sloane, who cited Merian's observations, said nothing about this aspect of the plant's virtues.[32] European mores and institutions suppressed the development of certain kinds of knowledge. Within Europe the demise of the midwife sounded the death knell of traditional knowledge of contraception—knowledge historically belonging to women. As late as 1600, two hundred contraceptives and abortifacients, both of a vegetable and a mechanical nature, were still in use.[33] European domestic and global expansion in the eighteenth and nineteenth centuries, however, encouraged pronatalist, mercantilist policies that targeted for extinction the midwife's and women's control of fertility.[34] In this climate, it is unlikely that naturalists would have collected additional knowledge about contraceptives from abroad, nor in the absence of women would it necessarily have occurred to them to do so. Male naturalists may also have lacked the training to understand what parts of plants served as contraceptives or abortifacients, or how to prepare and administer them.

It is difficult or even impossible to say how things might have been different. The point is to appreciate how knowledge has been molded historically. What I have tried to show is that knowledge was shaped by patterns of inclusion and exclusion from the scientific community and, more importantly, by the social and political struggles shaping those patterns. That Europeans modeled plant sexuality on culturally sanctioned heterosexual unions, saw mammals as essentially breasted, made the investigation of sexual and racial difference a priority of the medical sciences, cannot be blamed on the shortsightedness of a few individuals alone, but rather can be traced to broader social trends of which science was a part.

One often hears the argument that it does not matter who does science, that Newton's law of gravity will be true whether perceived by a woman, an African man, or a Euro-American man. There is a kernel of truth to this. Scientific knowledge is empirically grounded in sensory input from the natural world. But there are also important ways in which it can and does matter who does science. Human knowledge develops through conversations, observations, and exchanges—both private and public. These exchanges guide scientific research—pushing forward certain projects and setting limits to what is conceivable. Had Africans become a regular part of the European scholarly community, would (could) Europeans have debated for nearly two centuries their proximity to apes? Would Cuvier have so freely compared Sarah Bartmann to the apes had he imagined he would have to discuss the matter with her or another South African woman?

We have seen how gender—often invisible to eighteenth-century eyes and sensibilities—actively molded science. I have shown in very specific ways that eighteenth-century natural historians had choices, that outcomes could have been different. There was, for example, no overwhelming empirical reason to call mammals mammals; other gender-neutral terms could have captured equally well the natural affinities of this group. The fact that we are called mammals—and that this has not been questioned for over two hundred years—has as much to do with the question of women's place in science and society as with the evolutionary genealogy of this group of animals.

In recent years, we have become painfully aware of the legacies of eighteenth-century sexual science in which European male bodies came to represent the fully developed human type—while diverse and sundry females were studied only for their deviations from that norm, as a sexual subset of the universal human. Today, with a new awareness of gender, researchers are beginning to discover that many medical therapies have been designed specifically for male bodies. Some drugs used to treat heart attacks, for example, while beneficial to many men, turn out to cause dangerously low blood pressure in many women. Statistical studies have shown that women are ten times more likely as men to die after angioplasty, a technique designed to reopen clogged arteries. In 1986 the U.S. National Institutes of Health initiated a requirement that grant applications include female subjects in medical testing and research.

There is a certain irony, however, in current concerns about inadequate knowledge of the female body. Though many scientists have tended to slight research concerning women's health, they have too often been quick to jump to reductionistic, biologistic explanations of human inequality. It is not incidental to our problem that the double-edged sword of sexual science—the simultaneous exaggeration of sexual differences to the detriment of women, and the neglect of research potentially beneficial to women—has been wrought in institutions dominated by men. In regard to women, science is not a neutral culture. In the modern sexual division of labor that crystallized in the eighteenth century, science was part of the terrain that fell to the male sex. Scientists sought to distance themselves from things defined as feminine, including women.

We are just beginning to unravel how deeply gender has been worked into nature's body. Historical exposé, of course, is not enough, for like a variant on Penelope's thread, what we unravel by night is often rewoven by day in ongoing workaday institutions of science. Science—its methods, priorities, and institutions—must be recast to allow women and their concerns to fit comfortably within it. Scientists need to become aware not just of how history shapes the present, but also how what is studied—and what has been neglected—grows out of who is doing the studying, and for what ends.

Notes

Introduction

1. Priapus is the Greco-Roman god of procreation and personification of the erect phallus. According to Webster, an image of this god was often used as a scarecrow in ancient gardens.
2. Pliny the Elder, *Natural History*, trans. H. Rackham (Cambridge, Mass.: Harvard University Press, 1942), VIII, xliv, p. 77.
3. Aristotle, *Historia animalium*, in *The Works of Aristotle*, trans. D'arcy Thompson (Oxford: Clarendon Press, 1910), vol. 4, p. 572a. See also Nancy Cott, "Passionlessness: An Interpretation of Victorian Sexual Ideology, 1790–1850," *Signs: Journal of Women in Culture and Society* 4 (1978): 219–236.
4. William Smellie, *The Philosophy of Natural History* (Edinburgh, 1790), vol. 1, p. 238.
5. Julien Offray de La Mettrie, *L'homme plante* (Potsdam, 1748), p. 29.
6. Georg W. F. Hegel compared the male mind to an animal that acquires knowledge only through much struggle and technical exertion. The female mind, by contrast, does not (cannot) rise above its plantlike existence and remains rooted in its *an sich* existence (*Grundlinien der Philosophie des Rechts* [1821] in his *Werke*, ed. Eva Moldenhauer and Karl Michel [Frankfurt: Suhrkamp, 1969–1971], vol. 7, pp. 319–320).
7. David Noble, *A World without Women: The Christian Clerical Culture of Western Science* (New York: Alfred A. Knopf, 1992).
8. For critiques of biological studies of women, see, for example, Anne Fausto-Sterling, *Myths of Gender: Biological Theories about Women and Men* (New York: Basic Books, 1985); and Ruth Hubbard, *The Politics of Women's Biology* (New Brunswick: Rutgers University Press, 1990).

9. Literature on gender in science is voluminous. See, for example, Sandra Harding, *Whose Science? Whose Knowledge? Thinking from Women's Lives* (Ithaca: Cornell University Press, 1991); Sandra Harding and Jean O'Barr, eds., *Sex and Scientific Inquiry* (Chicago: University of Chicago Press, 1987); Ludmilla Jordanova, *Sexual Visions: Images of Gender in Science and Medicine between the Eighteenth and Twentieth Centuries* (Madison: University of Wisconsin Press, 1989); Donna Haraway, *Primate Visions: Gender, Race, and Nature in the World of Modern Science* (New York: Routledge, 1989); and Helen Longino, *Science as Social Knowledge: Values and Objectivity in Scientific Inquiry* (Princeton: Princeton University Press, 1990). For general histories of women in science, see Margaret Alic, *Hypatia's Heritage: A History of Women in Science from Antiquity to the Late Nineteenth Century* (London: Women's Press, 1986); Margaret Rossiter, *Women Scientists in America: Struggles and Strategies to 1940* (Baltimore: Johns Hopkins University Press, 1982); and Pnina Abir-Am and Dorinda Outram, eds., *Uneasy Careers and Intimate Lives: Women in Science, 1789–1979* (New Brunswick: Rutgers University Press, 1987). For biographies, see Evelyn Fox Keller, *A Feeling for the Organism: The Life and Work of Barbara McClintock* (New York: W. H. Freeman, 1983); Louis Bucciarelli and Nancy Dworsky, *Sophie Germain: An Essay in the History of the Theory of Elasticity* (Dordrecht: Reidel, 1980); Elizabeth Patterson, *Mary Somerville and the Cultivation of Science, 1815–1840* (The Hague: Nijhoff, 1983); Ann Hibner Koblitz, *A Convergence of Lives, Sofia Kovalevskaia: Scientist, Writer, Revolutionary* (Boston: Birkhäuser, 1983); and Geneviève Fraisse, *Clémence Royer: Philosophe et femme de science* (Paris: La Decouverte, 1985). For autobiographies, see *Cecilia Payne-Gaposchkin: An Autobiography and Other Recollections*, ed. Katherine Haramundanis (Cambridge: Cambridge University Press, 1984); Sara Ruddick and Pamela Daniels, eds., *Working It Out: 23 Women Writers, Artists, Scientists, and Scholars Talk about Their Lives and Work* (New York: Pantheon, 1977); Derek Richter, ed., *Women Scientists: The Road to Liberation* (London: Macmillan, 1982); and Vivian Gornick, *Women in Science: Portraits from a World in Transition* (New York: Simon and Schuster, 1983).

10. Carolyn Merchant, *The Death of Nature: Women, Ecology, and the Scientific Revolution* (San Francisco: Harper & Row, 1980).

11. Evelyn Fox Keller, *Reflections on Gender and Science* (New Haven: Yale University Press, 1985), p. 3. See also her *Secrets of Life, Secrets of Death: Essays on Language, Gender and Science* (New York: Routledge, 1992).

12. Londa Schiebinger, *The Mind Has No Sex? Women in the Origins of Modern Science* (Cambridge, Mass.: Harvard University Press, 1989).

13. Robert Proctor, *Value-Free Science? Purity and Power in Modern Knowledge* (Cambridge, Mass.: Harvard University Press, 1991).

14. Jacques-Christophe Valmont de Bomare, *Dictionnaire raisonné universel d'histoire naturelle* (Lyon, 1791), vol. 6, p. 633. David E. Allen, *The Naturalist in Britain: A Social History* (1976; Harmondsworth, Middlesex: Penguin Books, 1978), pp. 30–31.

15. Marie-Jean-Antoine-Nicolas de Caritat, marquis de Condorcet, "Eloge de M. de Linné," in *Histoire de l'Académie Royale des Sciences* (Paris, 1778), p. 78.

16. The value of the gold, silver, and precious stones shipped from the East Indies to England in a four-year period from 1759 to 1763 amounted to £600,000. Fernand Braudel, *The Wheels of Commerce*, trans. Siân Reynolds (1979; New York: Harper & Row, 1982), p. 222.
17. Louis-Antoine de Bougainville, *A Voyage round the World*, trans. John Forster (London, 1772), p. viii.
18. Edward Long, *The History of Jamaica* (London, 1774), vol. 2, p. 364.
19. Proctor, *Value-Free Science?*
20. Dorinda Outram, *The Body and the French Revolution: Sex, Class and Political Culture* (New Haven: Yale University Press, 1989), p. 75; also Joan Scott, "French Feminists Claim the Rights of 'Man,'" (Washington University Publication, April 1991).
21. Schiebinger, *Mind Has No Sex?*
22. Olympe de Gouges, *Réflexions sur les hommes nègres* (Paris, 1788), p. 95.

1. The Private Lives of Plants

1. Alexandre Koyré, *From the Closed World to the Infinite Universe* (Baltimore: Johns Hopkins Press, 1957), pp. vii–viii. See, for example, Robert Merton, *Science, Technology and Society in Seventeenth Century England* (1938; New York: Harper, 1970); Paul Feyerabend, *Against Method* (1975; London: Verso, 1988); and A. R. Hall, *From Galileo to Newton* (New York: Harper, 1962).
2. Linnaeus devised a system of binary nomenclature that was universally adopted for both plants and animals and still serves today as the backbone of biological classification. In 1905 the *International Code of Botanical Nomenclature* designated Linnaeus's *Species plantarum* of 1753 the starting point for botanical nomenclature. See Frans A. Stafleu, *Linnaeus and the Linnaeans: The Spreading of Their Ideas in Systematic Botany, 1735–1789* (Utrecht: A. Oosthoek's Uitgeversmaatschappij, 1971), p. 110.
3. See Christoph Trew, *Vermehrtes und verbessertes Blackwellisches Kräuter-Buch* (Nuremberg, 1750), preface; and Karen Reeds, "Botany in Medieval and Renaissance Universities" (Ph.D. diss., Harvard University, 1975). This transition was gradual. Agnes Arber has pointed out, of course, that from the time of Aristotle plants had been studied from two diverse viewpoints: as a branch of natural philosophy and as a by-product of medicine or agriculture; see her *Herbals: Their Origin and Evolution, a Chapter in the History of Botany, 1470–1670*, 3d ed. (Cambridge: Cambridge University Press, 1986), p. xxv and chap. 1.
4. Alice Stroup, *A Company of Scientists: Botany, Patronage, and the Community at the Seventeenth-Century Parisian Royal Academy of Sciences* (Berkeley and Los Angeles: University of California Press, 1990), p. 70.
5. Historians of botany traditionally have emphasized the break between herbalism and modern botany. This change, it should be noted, was gradual and many of those today recognized as the founders of modern botany continued to write about the medicinal virtues of plants. Linnaeus, for example, continued to search for new medicinal plants throughout his life.

6. Thomas Martyn, cited in David E. Allen, *The Naturalist in Britain: A Social History* (1976; Harmondsworth, Middlesex: Penguin Books, 1978), p. 39.

7. Carl Linnaeus, *Systema naturae* (1735), ed. M. S. J. Engel-Ledeboer and H. Engel (Nieuwkoop: B. de Graaf, 1964), "Observationes in regnum vegetabile," no. 7.

8. Linnaeus's ultimate goal was to devise a natural system, but until that time an artificial system that could group the plants in an orderly fashion was required. Ibid., no. 12. See also Linnaeus to Haller, 3 April 1737, in *The Correspondence of Linnaeus*, ed. James E. Smith (London, 1821), vol. 2, p. 229. Linnaeus's system was artificial but it was neither arbitrary nor heterodox. See James Larson's discussion in his *Reason and Experience: The Representation of Natural Order in the Work of Carl von Linné* (Berkeley and Los Angeles: University of California Press, 1971), pp. 61–62.

9. See Julius von Sachs, *Geschichte der Botanik vom XVI. Jahrhundert bis 1860* (Munich, 1876), pp. 82–83.

10. For a history of binomial nomenclature, see John Heller, *Studies in Linnaean Method and Nomenclature* (Frankfurt: Peter Lang, 1983), pp. 41–75.

11. Suzanne Kessler, "The Medical Construction of Gender: Case Management of Intersexed Infants," *Signs: Journal of Women in Culture and Society* 16 (1990): 3–26. See also Anne Fausto-Sterling, "The Five Sexes: Why Male and Female Are Not Enough," *The Sciences* (March/April 1993): 20–25.

12. *Science* (28 February 1992): 1073.

13. Though the Greeks were aware that some plants reproduce sexually, it was not the focus of their attention.

14. Pliny the Elder, *Natural History*, trans. H. Rackham (Cambridge, Mass.: Harvard University Press, 1942), XII, xxxii, p. 45. A. G. Morton, *History of Botanical Science: An Account of the Development of Botany from Ancient Times to the Present Day* (New York: Academic Press, 1981), pp. 28, 38.

15. William Smellie, "Botany," *Encyclopaedia Britannica* (Edinburgh, 1771), vol. 1, p. 646.

16. *Dictionarium Britannicum*, ed. G. Gordon, P. Miller, and N. Bailley (London, 1730), s.v. "pistillum." Joseph Pitton de Tournefort in 1694 standardized the modern usage of the term pistil (*pistile*) to designate the ovary, style, and stigma of the flower; the term was introduced into botanical usage in England in the 1750s. The use of the term stamen is much older; Pliny referred to the stamen of the lily. The technical use of the word in botany, however, dates to about 1625.

17. Morton, *History of Botanical Science*, p. 213.

18. Jacques Rousseau, "Sébastien Vaillant: An Outstanding Eighteenth-Century Botanist," *Regnum Vegetabile* 71 (1970): 195–228. Giulio Pontedera powerfully rejected the entire notion of plant sexuality in 1720 (*Anthologia, sive De floris natura*).

19. "The Prize Dissertation of the Sexes of Plants by Carolus von Linnaeus," in Robert Thornton, *A New Illustration of the Sexual System of Carolus von Linnaeus* (London, 1799–1807).

20. Smellie, "Botany," p. 646. Rudolph Camerarius experimented with fertilization (*De sexu plantarum epistola* [Tübingen, 1694], pp. 80–84).

21. Claude Geoffroy, "Observations sur la structure et l'usage des principales parties des fleurs," *Mémoires de l'Académie Royale des Sciences* (1711): 211.

22. Nehemiah Grew, *The Anatomy of Plants* (London, 1682), pp. 170–172.

23. Much has been written about the debates between the sexualists and antisexualists in this regard. See especially Sachs, *Geschichte der Botanik*; and François Delaporte, *Nature's Second Kingdom: Explorations of Vegetality in the Eighteenth Century*, trans. Arthur Goldhammer (1979; Cambridge, Mass.: MIT Press, 1982).

24. Carl Linnaeus, *Praeludia sponsaliorum plantarum* (1729), reprinted in *Smärre Skrifter af Carl von Linné*, ed. N. H. Lärjungar and T. Fries (Uppsala: Almquist & Wiksells, 1908), vol. 1, pp. 13–14, section 15. Linnaeus drew this information from Vaillant. See also Jean-Jacques Rousseau, *Dictionnaire des termes d'usage en botanique*, in *Botany: A Study of Pure Curiosity* (London: Michael Joseph, 1979), s.v. "pistil."

25. Julien Offray de La Mettrie, *L'homme plante* (Potsdam, 1748).

26. Frederick Churchill, "Sex and the Single Organism: Biological Theories of Sexuality in Mid-Nineteenth Century," in *Studies in History of Biology*, vol. 3, ed. William Colemann and Camille Limoges (Baltimore: Johns Hopkins University Press, 1979), p. 141.

27. Geoffroy, "Observations sur la structure," p. 212; Sébastien Vaillant, *Discours sur la structure des fleurs* (Leiden, 1718), p. 10.

28. Ibid., p. 14.

29. Homosexual relations among the lower vertebrates, such as female whiptail lizards of the American Southwest, have only recently been studied. Though an isolated female whiptail is capable of reproducing on her own, paired females produce more eggs more frequently (Bettyann Kevles, *Females of the Species: Sex and Survival in the Animal Kingdom* [Cambridge, Mass.: Harvard University Press, 1986], pp. 201–203).

30. As Frederick Churchill has shown, the sexual model of reproduction has had its historic ups and downs. By the 1860s the assumed uniqueness of sexual reproduction was in decline, only to be bolstered again with the rise of the theory of evolution which promoted sexuality as the "engine" for generating variation (Churchill, "Sex and the Single Organism," p. 169). Now again, however, the central importance ascribed to sexuality is being questioned. Lynn Margulis and Dorion Sagan have argued, for example, that biparental sex does not immediately confer any great advantage upon organisms (*Origins of Sex: Three Billion Years of Genetic Recombination* [New Haven: Yale University Press, 1986]).

31. I thank Paul Harvey for this information.

32. Linnaeus, *Praeludia sponsaliorum plantarum*, section 16. Also cited in James Larson, "Linnaeus and the Natural Method," *Isis* 58 (1967): 304–320, especially 306.

33. Jeffrey Merrick, "Royal Bees: The Gender Politics of the Beehive in Early Modern Europe," *Studies in Eighteenth-Century Culture* 18 (1988): 7–37.

34. Erasmus Darwin, *The Loves of the Plants* (1789), part II of *The Botanic Garden: A Poem in Two Parts* (New York: Garland Publishing, Inc., 1978), vol. 2, pp. 14–15.

35. Nancy Leys Stepan, "Race and Gender: The Role of Analogy in Science," *Isis* 77 (June 1986): 261–277. See also Mary Hesse, *Models and Analogies in Science* (Notre Dame, Ind.: University of Notre Dame Press, 1966); Alan Gross, *The Rhetoric of Science* (Cambridge, Mass.: Harvard University Press, 1990); Lawrence Prelli, *A Rhetoric of Science: Inventing Scientific Discourse* (Columbia: University of South Carolina Press, 1989); and Peter Dear, ed., *The Literary Structure of Scientific Argument* (Philadelphia: University of Pennsylvania Press, 1991).

36. See, for example, William T. Stearn, cited in Wilfrid Blunt, *The Compleat Naturalist: A Life of Linnaeus* (London: William Collins Sons & Co., 1971), p. 244.

37. John Farley, *Gametes and Spires: Ideas about Sexual Reproduction, 1750–1914* (Baltimore: Johns Hopkins University Press, 1982).

38. As suggested in Delaporte, *Nature's Second Kingdom*, p. 143.

39. Desmond King-Hele, *Erasmus Darwin* (New York: Charles Scribner's Sons, 1963), p. 114.

40. On clandestine marriage, see Lawrence Stone, *Road to Divorce: England, 1530–1987* (Oxford: Oxford University Press, 1990), pp. 96–120.

41. Lawrence Stone, *The Family, Sex and Marriage in England, 1500–1800* (New York: Harper & Row, 1977).

42. Blunt, *Compleat Naturalist*, pp. 85, 167.

43. Margaret Jacob, "The Materialist World of Pornography," paper delivered at the New York Area French History Seminar, September 1992.

44. Blunt, *Compleat Naturalist*, pp. 176–177.

45. Ibid.

46. Bernard de Jussieu to Linnaeus, 30 January 1749, in *The Correspondence of Linnaeus*, ed. Smith, vol. 2, p. 221.

47. Blunt, *Compleat Naturalist*, pp. 165–166.

48. *Oxford English Dictionary*, s.v. "gamete."

49. See Wolf Lepenies, *Das Ende der Naturgeschichte: Wandel kultureller Selbstverständlichkeiten in den Wissenschaften des 18. und 19. Jahrhunderts* (Frankfurt: Suhrkamp, 1978); and Ludmilla Jordanova, ed., *Languages of Nature* (New Brunswick: Rutgers University Press, 1986).

50. Cited by Ronald King in Robert Thornton, *The Temple of Flora* (1799; Boston: New York Graphic Society, 1981), p. 19. See also Sten Lindroth, "The Two Faces of Linnaeus," in *Linnaeus: The Man and His Work*, ed. Tore Frängsmyr (Berkeley and Los Angeles: University of California Press, 1983), pp. 8, 35.

51. Linnaeus loved the great poets of Rome, especially Virgil and Ovid. In addition to classical mythology, Linnaeus also used images from traditional wedding poetry and the Book of Psalms in the Bible. See Lindroth, "The Two Faces of Linnaeus," p. 10. See also John Heller, "Classical Mythology in the *Systema naturae* of Linnaeus," *Transactions and Proceedings of the American Philological Association* 76 (1945): 333–347.

52. Anna Seward, *Memoirs of the Life of Dr. Darwin* (Philadelphia, 1804), p. 95. Darwin also found the Rosicrucian doctrine of gnomes, sylphs, nymphs, and salamanders proper machinery for a botanic poem. He saw hieroglyphics as embodying in allegory many truths of nature known to the Egyptians which were later carried into the mythology of Greece and Rome. Darwin, *Botanic Garden*, Apology, vii–viii.

53. It has been argued that Linnaeus was essentially a scholastic who ordered plants into classes, orders, genera, and species along the same lines as the learned doctors of the Middle Ages. Lindroth follows Julius von Sachs in this interpretation; see Lindroth, "Two Faces of Linnaeus," pp. 33–37.

54. Mary F. Willson and Nancy Burley, *Mate Choices in Plants* (Princeton: Princeton University Press, 1983), pp. 3–4.

55. Vaillant, *Discours sur la structure des fleurs*. Also Sébastien Vaillant, *Botanicon Parisiense* (Leiden and Amsterdam, 1727), preface by Herman Boerhaave. Linnaeus read a review of this work in the *Actis Lipsienibus* (Benjamin Jackson, *Linnaeus* [London: H. F. & G. Witherby, 1923], p. 45). Linnaeus hurriedly prepared his *Praeludia sponsaliorum plantarum* after the appearance of a dissertation supervised by G. Wallin entitled "The Marriage of Plants."

56. Georges-Louis Leclerc, comte de Buffon, *Histoire naturelle, générale et particulière* (Paris, 1749), vol. 1, pp. 13–20.

57. Allen, *Naturalist in Britain*, chaps. 1 and 2.

58. John Miller, *An Illustration of the Sexual System of Carolus von Linnaeus* (London, 1777); James E. Smith, trans., *A Dissertation on the Sexes of Plants* (London, 1786); and Thornton, *New Illustration of the Sexual System of Carolus von Linnaeus*.

59. Charles Alston, "A Dissertation on the Sexes of Plants," *Essays and Observations Physical and Literary Read before the Philosophical Society of Edinburgh* (1754; Edinburgh, 1771), vol. 1, pp. 315–318.

60. Smellie, "Botany," pp. 627–653; and William Smellie, *The Philosophy of Natural History* (Edinburgh, 1790), vol. 1, pp. 245–263, especially p. 246. In 1790 John Rotheram published *The Sexes of Plants Vindicated* as a reply to Smellie's scientific objections but he did not mention the matter of morals.

61. Smellie, "Botany," p. 653.

62. William Withering, *A Botanical Arrangement of British Plants*, 2 vols. (Birmingham, 1787), vol. 1, p. xv. Ludwig of Leipzig also avoided sexual terms in his explication of Linnaeus's classes and orders by substituting the more straightforward botanical terms anther and style for Linnaeus's andria and gynia. Linnaeus's first class was thus rendered "monatherae" and his first order "monostylae," and so on. Richard Pulteney, *A General View of the Writings of Linnaeus*, 2d ed. (London, 1805), p. 243.

63. Johann Siegesbeck, *Verioris brevis sciagraphia* (St. Petersburg, 1737), p. 49.

64. Amman to Linnaeus, 15 November 1737, in *Correspondence of Linnaeus*, ed. Smith, vol. 2, p. 193.

65. Cited by Stearn in Blunt, *Compleat Naturalist*, p. 245.

66. It is also curious that Jean-Jacques Rousseau, Europe's greatest advocate of

sexual complementarity, did not indulge in heavy-handed sexual imagery. Botany, Rousseau was fond of teaching, soothes—rather than inflames—the passions. His letters on botany addressed to Madame Etienne Delessert, in which he introduced mother and daughter to the Linnaean system, are remarkable for their neglect of sexual reproduction in plants. J.-J. Rousseau, "Lettres sur la botanique," in *Oeuvres complètes*, ed. Bernard Gagnebin and Marcel Raymond (Paris: Gallimard, 1959–1969), vol. 4.

67. Darwin, *Loves of the Plants*, canto I.

68. Erasmus Darwin, *Zoonomia; or, The Laws of Organic Life* (London, 1794), vol. 1, p. 147.

69. Seward, *Memoirs of the Life of Dr. Darwin*. For a different view see King-Hele, *Erasmus Darwin*, pp. 116–117.

70. James Logan, "The Poetry and Aesthetics of Erasmus Darwin," *Princeton Studies in English* 15 (1936): 114.

71. *The Monthly Review* 9 (June 1793): 183. The French translator of Darwin's poem gives a genealogy of botanic poetry stretching from Ovid to Paul Contant's 1609 *Jardin et cabinet poétique*; see also J.-P.-F. Deleuze, *Les amours des plantes* (Paris, 1800), preface.

72. Letter to James Watt, 20 November 1789, reprinted in *The Letters of Erasmus Darwin*, ed. Desmond King-Hele (Cambridge: Cambridge University Press, 1981), pp. 196, 206, 225. Darwin sold his *Loves of the Plants* for £800 and his *Botanic Garden* for £900.

73. Letter to Joseph Johnson, 23 May 1784, reprinted in ibid., pp. 139–140.

74. Seward, *Memoirs of the Life of Dr. Darwin*, p. 95.

75. Darwin, *Botanic Garden*, vol. 1, p. v.

76. Letter to James Watt, 20 November 1789, reprinted in *Letters of Erasmus Darwin*, ed. King-Hele, p. 196.

77. King-Hele, *Erasmus Darwin*, pp. 116–117.

78. Seward, *Memoirs of the Life of Dr. Darwin*, pp. 124–125, 157. In the whole of *The Botanic Garden*, Seward found only one objectionable passage, that of a tale retold from Homer in which azoic gas is personified as Mars and made lover to the virgin air (Venus) with fire (Vulcan) the jealous rival. Here Darwin, Seward judged, had overstepped, like Homer before him, the bounds of propriety with his libertine and unjust deities.

79. Maureen McNeil, *Under the Banner of Science: Erasmus Darwin and His Age* (Manchester: Manchester University Press, 1987), pp. 64–66.

80. See his celebration of the French Revolution in his *Economy of Vegetation*, in *The Poetical Works of Erasmus Darwin* (London, 1806), vol. 1, pp. 106–107.

81. Norton Garfinkle, "Science and Religion in England, 1790–1800: The Critical Responses to the Work of Erasmus Darwin," *Journal of the History of Ideas* 16 (1955): 378.

82. Ibid., p. 380; see also McNeil, *Under the Banner of Science*, pp. 133–135.

83. Roy Porter, "Mixed Feelings: The Enlightenment and Sexuality in Eighteenth-Century Britain," in *Sexuality in Eighteenth-Century Britain*, ed. Paul-Gabriel Boucé (Manchester: University of Manchester Press, 1982), pp. 1–27.

84. Ibid., pp. 8–15, 19–20.

85. McNeil, *Under the Banner of Science*, pp. 80–84. See also William Withering's account in *Miscellaneous Tracts* (London, 1822), vol. 2, pp. 115–123.

86. *The Anti-Jacobin; or, Weekly Examiner* 23 (April 1798): 180–182; 24 (April 1798): 188–189; and 26 (May 1789): 204–206. Darwin apparently pretended that he had never heard of this satire. Geometry may have been chosen as the satiric vehicle in this case because geometric lines were at this time divided into gender, class, or order according to the number of dimensions of an equation expressing the relation between the ordinates and the abscissas. *Dictionarium Britannicum*, s.v. "gender." The same dictionary defines "man" as a creature endowed with reason, and though an etymology is given for woman ("pamb" or womb plus man), "woman" is not defined.

87. Richard Polwhele, *The Unsex'd Females; a Poem* (1798; New York, 1800), pp. 33–34.

88. Ibid, pp. 10–20.

89. Erasmus Darwin, *A Plan for the Conduct of Female Education in Boarding Schools* (London, 1797).

90. See Desmond King-Hele, *Doctor of Revolution: The Life and Genius of Erasmus Darwin* (London: Faber & Faber, 1977), pp. 234–237. King-Hele has incorrectly emphasized the radical nature of Darwin's tract.

91. Polwhele considered Erasmus Darwin's *Botanic Garden*, where "lustful boys anatomize a plant," a prime source of moral decay. Polwhele also took Emma Crewe to task for overstepping the modesty of nature in her portrayal of Cupid in the frontispiece to Darwin's *Loves of the Plants* (*Unsex'd Females*, p. 27).

92. Robert Thornton, *The Politician's Creed* (London, 1795–1799), title page and introduction.

93. Priscilla Wakefield, *Introduction to Botany* (London, 1796).

94. On botany as a science particularly suitable for women, see Londa Schiebinger, *The Mind Has No Sex? Women in the Origins of Modern Science* (Cambridge, Mass.: Harvard University Press, 1989), pp. 241–244. See also Ann Shteir, "Linnaeus's Daughters: Women and British Botany," in *Women and the Structure of Society*, ed. Barbara Harris and Jo Ann McNamara (Durham: Duke University Press, 1984); and Ann Shteir, "Botany in the Breakfast Room: Women in Early Nineteenth-Century British Plant Study," in *Uneasy Careers and Intimate Lives: Women in Science, 1789–1979*, ed. Pnina G. Abir-Am and Dorinda Outram (New Brunswick: Rutgers University Press, 1987), pp. 31–44.

95. For a fuller discussion of the scientific revolution in views of sexual difference, see my *Mind Has No Sex?* chaps. 6 and 7.

96. Thomas Laqueur, *Making Sex: Body and Gender from the Greeks to Freud* (Cambridge, Mass.: Harvard University Press, 1990). See also the critical evaluation of Laqueur's work by Katharine Park and Robert Nye, "Destiny Is Anatomy," *The New Republic* (18 February 1991): 53–57.

97. See Aristotle, *Generation of Animals*, trans. A. L. Peck (Cambridge, Mass.: Harvard University Press, 1953), I, i–ii, pp. 11–15, IV, vi, p. 459. See also Sarah Pomeroy, *Goddesses, Whores, Wives, and Slaves* (New York: Schocken, 1975);

M. C. Horowitz, "Aristotle and Woman," *Journal of the History of Biology* 9 (1976): 183–213; Danielle Jacquart and Claude Thomasset, *Sexuality and Medicine in the Middle Ages*, trans. Matthew Adamson (Cambridge: Polity Press, 1988); and Evelyne Berriot-Salvadore, "Le discours de la médecine et de la science," in *Histoire des femmes en Occident*, ed. Natalie Davis and Arlette Farge (Paris: Plon, 1991), vol. 3, pp. 359–395.

98. Londa Schiebinger, "Skeletons in the Closet: The First Illustrations of the Female Skeleton in Eighteenth-Century Anatomy," *Representations* 14 (1986): 42–82.

99. Marlene LeGates, "The Cult of Womanhood in Eighteenth-Century Thought," *Eighteenth-Century Studies* 10 (1976): 21–39; Ruth Bloch, "Untangling the Roots of Modern Sex Roles: A Survey of Four Centuries of Change," *Signs: Journal of Women in Culture and Society* 4 (1978): 237–257; Susanne Risse-Stumbries, *Erziehung und Bildung der Frau in der zweiten Hälfte des 18. Jahrhunderts* (Frankfurt: R. G. Fischer, 1980); Karin Hausen, "Die Polarisierung der 'Geschlechtscharaktere,'" in *Sozialgeschichte der Familie in der Neuzeit Europas*, ed. Werner Conze (Stuttgart: Klett, 1976); Randolph Trumbach, *The Rise of the Egalitarian Family: Aristocratic Kinship and Domestic Relations in Eighteenth-Century England* (New York: Academic Press, 1978); Susan Okin, "Women and the Making of the Sentimental Family," *Philosophy & Public Affairs* 11 (1982): 65–88; and Linda Pollock, *Forgotten Children: Parent-Child Relations from 1500 to 1900* (Cambridge: Cambridge University Press, 1983). More recently, scholars have emphasized how the remaking of the family was critical to the founding of political authority. See Alan Macfarlane, *The Origins of English Individualism: The Family, Property and Social Transition* (Cambridge: Cambridge University Press, 1979); Carole Pateman, *The Sexual Contract* (Stanford: Stanford University Press, 1988); and Lynn Hunt, *The Family Romance of the French Revolution* (Berkeley and Los Angeles: University of California Press, 1992).

2. Why Mammals Are Called Mammals

1. The tenth edition of Linnaeus's *Systema naturae* and Carl Clerck's *Aranei Svecici* together form the starting point of modern zoological nomenclature. See *International Code of Zoological Nomenclature*, ed. W. D. Ride (London: British Museum, 1985), I.3. The term *Mammalia* first appeared in a student dissertation, *Natura pelagi*, in 1757 but was not published until 1760 (*Amoenitates academicae* [Erlangen, 1788], vol. 5, pp. 68–77).

2. Literature on Linnaeus is voluminous. See, for example, *A Catalogue of the Works of Linnaeus* (London: British Museum, 1933); Henri Daudin, *De Linné à Jussieu: Méthodes de la classification* (Paris: Félix Alcan, 1926); Ernst Mayr, *The Growth of Biological Thought: Diversity, Evolution, and Inheritance* (Cambridge, Mass.: Harvard University Press, 1982); Heinz Goerke, *Linnaeus*, trans. Denver Lindley (New York: Charles Scribner, 1973); and Gunnar Broberg, ed., *Linnaeus: Progress and Prospects in Linnaean Research* (Stock-

holm: Almquist & Wiksell International, 1980). Broberg's *Homo sapiens L.: Studier i Carl von Linnés naturuppfattning och människolära* (Stockholm: The Swedish History of Science Society, 1975), by contrast, considers broader contexts.

3. Broberg, *Linnaeus*, p. 34.

4. W. T. Stearn, "The Background of Linnaeus's Contributions to the Nomenclature and Methods of Systematic Biology," *Systematic Zoology* 8 (1959): 4–22; and E. G. Linsley and R. L. Usinger, "Linnaeus and the Development of the International Code of Zoological Nomenclature," ibid., pp. 39–46.

5. Carl Linnaeus, *Systema naturae per regna tria naturae*, 10th ed. (Stockholm, 1758).

6. Aristotle, *Historia animalium*, in *The Works of Aristotle*, trans. D'arcy Thompson (Oxford: Clarendon Press, 1910); G. E. R. Lloyd, *Science, Folklore and Ideology* (Cambridge: Cambridge University Press, 1983), p. 16; Aristotle, *Generation of Animals*, trans. A. L. Peck (Cambridge, Mass.: Harvard University Press, 1953), p. lxix; and Pierre Pellegrin, *Aristotle's Classification of Animals: Biology and the Conceptual Unity of the Aristotelian Corpus*, trans. Anthony Preus (Berkeley and Los Angeles: University of California Press, 1986).

7. Herman Frey, *Biblisch Thierbuch* (Leipzig, 1595). See Willy Ley, *Dawn of Zoology* (Englewood Cliffs, N.J.: Prentice-Hall, 1968), pp. 160, 164.

8. Despite these objections, the term figured prominently in the title of his book. In the text Ray bowed to tradition, leaving the cetaceans among fishes, "although they evidently agree with viviparous quadrupeds in everything except hair, feet and the element in which they live." John Ray, *Synopsis methodica animalium quadrupedum et serpentini generis* (London, 1693), p. 55. See also Charles Raven, *John Ray, Naturalist: His Life and Works* (Cambridge: Cambridge University Press, 1950).

9. Thomas Huxley, cited in Ernst Haeckel, *Das Menschen-Problem und die Herrentiere von Linné* (Frankfurt: Neuer Frankfurter Verlag, 1907), p. 8. Some historians have argued that it was the problem of how to classify the whale that led to Linnaeus's search for new terminology (see, for example, William Gregory, "The Orders of Mammals," *Bulletin of the American Museum of Natural History* 27 [1910]: especially 28).

10. Pierre Belon, *L'histoire de la nature des oyseaux* (Paris, 1555), pp. 40–41; Edward Tyson, *Orang-Outang, sive Homo sylvestris; or, The Anatomy of a Pygmie Compared with That of a Monkey, an Ape, and a Man* (London, 1699). See Maurice Daumas, *Histoire de la science* (Paris: Gallimard, 1957), p. 1352.

11. Carl Linnaeus, *Fauna Svecica* (Stockholm, 1746), preface.

12. See Londa Schiebinger, "The Gendered Ape: Early Representations of Primates in Europe," in *A Question of Identity: Women, Science, and Literature*, ed. Marina Benjamin (New Brunswick: Rutgers University Press, 1993).

13. Georges-Louis Leclerc, comte de Buffon, *Histoire naturelle générale et particulière* (Paris, 1749–1804), vol. 14, p. 18.

14. Cited by Jean Baptiste Bory de Saint-Vincent, *Dictionnaire classique d'histoire naturelle* (Paris, 1825), vol. 8, p. 270.

15. On this point see Gunnar Broberg's excellent *"Homo sapiens*: Linnaeus's Classification of Man," in *Linnaeus: The Man and His Work*, ed. Tore Frängsmyr (Berkeley and Los Angeles: University of California Press, 1983), pp. 156–194.

16. Ray, *Synopsis methodica*, "Animalium tabula generalis," p. 53. See also William Gregory, "Linnaeus as an Intermediary between Ancient and Modern Zoology," *Annals of the New York Academy of Sciences* 18 (1908): 21–31, especially 25. Ray's terms were used as adjectives, not nouns—an important distinction at a time when scholastics distinguished between essence and accident. Theodor Gill, "The Story of a Word—Mammal," *Popular Science Monthly* 61 (1902): 434–438.

17. Broberg, *"Homo sapiens,"* p. 175.

18. I have derived this term from Linnaeus's use of *"pilus"* in his catalogue of mammalian traits (*Systema naturae*, 10th ed., p. 12). In the early nineteenth century, Lorenz Oken suggested that the class of mammals might better be called *Pilosa* for the uniqueness of their hair. Haeckel, also arguing for this term, noted that cutaneous glands (either sweat or sebaceous) gave rise to mammary glands, suggesting that in mammalian evolution hair preceded mammary glands. Haeckel, *Menschen-Problem*, p. 19.

19. Broberg, *Homo Sapiens L.*, p. 176.

20. Carl Linnaeus, *Lachesis Lapponica; or, A Tour in Lapland*, trans. James E. Smith (London, 1811), vol. 1, p. 191, slightly modified.

21. The number of pig nipples, for example, varies from between eight and eighteen. Ernst Bresslau, *The Mammary Apparatus of the Mammalia in the Light of Ontogenesis and Phylogenesis* (London: Methuen, 1920), p. 98.

22. Gill, "Story of a Word," p. 435.

23. Stearn, "Background of Linnaeus's Contributions," p. 8.

24. Linnaeus's term *Primates* encountered more resistance. Notably, Blumenbach and Cuvier insisted on separating humans and apes into distinct orders—*Inermis* (meaning unarmed, Blumenbach) and *Bimanes* (Cuvier) for humans, and *Quadrumanes* (a term coined by Edward Tyson) for apes. Johann Blumenbach, *Handbuch der Naturgeschichte* (Göttingen, 1779), pp. 57–59; Georges Cuvier, *Le règne animal* (Paris, 1817), vol. 1. The idea of separating humans from apes ran so deep in Cuvier's thinking that, although he accepted humans' place among the mammals, he very often juxtaposed the terms *"l'homme"* and *"les mammifères"* as if humans were not mammals at all (*Leçons d'anatomie comparée* [Paris, 1800–1805]). Karl Illiger also made humans the sole inhabitants of his first order *Erecta*; apes were included in a second order, *Pollicata*.

25. Buffon, *Histoire naturelle*, vol. 1, pp. 38–40. C. Prévost, the author of "Mammifères" in the *Dictionnaire classique d'histoire naturelle*, noted that in this period it was commonly thought that male horses had no teats and consequently that breasts were not a universal characteristic of mammals (Paris, 1826, vol. 10, p. 74). As John Lyon and Phillip Sloan have pointed out, Buffon may have been thinking of stallions, which have no teats and usually only inconspicuous rudimentary mammary glands, but even these are not always

present (*From Natural History to the History of Nature: Readings from Buffon and His Critics* [Notre Dame: University of Notre Dame Press, 1981], p. 94 n. 8).

26. Buffon, *Histoire naturelle*, vol. 1, pp. 38–40. See also Phillip Sloan, "The Buffon-Linnaeus Controversy," *Isis* 67 (1976): 356–375; and James Larson, "Linné's French Critics," *Linnaeus*, ed. Broberg, pp. 67–79.

27. Henri de Blainville, "Prodrome: D'une nouvelle distribution systématique du règne animal," *Journal de physique* 83 (1816), p. 246. See also Toby Appel, "Henri de Blainville and the Animal Series: A Nineteenth-Century Chain of Being," *Journal of the History of Biology* 13 (1980): 291–319, especially 301.

28. John Hunter, *Essays and Observations on Natural History, Anatomy, Physiology, Psychology, and Geology*, ed. Richard Owen (London, 1861), vol. 1, p. 25.

29. Gill, "Story of a Word," pp. 436–437. See also *Dictionnaire pittoresque d'histoire naturelle* 4 (1836), s.v. "Mammifères."

30. Mamma meaning breast first appeared in English in 1579 (Henry Skinner, *The Origin of Medical Terms* [Baltimore: Williams & Wilkins Company, 1949], p. 223).

31. Blumenbach claimed that male hamsters and dormice do not have mammary glands but did not for this reason remove them from the class of mammals (*Handbuch der Naturgeschichte*, p. 46).

32. *Encyclopédie, ou Dictionnaire raisonné des sciences, des arts et des métiers* (Paris, 1751–1765), s.v. "Mamelle."

33. Aristotle, *Historia animalium*, p. 522a.

34. Buffon, *Histoire naturelle*, vol. 2, p. 543.

35. Hunter, *Essays and Observations on Natural History*, pp. 238–239. Males nursing infants was a popular theme. In the nineteenth century, travelers made the remarkable claim that Brazilian men nurse all infants ("Mammifères," *Dictionnaire classique d'histoire naturelle*, vol. 10, p. 105). Other travelers claimed that God had bestowed on the men of eastern Ethiopia "breasts of milk as amply supplied as those of the women." In Portugal, a man fifty years old was said to have suckled two orphans of a female relation (Joano dos Santos, "History of Eastern Ethiopia" in John Pinkerton, *A General Collection of the Best and Most Interesting Voyages and Travels in all Parts of the World* [London, 1808–1814], vol. 16, p. 697). Centuries earlier Aristotle had spoken of an androgynous race of people, their left breast being that of a man and their right breast that of a woman (Pliny the Elder, *Natural History*, trans. H. Rackham [Cambridge, Mass.: Harvard University Press, 1942], VII, ii, pp. 14–17).

36. Erasmus Darwin, *Zoonomia; or, The Laws of Organic Life* (London, 1794), vol. 1, p. 512.

37. G. Gegenbauer cited in Charles Darwin, *The Descent of Man and Selection in Relation to Sex* (1871; London: John Murray, 1913), p. 251 n. 29.

38. Ibid., pp. 249–253. Darwin cited Clémence Royer's *Origine de l'homme* (Paris, 1870). On Royer, see Joy Harvey, " 'Strangers to Each Other': Male and Female Relations in the Life and Work of Clémence Royer," in *Uneasy Careers*

and Intimate Lives: Women in Science, 1789–1979, ed. Pnina Abir-Am and Dorinda Outram (New Brunswick: Rutgers University Press, 1987), pp. 147–171.

39. Stephen Jay Gould, "Freudian Slip," *Natural History* (February 1987): 14–19.

40. My account of the platypus is taken from Harry Burrell's classic, *The Platypus* (Sydney: Angus & Robertson Limited, 1927), pp. 1–45.

41. Shaw's report is reprinted in Carl Linnaeus, *A General System of Nature*, trans. William Turton (London, 1806), vol. 1, pp. 30–32.

42. The German anatomist Friedrich Tiedemann left open the question of where to classify the platypus. Jean-Baptiste de Monet de Lamarck created a new class—*Prototheria* (he did not consider platypuses mammals because they had no mammary glands and were probably oviparous; they certainly were not birds, nor were they reptiles, since they possessed a four-chambered heart). Karl Illiger placed them in the division *Reptantia*, between reptiles and mammals. Burrell, *Platypus*, p. 30.

43. Ronald King in Robert Thornton, *The Temple of Flora* (1799; Boston: New York Graphic Society, 1981), p. 9. Linnaeus sometimes named new genera after friends and colleagues, intending to suggest a spiritual likeness between the individual and the plant or animal in question (Benjamin Jackson, *Linnaeus* [London: H. F. & G. Witherby, 1923], p. 278). He also ranked his colleagues as "Officers in Flora's Army" according to his evaluation of their scientific merit. His list was headed by "General Linnaeus"; the lowliest rank was assigned to his critic, Johann Siegesbeck (Heinz Goerke, *Linnaeus*, trans. Denver Lindley [New York: Charles Scribner's Sons, 1973], p. 108).

44. My project to identify historical trends molding taxonomy differs from Alan Gross's, where he makes the more general argument that rhetoric infuses most aspects of science, including taxonomy (*The Rhetoric of Science* [Cambridge, Mass.: Harvard University Press, 1990]).

45. Cuvier, *Règne animal*, vol. 1, p. 76.

46. The other characters are: (1) a jaw articulation formed by the squamosal and the dentary; (2) a chain of three bones, malleus, incus, and stapes connecting the tympanic membrane to the inner ear; (3) the presence of hair or fur; (4) the left aortic arch in the systemic arch; and (5) cheek teeth with divided roots. See D. M. Kermack and K. A. Kermack, *The Evolution of Mammalian Characters* (London: Croom Helm, 1984), p. vii; also T. S. Kemp, *Mammal-like Reptiles and the Origin of Mammals* (London: Academic Press, 1982); and Louis Guillette, Jr. and Nicholas Hotton, III, "The Evolution of Mammalian Reproductive Characteristics in Therapsid Reptiles," *The Ecology and Biology of Mammal-like Reptiles*, ed. Nicholas Hotton III, Paul MacLean, Jan Roth, and Carol Roth (Washington, D.C.: Smithsonian Institution Press, 1986), pp. 239–250, especially 244–246.

47. Scott Atran, *Cognitive Foundations of Natural History: Towards an Anthropology of Science* (Cambridge: Cambridge University Press, 1990), p. 316 n. 23–24.

48. Stephen Jay Gould, "A Quahog Is a Quahog," in *The Panda's Thumb: More Reflections in Natural History* (New York: Norton, 1980), pp. 204–207.

49. The cultural significance of the breast and mother's milk is a large topic, and

in this section I want to touch on only those aspects relevant to Linnaeus's work. Marina Warner's *Alone of All Her Sex: The Myth and the Cult of the Virgin Mary* (New York: Alfred A. Knopf, 1976) and her *Monuments and Maidens: The Allegory of the Female Form* (New York: Atheneum, 1985) along with Caroline Bynum's *Jesus as Mother: Studies in the Spirituality of the High Middle Ages* (Berkeley and Los Angeles: University of California Press, 1982) have been very helpful, though they focus primarily on the Middle Ages. Heinz Kirchhoff's "Die künstlerische Darstellung der weiblichen Brust als Attribut der Weiblichkeit und Fruchtbarkeit als auch der Spende der Lebenskraft und der Weisheit" (*Geburtshilfe und Frauenheilkunde* 50 [1990]: 234–243) is rich but written, like Erich Neumann's *Die grosse Mutter* (Zurich: Rhein Verlag, 1956), from a Jungian perspective and without attention to historical context. Helpful materials are also found in Anne Hollander, *Seeing through Clothes* (New York: Penguin Books, 1975) and in Françoise Borin, "Arrêt sur image," in *Histoire des femmes en Occident*, ed. Natalie Davis and Arlette Farge (Paris: Plon, 1991), vol. 3, pp. 213–219. See also the anecdotes collected by Gustave-Jules Witkowski in his *Les seins dans l'histoire* (Paris: A. Maloine, 1903). A good cultural history of the breast and mother's milk is much needed.

50. See Lynn Hunt, *Politics, Culture, and Class in the French Revolution* (Berkeley and Los Angeles: University of California Press, 1984), especially part 1; also Warner, *Monuments and Maidens*, chaps. 12, 13.

51. Broberg has shown that Linnaeus first used the term *sapiens* in 1753 to denote a species of monkey referred to as *Simia sapiens*—a species said to play a mean game of backgammon ("*Homo sapiens*," p. 176). Linnaeus wrote of "trivial names" in reference to botany: "I have put trivial names in the margin so that without more ado we can represent one plant by one name; these I have taken, it is true, without special choice, leaving this for another day. However, I would warn some solemnly all sensible botanists not to propose a trivial name without adequate specific distinction, lest the science fall back into its early crude state." Cited in John Heller, *Studies in Linnaean Method and Nomenclature* (Frankfurt: Peter Lang, 1983), p. 278.

52. Linnaeus saw reason as the principle characteristic distinguishing humans from other animals. In the preface to his *Fauna Svecica* (1746) he called reason "the most noble thing of all" that places humans above all others. See also H. W. Janson, *Apes and Ape Lore in the Middle Ages and the Renaissance* (London: The Warburg Institute, 1952), pp. 74–75.

53. Plato, *Timaeus*, 91c. Plato seemed uncertain whether woman should be classed with brute beasts or rational beings. Ian Maclean, *The Renaissance Notion of Woman: A Study in the Fortunes of Scholasticism and Medical Science in European Intellectual Life* (Cambridge: Cambridge University Press, 1980), p. 31.

54. Aristotle, *Historia animalium*, 500a, 521b, and 582a. Throughout the Middle Ages, there was little interest in mammae as a marker of sexual difference. See Joan Cadden, *The Meanings of Sexual Difference in the Middle Ages: Medicine, Natural Philosophy, and Culture* (Cambridge: Cambridge University Press, 1992).

55. Aristotle, *Generation of Animals*, 776a–777a. Aristotle saw milk production

as natural and good; he argued against Empedocles who saw milk as a whitish pus emanating from purified blood.

56. Warner, *Alone of All Her Sex*, p. 194.

57. Linnaeus also advocated suckling children by cows in order to improve survival rates as was done in certain villages in France. Carl Linnaeus, "Nutrix noverca," respondent F. Lindberg (1752), in *Amoenitates academicae* (Erlangen, 1787), vol. 3, pp. 262–263. Goats and other animals were used to suckle syphilitic children in foundling hospitals in the eighteenth century or when there was a shortage of human nurses. Valerie Fildes, *Wet Nursing: A History from Antiquity to the Present* (Oxford: Basil Blackwell, 1988), p. 147.

58. Mervyn Levy, *The Moons of Paradise: Some Reflections on the Appearance of the Female Breast in Art* (London: Arthur Barker Limited, 1962), p. 55. William Godwin, *Memoirs of the Author of a Vindication of the Rights of Woman* (London, 1798), p. 183.

59. Hermann Ploss, Max Bartels, and Paul Bartels, *Woman: An Historical Gynecological and Anthropological Compendium*, ed. Eric Dingwall (St. Louis: C. V. Mosby Company, 1936), vol. 3, p. 211.

60. Petrus Camper did not explain why he used a female figure to illustrate the art of transforming "a quadruped into the human figure" (*The Works of the Late Professor Camper on the Connexion between the Science of Anatomy and the Arts of Drawing, Painting, Statuary, etc.*, trans. T. Cogan [London, 1794], plate 7, fig. 13).

61. Carolyn Merchant, *The Death of Nature: Women, Ecology, and the Scientific Revolution* (San Francisco: Harper & Row, 1980).

62. On Maier's images, see Sally Allen and Joanna Hubbs, "Outrunning Atalanta: Feminine Destiny in Alchemical Transmutation," in *Sex and Scientific Inquiry*, ed. Sandra Harding and Jean O'Barr (Chicago: University of Chicago Press, 1987), pp. 79–98.

63. Charles Cochin and Hubert-François Gravelot, *Iconologie par figures, ou Traité complet des allégories, emblèmes, &c.* (1791; Geneva: Minkoff Reprint, 1972), s.v. "Nature." Erasmus Darwin also portrayed "Nature" as multi-breasted in *The Temple of Nature* (London, 1803), frontispiece.

64. Linnaeus, *Fauna Svecica*, frontispiece. Otto Gertz has suggested that Linnaeus provided the engraver with the initial design for this frontispiece ("Artemis och Hinden: Frontispisplanschen i Linnés *Fauna Svecica*," *Svenska Linné-Sällskapets Årsskrift* 31 [1948]: 20).

65. Neumann, *Grosse Mutter*, p. 128.

66. Robert Fleischer, *Artemis von Ephesos und verwandte Kultstatuen aus Anatolien und Syrien* (Leiden: E. J. Brill, 1973); George Elderkin, "Diana of the Ephesians," *Art in America* 25 (1937): 54–63; and Hermann Thiersch, *Artemis Ephesia: Eine archäologische Untersuchung* (Berlin: Weidmannsche Buchhandlung, 1935). Linnaeus's epithet "Nosce te ipsum" (know thyself) appended to *Homo* in the first edition of his *Systema naturae* was also found on the Temple of Diana. Jane Sharp, the English midwife, noted that polymastia occasionally occurs in women (*The Midwives Book* [London, 1671], p. 336).

67. Warner, *Alone of All Her Sex*, pp. 192, 200; Warner, *Monuments and Maidens*,

p. 283. Whether the Virgin menstruated was much discussed in the Middle Ages; theologians, committed to a new emphasis on Incarnation, argued that she did. Cadden, *Meanings of Sexual Difference in the Middle Ages*, pp. 174–175.

68. Bynum, *Jesus as Mother*, p. 115. See also Erwin Panofsky, *Abbot Suger* (Princeton: Princeton University Press, 1946), pp. 30–31. Sander Gilman has discussed how the traditional image of the Virgin Mary as the nursing Mother was transformed into an emblem of excess in Luca Giordano's 1664 "Allegory of Syphilis" (*Sexuality: An Illustrated History* [New York: John Wiley & Sons, 1989], p. 144).

69. Warner, *Alone of All Her Sex*, p. 194.

70. The pictorial representation of *sapientia lactans* dates to the early fifteenth century. *Sapientia lactans* was incorporated into the seal of Cambridge University, which shows the naked *Alma Mater Cantabrigia* with milk streaming from her breasts (W. S. Heckscher, "Spiritualia sub metaphoris corporalium," *University of Toronto Quarterly* 16 [1946–1947]: 212 n. 9). See also Peter Dronke, "Bernard Silvestris, Natura, and Personification," *Journal of the Warburg and Courtauld Institutes* 43 (1980): 16–31, especially 28–29; Klaus Lange, "Geistliche Speise," *Zeitschrift für deutsches Altertum* 95 (1966): 81–122; and Lieselotte Möller, "Nährmutter Weisheit," *Deutsche Vierteljahrsschrift* 24 (1950): 347–359.

71. Johann Wolfgang Goethe, *Faust: Eine Tragödie* (1808–1832; Munich: Deutscher Taschenbuch Verlag, 1962), p. 19. Alexander von Humboldt dedicated to Goethe his frontispiece showing the spirit of poetry unveiling "the mystery of nature." Nature is personified as the multimammae Diana. See Alexander von Humboldt, *Reise von Alexander von Humboldt und Aimé Bonpland* (Tübingen, 1807). I thank David Hull for calling this to my attention. In the Middle Ages, it was thought that fundamental causes could be discovered "in the most secret recesses of Natura's breasts" (Dronke, "Bernard Silvestris," p. 25). The nineteenth-century statue, "Nature Unveiling before Science," featured in the foyer of the Paris medical faculty, reveals only her breasts and face. See Merchant, *Death of Nature*, fig. 17; also Ludmilla Jordanova, *Sexual Visions: Images of Gender in Science and Medicine between the Eighteenth and Twentieth Centuries* (Madison: University of Wisconsin Press, 1989), chap. 5.

72. Ploss and Bartels, *Woman*, vol. 3, pp. 233–234.

73. Kirchhoff, "Künstlerische Darstellung der weiblichen Brust," p. 240.

74. On Amazons, see J. A. Fabricius, "Dissertatio critica," cited in Thomas Bendyshe, "The History of Anthropology," *Memoirs Read Before the Anthropological Society of London* 1 (1865): 415–416. Saints Agnes and Barbara were shown having their breasts cut off as a form of torture in grotesque art of the late Middle Ages (Margaret Miles, *Carnal Knowing: Female Nakedness and Religious Meaning in the Christian West* [Boston: Beacon Press, 1989], p. 156).

75. Warner, *Monuments and Maidens*, p. 281. In eighteenth-century France, Charity appeared in propaganda to encourage maternal nursing. T. G. H.

Drake, "The Wet Nurse in France in the Eighteenth Century," *Bulletin of the History of Medicine* 8 (1940): 944.

76. The paintings of Peter Paul Rubens are prime examples of the appreciation of voluptuous breasts. In the seventeenth century all across Europe, breasts were shown to be larger and rounder than in the previous century. Anne Hollander has traced changing ideals of the breast, showing that the bared breast, a symbol of maternal self-sacrifice in the fourteenth century and of Amazonian heroism in the fifteenth century, became in the seventeenth and eighteenth centuries a sexual ornament and expression of pure eroticism (*Seeing through Clothes*, chap. 3). See, for example, Bernard Mandeville, *The Virgin Unmask'd; or, Female Dialogues Betwixt an Elderly Maiden Lady, and Her Niece* (London, 1709).

77. Sharp, *Midwives Book*, p. 360.

78. Pinkerton, *General Collection of . . . Voyages*, vol. 11, p. 194.

79. Mary Lindemann, "Love for Hire: The Regulation of the Wet-Nursing Business in Eighteenth-Century Hamburg," *Journal of Family History* 6 (1981): 382. Midwives, such as Jane Sharp, were concerned that overly large breasts might become cancerous (Sharp, *Midwives Book*, p. 337). Sharp's concern was with milk production, not the beauty of the breast.

80. Barbara Gelphi, *Shelley's Goddess: Maternity, Language, Subjectivity* (New York: Oxford University Press, 1992), pp. 43–60. See also Jean Block, "Women and Reform of the Nation," in *French Women and the Age of Enlightenment*, ed. Samia Spencer (Bloomington: University of Indiana Press, 1984), pp. 3–18.

81. Ploss and Bartels, *Woman*, vol. 1, pp. 398–399. Witches were also portrayed with heavy, pendulous breasts during the European witch craze (Miles, *Carnal Knowing*, pp. 136–138). These types of associations led early modern Europeans to doubt that the elaborate breasts adorning the Diana of the Ephesians were the breasts of a woman. Their pendulous fullness suggested rather the udders of beasts. Furthermore, they had no nipples, a curiosity leading one twentieth-century art historian to conjecture that Diana's overfull mammae were not breasts at all but indeed bull scrota—the bull also being an ancient symbol of fertility (Kirchhoff, "Künstlerische Darstellung der weiblichen Brust," p. 236).

82. John Gabriel Stedman, *Narrative of a Five Years Expedition against the Revolted Negroes of Surinam* (1796; Baltimore: Johns Hopkins University Press, 1988), p. 89.

83. Charles White, *An Account of the Regular Gradation in Man and in Different Animals and Vegetables* (London, 1796), p. 134. Cited also in William Stanton, *The Leopard's Spots: Scientific Attitudes toward Race in America, 1815–59* (Chicago: The University of Chicago Press, 1960), p. 17.

84. Dissatisfaction with wet-nursing began in the 1680s, however, the height of the campaign came in the eighteenth century. See Sharp, *Midwives Book*, pp. 353, 361–362; Valerie Fildes, *Breasts, Bottles and Babies: A History of Infant Feeding* (Edinburgh: Edinburgh University Press, 1986); and Randolph Trumbach, *The Rise of the Egalitarian Family: Aristocratic Kinship and Domestic*

Relations in Eighteenth-Century England (New York: Academic Press, 1978). Dry-nursing under the mother's direct supervision was also advocated but led to even higher infant mortality.

85. George Sussman, *Selling Mothers' Milk: The Wet-Nursing Business in France, 1715–1914* (Urbana: University of Illinois Press, 1982), p. 20; see also Nancy Senior, "Aspects of Infant Feeding in Eighteenth-Century France," *Eighteenth-Century Studies* 16 (1983): 367; Mary Sheriff, "Fragonard's Erotic Mothers and the Politics of Reproduction," in *Eroticism and the Body Politic*, ed. Lynn Hunt (Baltimore: Johns Hopkins University Press, 1991), pp. 14–40.

86. Figures collected by Maxime de Sarthe-Lenoir, Lieutenant Général de Police for Paris, in the 1770s cited in Senior, "Aspects of Infant Feeding," pp. 367–368. See also George Sussman, "Parisian Infants and Norman Wet-Nurses in the Early Nineteenth Century," *Journal of Interdisciplinary History* 7 (1977): 637.

87. Joseph Raulin, *De la conservation des enfans* (Paris, 1768), vol. 1, "épître au roi."

88. See, for example, ibid.; J. E. Gilibert, "Dissertation sur la dépopulation, causée par les vices, les préjugés et les erreurs des nourrices mercénaires," preface, *Les chefs-d'oeuvres de Monsieur de Sauvages* (Lyon, 1770), vol. 2; and Johann Frank, *System einer vollständigen medicinischen Polizey* (Mannheim, 1779), vol. 1. In an attempt to curb abuses and decrease infant mortality, wet-nursing in France was regulated by law in 1715 (Sussman, *Selling Mothers' Milk*, p. 38).

89. Linnaeus, "Nutrix noverca," trans. by J. E. Gilibert as "La nourrice marâtre, ou Dissertation sur les suites funestes du nourrissage mercénaire," in *Les chefs-d'oeuvres de Monsieur de Sauvages*, vol. 2, pp. 215–244. See also William Cadogan, *An Essay upon Nursing and the Management of Children* (London, 1748); and Jean-Jacques Rousseau, *Emile, ou De l'éducation* (1762), in *Oeuvres complètes*, ed. Bernard Gagnebin and Marcel Raymond (Paris: Gallimard, 1959–1969), vol. 4, pp. 254–264.

90. Linnaeus, "Nutrix noverca," p. 258.

91. This argument dates at least to the seventeenth century (Guérin, 1675). See Senior, "Aspects of Infant Feeding," pp. 378–379. On the theme of women following the example of beasts in suckling their young, see also Cadogan, *Essay upon Nursing*, p. 7; Raulin, *De la conservation des enfans*, vol. 1, pp. xxv–xxviii; Jacques Ballexserd, *Dissertation sur cette question: Quelles sont les principes de la mort d'un aussi grand nombre d'enfans* (Geneva, 1775), p. 64; and *Der Patriot*, 27 January 1724, cited in Lindemann, "Love for Hire," p. 381. The anonymous "Sophia" used a similar argument to try to convince men to let their wives breast-feed (*Woman not Inferior to Man* [London, 1739], cited in Vivien Jones, ed., *Women in the Eighteenth Century: Constructions of Femininity* [New York: Routledge, 1990], p. 225).

92. Charles Whitlaw, *New Medical Discoveries, with a Defence of the Linnaean Doctrine* (London, 1829), vol. 1, p. 233.

93. Marie-Angélique Anel le Robours, *Avis aux mères qui veulent nourrir leurs enfans*, 3d ed. (Paris, 1775), especially pp. ix, 53, 92–93. See also Gilibert, "Dissertation sur la dépopulation," pp. 255–256, 264. European women were

also encouraged to follow the example of "primitive mothers" (Africans and Native Americans), for whom milk was said to form "the natural bond that unites mother and child." Cited in D. G. Charlton, *New Images of the Natural in France* (Cambridge: Cambridge University Press, 1984), p. 156.

94. Cited in Jones, *Women in the Eighteenth Century*, p. 85.

95. Abuses related to financial concerns were greater in France than in England. Fiona Newall, "Wet Nursing and Child Care in Aldenham, Hertfordshire, 1595–1726," in *Women as Mothers in Pre-Industrial England*, ed. Valerie Fildes (London: Routledge, 1990), p. 129.

96. Linnaeus, "Nutrix noverca," p. 265. Though this argument was heard less frequently, it was still prominent in the eighteenth century.

97. Cadogan, *Essay upon Nursing*, p. 7.

98. Fildes, *Wet Nursing*, p. 193. A few medical men noted the high mortality rates among wet-nurses' own children (for example, Linnaeus, "Nutrix noverca," p. 264; see also James Lehning, "Family Life and Wetnursing in a French Village," *Journal of Interdisciplinary History* 12 [1982]: 651). In some cases, it was claimed that wet-nursing was responsible for depopulating entire villages (Lindemann, "Love for Hire," p. 380). By and large, however, concern was focused on the physical and moral well-being of middle- and upper-class children.

99. See Jean Donnison, *Midwives and Medical Men: A History of Inter-Professional Rivals and Women's Rights* (London: Heinemann, 1977); Ornella Moscucci, *The Science of Woman: Gynaecology and Gender in England, 1800–1929* (Cambridge: Cambridge University Press, 1990), pp 42–57.

100. Cadogan, *Essay upon Nursing*, pp. 3, 24.

101. Edward Long, *The History of Jamaica* (London, 1774), vol. 2, p. 276.

102. Rousseau, *Emile*, pp. 254–264. See also Mary Jacobus, "Incorruptible Milk: Breast-feeding and the French Revolution, in *Rebel Daughters: Women and the French Revolution*, ed. Sara Melzer and Leslie Rabine (New York: Oxford University Press, 1992), p. 62.

103. Lindemann, "Love for Hire," p. 391.

104. *Allgemeines Landrecht* (1794), part II, title II, art. 67, in Susan Bell and Karen Offen, eds. *Women, the Family and Freedom: The Debate in Documents 1750–1880* (Stanford: Stanford University Press, 1983), vol. 1, p. 39. See also Doris Alder, "Im 'Wahren Paradies der Weiber': Naturrecht und rechtliche Wirklichkeit der Frauen im Preussischen Landrecht," in *Sklavin oder Bürgerin: Französische Revolution und neue Weiblichkeit, 1760–1830*, ed. Viktoria Schmidt-Linsenhoff (Frankfurt: Jonas Verlag, 1989), pp 206–222.

105. Jean-Jacques Rousseau, *The Confessions of Jean-Jacques Rousseau*, trans. J. Cohen (Harmondsworth, Middlesex: Penguin, 1953), p. 333. See also William Kessen, "Rousseau's Children," *Daedalus* 107 (1978): 155; ironically, Emile was brought up by a wet nurse in the country (Senior, "Aspects of Infant Feeding," p. 385). See also Carol Blum, *Rousseau and the Republic of Virtue: The Language of Politics in the French Revolution* (Ithaca: Cornell University Press, 1986), pp. 74–92.

106. Rousseau, *Emile*, p. 255.

107. Ibid., p. 258.
108. Jordanova, *Languages of Nature*, p. 97; Warner, *Monuments and Maidens*, p. 282.
109. See Hunt, *Politics, Culture, and Class in the French Revolution*, chaps. 2, 3.
110. Darline Levy, Harriet Applewhite, and Mary Johnson, eds., *Women in Revolutionary Paris 1789–1795* (Urbana: University of Illinois Press, 1979), p. 219. See also Outram, *The Body and the French Revolution*.
111. Claudette Hould, *Images of the French Revolution* (Québec: Les Publications du Québec, 1989), pp. 378–379. See also Mona Ozouf, *Festivals and the French Revolution*, trans. Alan Sheridan (Cambridge, Mass.: Harvard University Press, 1988), p. 84; and Viktoria Schmidt-Linsenhoff, "Frauenbilder der Französische Revolution," in *Sklavin oder Bürgerin*, ed. Schmidt-Linsenhoff, pp. 451–452. A multibreasted Diana, signifying nature and its bounty, also accompanied a heroic female "Egalité" holding the *Declaration of the Rights of Man and Citizen* in an engraving after J. G. Moitte (François Furet and Mona Ozouf, eds., *A Critical Dictionary of the French Revolution*, trans. Arthur Goldhammer [Cambridge, Mass.: Harvard University Press, 1989], plates following p. 746). Honoré Daumier's *Republic*, drawn for a competition for an image of the French Republic in 1848, featured a powerful nude holding a flag and nursing two male infants (Maurice Agulhon, *Marianne into Battle: Republican Imagery and Symbolism in France, 1789–1880*, trans. Janet Lloyd [Cambridge: Cambridge University Press, 1981], pp. 78, 83).
112. Lynn Hunt, *The Family Romance of the French Revolution* (Berkeley and Los Angeles: University of California Press, 1992), pp. 151–191, especially 153–155. Mary Jacobus has argued that David presented an allegory of the state as "Mother Republic" whose virtuous milk participated in "a fantasy of incorruptible signs" designed to undergird the centralized Jacobin state ("Incorruptible Milk," in *Rebel Daughters*, ed. Melzer and Rabine, pp. 66–68). See also Carol Duncan, "Happy Mothers and Other New Ideas in Eighteenth-Century French Art," in *Feminism and Art History: Questioning the Litany*, ed. Norma Broude and Mary Garrand (New York: Harper & Row, 1982), pp. 200–219.
113. On working-class women, see Brigit Hill, *Women, Work, and Sexual Politics in Eighteenth-Century England* (Oxford: Basil Blackwell, 1989).

3. The Gendered Ape

1. Arthur Lovejoy, *The Great Chain of Being: A Study of the History of an Idea* (1933; Cambridge, Mass.: Harvard University Press, 1964). The ancients were acquainted with apes but made few attempts to explain the relationship between apes and humans. H. W. Janson, *Apes and Ape Lore in the Middle Ages and the Renaissance* (London: The Warburg Institute, 1952), p. 73.
2. See, for example, Arthur Lovejoy, "Monboddo and Rousseau," *Modern Philology* 30 (1932–1933): 275–296; Janson, *Apes and Ape Lore*; Franck Tinland, *L'homme sauvage, Homo ferus et Homo sylvestris, de l'animal à l'homme* (Paris: Payot, 1968); Edward Dudley and Maximillian Novak, eds., *The Wild*

Man Within: An Image in Western Thought from the Renaissance to Romanticism (Pittsburgh: University of Pittsburgh Press, 1972); and Robert Wolker, "Tyson and Buffon on the Orang-utan," *Studies on Voltaire and the Eighteenth Century* 155 (1976): 2301–2319.

3. Claude-Nicolas Le Cat, *Traité de l'existance du fluide des nerfs* (Berlin, 1765), plate 1, p. 35.

4. Jean-Jacques Rousseau, "Discours sur l'origine et les fondements de l'inégalité parmi les hommes," in *Oeuvres complètes,* ed. Bernard Gagnebin and Marcel Raymond (1755; Paris: Gallimard, 1959–1969), vol. 3, p. 212.

5. On this contrast, see C. D. O'Malley and H. W. Magoun, "Early Concepts of the Anthropomorpha," *Physis: Rivista di storia della scienza* 4 (1962): 39–63, especially 46. See also Janson, *Apes and Ape Lore,* chap. 9.

6. Roger Lewin, *Human Evolution,* 2d ed. (Boston: Blackwell Scientific Publications, 1989), p. 1.

7. Carl Linnaeus, *Systema naturae per regna tria naturae,* 10th ed. (Stockholm, 1758), vol. 1, p. 21. *Primate* also carried religious connotations, denoting a bishop of highest rank in a province or country.

8. Nicolaas Tulp, *Observationum medicarum libri tres* (Amsterdam, 1641); for *quimpezé,* see M. de la Brosse, cited in Georges-Louis Leclerc, comte de Buffon, *Histoire naturelle, générale et particulière* (Paris, 1749–1804), vol. 14, p. 51; for chimpanzee, see Gerard Scotin, "Chimpanzee, Scotin sculp. A.D. 1738"; for gibbon, see Buffon, *Histoire naturelle,* vol. 14, pp. 96–113; and for gorilla, see Thomas Savage, "Notice Describing the External Character and Habits of a New Species of Troglodytes (T. *gorilla,* Savage)," *Proceedings of the Boston Society of Natural History* 2 (1848): 245–247. See also Robert and Ada Yerkes, *The Great Apes: A Study of Anthropoid Life* (New Haven: Yale University Press, 1929), pp. 36–40.

9. According to Johann Blumenbach, "orangutan" is better translated "intelligent being" (*On the Natural Varieties of Mankind,* trans. Thomas Bendyshe [1865; New York: Bergman, 1969], p. 95 n. 2). Some European voyagers claimed that natives considered chimpanzees and orangutans human—both terms mean "wild man." Bontius reported this of the Javanese. Daniel Beeckman stated that the natives of Borneo believed that orangutans were once people but had been transformed into beasts because of their blasphemy (*A Voyage to and from the Island of Borneo* [London, 1718], p. 37). Savage asserted that the native people of Gabon believed chimpanzees to be "degenerated human beings" ("Notice Describing the External Character," p. 246). See also O'Malley and Magoun, "Early Concepts of the Anthropomorpha," pp. 58–59.

10. Robert Visser, *The Zoological Work of Petrus Camper 1722–1789* (Amsterdam: Rodopi, 1985), p. 39.

11. Petrus Camper, "De l'orang-outang et de quelques autres espèces de singes," in *Oeuvres de Pierre Camper* (Paris, 1803), vol. 1. See also Visser, *Zoological Work of Petrus Camper,* pp. 34–35. See Alan Jenkins, *The Naturalists* (New York: Mayflower Books, 1978), p. 108.

12. See text accompanying Gerard Scotin's illustration of the 1738 London chimpanzee; also Pons Alletz, *Histoire des singes, et autres animaux curieux* (Paris, 1752), p. 38. Stephen Jay Gould, "Chimp on the Chain," *Natural History* (December (1983): 18–26, especially 24. James Prichard, *Researches into the Physical History of Mankind* (London, 1841), vol. 1, p. 286.

13. Edward Tyson, *Orang-Outang, sive Homo Sylvestris; or, The Anatomy of a Pygmie Compared with that of a Monkey, an Ape, and a Man* (London, 1699), pp. 92–95. William Cowper executed all of Tyson's plates. On Tyson, see M. F. Ashley Montagu, *Edward Tyson and the Rise of Human and Comparative Anatomy in England* (Philadelphia: American Philosophical Society, 1943). The skeleton of Tyson's chimp became a family heirloom. Tyson's granddaughter brought it as part of her dowry to her marriage to Dr. Allardyce, who in turn gave it to the Cheltenham Museum. Thomas Huxley, *Man's Place in Nature and Other Anthropological Essays* (1896; New York: Greenwood Press, 1968), pp. 13–14. The skeleton is now displayed in the gift shop of the Natural History Museum, London.

14. Buffon, *Histoire naturelle*, vol. 14, p. 30.

15. Lovejoy, *Great Chain of Being*, p. 233; and Charles Bonnet, *Contemplation de la nature* in *Oeuvres complètes* (Neuchâtel, 1779–1783), vol. 7, 174. See also Lorin Anderson, *Charles Bonnet and the Order of the Known* (Dordrecht, Holland: D. Reidel Publishing Co., 1982), pp. 34–58.

16. Carl Linnaeus, "Anthropomorpha," respondent C. E. Hoppius (1760), in *Amoenitates academicae* (Erlangen, 1789), vol. 6, p. 66; also his *Fauna Svecica* (Stockholm, 1746), preface. Linnaeus considered theses written under his direction to be his own work (the student's name appears as the respondent). He collected and published them under the title *Amoenitates academicae* (1749–1790). Pieter Smit, "The Zoological Dissertations of Linnaeus," *Linnaeus: Progress and Prospects in Linnean Research*, ed. Gunnar Broberg (Stockholm: Almquist & Wiksell International, 1980), pp. 118–136.

17. Linnaeus, "Anthropomorpha," pp. 72–76. Linnaeus also sometimes considered *Homo caudatus* a third species of humans. On Linnaeus's *Homo troglodytes*, see Broberg's excellent "*Homo sapiens*: Linnaeus's Classification of Man," in *Linnaeus: The Man and His Work*, ed. Tore Frängsmyr (Berkeley and Los Angeles: University of California Press, 1983), pp. 185–186.

18. See Lovejoy, "Monboddo and Rousseau"; and Robert Wolker, "Perfectible Apes in Decadent Cultures: Rousseau's Anthropology Revisited," *Daedalus* 107 (1978): 107–134. Darwin demonstrated our common ancestry with the apes, though today the great apes are considered members of a side branch in human evolution, not our immediate ancestors (Gould, "Chimp on the Chain," p. 20). The notion remains that humans are special. In 1958, Julian Huxley suggested that our great intellect warrants placing humans in a separate kingdom: the Psychozoan (Lewin, *Human Evolution*, pp. 4, 27–28). While early modern naturalists considered the generic orangutan the most humanlike of the anthropoid apes, the true orangutan is in fact the ape most distantly related to humans. The chimpanzee is our nearest relative.

19. See Keith Thomas, *Man and the Natural World: A History of the Modern Sensibility* (New York: Pantheon Books, 1983), pp. 30–36. There were many other points of comparison between humans and animals. Erasmus Darwin argued, for example, that, like humans, animals also make contracts (*Zoonomia; or, The Laws of Organic Life* [London, 1794], vol. 1, p. 171).

20. Janson, *Apes and Ape Lore*, pp. 73–106.

21. Ibid., p. 89.

22. Tyson, *Orang-Outang, sive Homo Sylvestris*, p. 55.

23. John Locke, *An Essay Concerning Human Understanding* (1706; New York: Dutton, 1961), vol. 1, pp. 124–127 (II, xi, 5–12). See also Thomas, *Man and the Natural World*, p. 125.

24. David Hume, *Essays Moral, Political, etc.*, ed. T. H. Green (London, 1882), vol. 2, pp. 85–88.

25. Rousseau and Monboddo held that the generic orangutan had the same mental faculties as humans but had failed to perfect them. See Lovejoy, "Monboddo and Rousseau," p. 278.

26. Tyson, *Orang-Outang, sive Homo Sylvestris*, p. 55; Buffon, *Histoire naturelle*, vol. 14, p. 32.

27. Blumenbach, *On the Natural Varieties of Mankind*, pp. 182–183. For Linnaeus, see especially *Fauna Svecica*, preface.

28. Margaret Cavendish, Duchess of Newcastle, *Philosophical Letters* (London, 1664), pp. 40–41, 43. On Cavendish, see Douglas Grant, *Margaret the First: A Biography of Margaret Cavendish, Duchess of Newcastle, 1623–1673* (London: Hart-Davis, 1957); Henry Ten Eyck Perry, *The First Duchess of Newcastle and her Husband as Figures in Literary History* (Boston: Ginn and Company, 1918); R. W. Goulding, *Margaret (Lucas) Duchess of Newcastle* (London: Lincolnshire Chronicle, 1925); Virginia Woolf, "The Duchess of Newcastle," in *The Common Reader* (London: Hogarth Press, 1929), pp. 98–109; Lisa Sarasohn, "A Science Turned Upside Down: Feminism and the Natural Philosophy of Margaret Cavendish," *The Hunting Library Quarterly* 47 (1984): 289–307; and Londa Schiebinger, *The Mind Has No Sex? Women in the Origins of Modern Science* (Cambridge, Mass.: Harvard University Press, 1989), pp. 47–59. On Montaigne, see Georg Boas, *The Happy Beast in French Thought of the Seventeenth Century* (Baltimore: Johns Hopkins University Press, 1933), pp. 3–17.

29. Denis Diderot, *Oeuvres complètes de Diderot*, ed. J. Assézat (Paris, 1875), vol. 2, p. 190. See also Wolker, "Tyson and Buffon on the Orang-utan," p. 2308.

30. Broberg, "*Homo sapiens*," p. 161.

31. Claude Perrault, *Mémoires pour servir à l'histoire naturelle des animaux* (Paris, 1676). Petrus Camper dissected the larynx of an orangutan in 1799 and concluded (incorrectly) that these animals were physically incapable of speech ("Account of the Organs of Speech of the Orang Outang," *Philosophical Transactions of the Royal Society of London* 69, pt. 1 [1779]: 139–159). See also Camper, "De l'orang-outang et de quelques autres espèces de singes"; Visser, *Zoological Work of Petrus Camper*, pp. 33–39; and Wolker, "Tyson and Buffon on the Orang-utan," pp. 2308–2309.

32. Linnaeus, *Systema naturae*, 10th ed., p. 24; also his "Anthropomorpha," p. 74.

33. Jacob Bontius, *Historiae naturalis & medicae Indiae Orientalis libri sex* (Amsterdam, 1658), p. 85; also Buffon, *Histoire naturelle*, vol. 14, p. 59.

34. Rousseau, "Discours sur l'origine," p. 162.

35. Buffon, *Histoire naturelle*, vol. 14, pp. 36, 46.

36. Blumenbach, *On the Natural Varieties of Mankind*, p. 83. Bontius and Tyson also emphasized the humanlike emotions expressed by apes. Tyson's pygmie cried "like a child" (*Orang-Outang, sive Homo Sylvestris*, p. 25).

37. Plato, *Timaeus*, 90a.

38. Rousseau, "Discours sur l'origine," p. 197. He might have noted that apes' breasts are similarly placed, but he did not.

39. Tyson, *Orang-Outang, sive Homo Sylvestris*, p. 13. Early modern naturalists were still greatly influenced by the ancients who portrayed apelike creatures (mostly imaginary) walking erect with staffs ([Jonathan Swift], *Miscellanies in Prose and Verse* [London, 1732], vol. 3, p. 101). In anatomical illustrations of this period, ape and monkey were commonly drawn standing erect. Richard Bradley, for example, in comparing the skeleton of a monkey to a human drew the monkey in an unnaturally erect posture, thus heightening its human appearance (*A Philosophical Account of the Works of Nature* [London, 1721], plate XIX). In the English translation of Georges Cuvier's *Le règne animal*, the skeleton of the chimpanzee is also drawn perfectly erect (Baron Cuvier, *The Animal Kingdom* [London, 1827], vol. 1, following p. 252).

40. J.-B. Audebert, *Histoire naturelle des singes et des makis* (Paris, 1800), p. 16. He is referring to the illustration in Buffon, *Histoire naturelle*, supplement, vol. 7, p. 2.

41. Blumenbach, *On the Natural Varieties of Mankind*, pp. 171–172. Despite his desire to see apes as bipedal, Tyson had suggested early on that they be called *Quadru-manus* because their hind feet resembled hands (*Orang-Outang, sive Homo Sylvestris*, p. 13).

42. Duarte Lopez (1578), cited in O'Malley and Magoun, "Early Concepts of the Anthropomorpha," p. 39.

43. Buffon, *Histoire naturelle*, vol. 14, pp. 53–54.

44. La Brosse cited in Buffon, *Histoire naturelle*, vol. 14, p. 55; Tulp, *Observationum medicarum libri tres*, pp. 274–279; "A Narrative . . . sent by John Maatzuyker de Baden," in Jan Nieuhof, *An Embassy from the East-India Company of the United Provinces to the Grand Tartar Cham Emperour of China*, trans. J. Ogilby (London, 1669), p. 91.

45. Lawrence Stone, *The Family, Sex and Marriage in England, 1500–1800* (New York: Harper & Row, 1977), p. 221. See also Susan Okin, "Women and the Making of the Sentimental Family," *Philosophy & Public Affairs* 11 (1982): 65–88.

46. James Burnet, Lord Monboddo, *Of the Origin and Progress of Language* (Edinburgh, 1773–1792), vol. 1, pp. 287–288.

47. Linnaeus, "Anthropomorpha," p. 76. Rousseau, "Discours sur l'origine," p. 211. Priscilla Wakefield, *Instinct Displayed* (1816; London, 1821), pp. 225, 233. Rousseau also reported that apes buried their dead. He drew his remarks

from Andrew Battell's report published in the seventeenth century (Samuel Purchas, *Hakluytus posthumus; or, Purchas his Pilgrimes* [London, 1625], vol. 2, pp. 981–982). Monboddo, *Of the Origin and Progress of Language*, vol. 1, p. 290.

48. Jean-Jacques Rousseau, *Emile, ou De l'éducation* (1762), in *Oeuvres complètes*, ed. Bernard Gagnebin and Marcel Raymond (Paris: Gallimard, 1959–1969), vol. 4, pp. 693–697. See also Margaret Miles, *Carnal Knowing: Female Nakedness and Religious Meaning in the West* (Boston: Beacon Press, 1989), pp. 155–159.

49. Blumenbach, *On the Natural Varieties of Mankind*, p. 182; and Buffon, *Histoire naturelle*, vol. 14, p. 60. Foucher d'Obsonville was, to my knowledge, the only naturalist to suggest that one might investigate the peculiarities of the human penis for purposes of classification. Nonetheless he concluded that "the lesser or greater extension of the membranes or teguments of such parts appears to be indifferent to the classification of the species" (*Essais philosophiques sur les moeurs de divers animaux étrangers* [Paris, 1783], p. 369).

50. Camper, "De l'orang-outang," pp. 108–112; also Petrus Camper, *The Works of the Late Professor Camper on the Connexion between the Science of Anatomy and the Arts of Drawing, Painting, Statuary, etc.*, trans. T. Cogan (London, 1794), p. 32.

51. Aristotle, *Historia animalium*, 502b; Perrault, *Mémoires pour servir à l'histoire naturelle des animaux*; see also Tyson, *Orang-Outang, sive Homo Sylvestris*, pp. 14, 44. Late in the eighteenth century, Camper continued to teach that ape's organs of generation were similar to canine's (*Works*, p. 32).

52. *Encyclopédie, ou Dictionnaire raisonné des sciences, des arts et des métiers*, (Paris, 1751–1765), s.v. "Hymen."

53. Aristotle, *Generation of Animals*, trans. A. L. Peck (Cambridge, Mass.: Harvard University Press, 1953), 728b.

54. Pliny the Elder, *Natural History*, trans. H. Rackham (Cambridge, Mass.: Harvard University Press, 1942), VII, xv, pp. 63–66.

55. Albertus Magnus, for example, stated incorrectly that only women had menstrual cycles. In Hildegard's *Physica*, cited in Janson, *Apes and Ape Lore*, pp. 77–78.

56. Blumenbach, *On the Natural Varieties of Mankind*, p. 182.

57. Buffon, *Histoire naturelle*, vol. 14, p. 136.

58. Ibid., pp. 182, 272–273. Henri Grégoire, *De la littérature des nègres, ou Recherches sur leurs facultés intellectuelles, leurs qualités morales et leur littérature* (Paris, 1808), pp. 33–34. Female Greenlanders were also reported to be devoid of menstrual flux (Buffon, *Histoire naturelle*, vol. 3, p. 373).

59. Charles White, *An Account of the Regular Gradation in Man and in Different Animals and Vegetables* (London, 1796), pp. 58–59. Thomas Winterbottom pointed out that White may have had this impression from the menorrhagia common among African slaves caused by poor diet and wretched conditions (*An Account of the Native Africans in the Neighbourhood of Sierra Leone* (1803; London: Frank Cass, 1969), vol. 2, p. 272).

60. Linnaeus, *Systema naturae*, 10th ed., p. 25. For the history of the discovery of the clitoris in humans, see Thomas Laqueur, *Making Sex: Body and Gender from the Greeks to Freud* (Cambridge, Mass.: Harvard University Press, 1990), pp. 66–68.

61. Tyson, reporting Perrault's findings, *Orang-Outang, sive Homo Sylvestris*, p. 46.

62. Blumenbach, *On the Natural Varieties of Mankind*, p. 171.

63. Aristotle, *Historia animalium*, 502a.

64. Linnaeus, *Systema naturae*, 10th ed., p. 20.

65. Tyson, *Orang-Outang, sive Homo Sylvestris*, p. 11.

66. Alvin Rodin and Jack Key, *Medicine, Literature and Eponyms* (Malabar, Florida: R. E. Krieger Publishing Co., 1989), s.v. "hymen."

67. Ephraim Chambers, *Cyclopaedia; or, An Universal Dictionary of Arts and Sciences* (London, 1741), s. v. "hymen."

68. Midwives had traditionally acted as judge and jury in questions of women's morality; the statutes of the Parisian midwives laid down fourteen criteria for judging whether or not a woman was still a virgin. As midwifery was increasingly taken over by male physicians, however, the reality of the hymen was called into question (Esther Fischer-Homberger, *Krankheit Frau und andere Arbeiten zur Medizingeschichte der Frau* [Bern: Hans Huber Verlag, 1979], pp. 85–105).

69. Buffon, *Histoire naturelle*, vol. 2, pp. 493–496.

70. Blumenbach, *On the Natural Varieties of Mankind*, pp. 89–90, 170. The origin of the hymen is still a matter of debate among biologists (see Bettyann Kevles's review of Lynn Margulis and Dorion Sagan's *Mystery Dance: On the Evolution of Human Sexuality* in the *New York Times Book Review*, 25 August 1991, p. 11).

71. Jacques Moreau de la Sarthe, *Histoire naturelle de la femme* (Paris, 1803), vol. 1, p. 53.

72. Georges Cuvier, *Leçons d'anatomie comparée* (Paris, 1800–1805), vol. 5, p. 131–132.

73. Moreau de la Sarthe, *Histoire naturelle de la femme*, vol. 1, p. 48.

74. Blumenbach, *On the Natural Varieties of Mankind*, pp. 169–170.

75. Janson, *Apes and Ape Lore*, p. 81.

76. "Abstract of a Letter from Stephen de Visme, Esp. at Canton, in China, to Henry Baker. . . ." *Philosophical Transactions of the Royal Society of London* 59 (1769): 71–73.

77. Foucher d'Obsonville, *Essais philosophiques*, p. 371.

78. Cited in William Cohen, *The French Encounter with Africans: White Responses to Blacks, 1530–1800* (Bloomington: Indiana University Press, 1980), p. 242. As Cohen pointed out, this was a rumor started by the English.

79. According to Dapper, the native Africans he encountered found silly the notion that "orangs" were the progeny of a union of woman and ape. Cited in Antoine Prévost, *Histoire générale des voyages* (The Hague, 1747), vol. 6, p. 411.

80. Edward Topsell, *The History of Four-Footed Beasts Taken Principally from the Historiae Animalium of Conrad Gesner* (1658; New York: Da Capo Press, 1967), pp. 3, 8; Tulp, *Observationum medicarum*, pp. 274–279; and Buffon, *Histoire naturelle*, vol. 14, p. 135. Janson has traced this notion of the ape embodying male sexual rapacity to the sixteenth century (*Apes and Ape Lore*, p. 208).

81. Tyson, *Orang-Outang, sive Homo Sylvestris*, p. 42.

82. Buffon, *Histoire naturelle*, vol. 14, pp. 50–51.

83. Bontius, *Historiae naturalis*, p. 85.

84. Blumenbach, *On the Natural Varieties of Mankind*, p. 201; Blumenbach has this from Plutarch.

85. La Brosse, cited in Buffon, *Histoire naturelle*, vol. 14, p. 51.

86. Henri de Blainville noted that he was disinclined to believe this of Sarah Bartmann, but he nonetheless reported the incident in his "Sur une femme de la race hottentote," *Bulletin des sciences, par la Société Philomatique de Paris* (1816): 189.

87. Tyson, *Orang-Outang, sive Homo Sylvestris*, p. 2; Blumenbach, *On the Natural Varieties of Mankind*, p. 81; Buffon, *Histoire naturelle*, vol. 14, p. 31; and Lionel Wafer, *A New Voyage and Description of the Isthmus of America* (1699; Cleveland: Burrows Brothers Co., 1903), p. 113.

88. Rousseau, "Discours sur l'origine," p. 211.

89. Ruth Yeazell, *Fictions of Modesty: Women and Courtship in the English Novel* (Chicago: University of Chicago Press, 1991).

90. Bontius, *Historiae naturalis*, p. 84; and Tyson, *Orang-Outang, sive Homo Sylvestris*, p. 19, figure 16. A. Vosmaer also found that Bontius exaggerated the "marvels" of this animal (*Description d'un recueil exquis d'animaux rares* [Amsterdam, 1804], p. 4).

91. The modesty Europeans observed in these animals he judged to result from the fact that they were captives. "Is it astonishing," he asked, "that such habits have been observed in a state of servitude?" Foucher d'Obsonville was one of the very few to assert that modesty is a product of nurture, not nature (*Essais philosophiques*, pp. 373, 375).

92. Relian cited in Buffon, *Histoire naturelle*, supplément, vol. 7, p. 9.

93. Monboddo, *Of the Origin and Progress of Language*, vol. 1, pp. 291–292.

94. *London Magazine* (21 September 1738): 464–465.

95. [Thomas Boreman], *A Description of Some Curious and Uncommon Creatures* (London, 1739), p. 24.

96. Linnaeus, "Anthropomorpha," description of figure 1.

97. White, *Account of the Regular Gradation*, p. 134. On Tulp, see also William S. Heckscher, *Rembrandt's Anatomy of Dr. Nicolaas Tulp: An Iconological Study* (New York: New York University Press, 1958). An even more feminized copy of Tulp's orangutan appeared in Prévost, *Histoire générale des voyages*, vol. 6, facing p. 411.

98. William Smellie, *The Philosophy of Natural History* (Edinburgh, 1790), p. 238.

99. Desfontaines, cited in François Delaporte, *Nature's Second Kingdom: Explo-*

rations of Vegetality in the Eighteenth Century, trans. Arthur Goldhammer (Cambridge, Mass.: MIT Press, 1982), p. 129.

100. Wakefield, *Instinct Displayed*, pp. 238–239. I thank Ann Shteir for calling this passage to my attention. See also John Stedman, *Narrative of a Five Years Expedition against the Revolted Negroes of Surinam* (1796; Baltimore: John Hopkins University Press, 1988), p. 142.

101. Linnaeus, *Systema naturae*, 10th ed., p. 21. In the nineteenth century, there were those who believed women to be driven by animal desires and instincts to such an extent that they coupled freely with apes and monkeys. Havelock Ellis reported a woman living in the Amazon basin with a coati monkey husband. The German anthropologist Carl Vogt taught that women more nearly approach the animal type in all things (Bram Dijkstra, *Idols of Perversity: Fantasies of Feminine Evil in Fin-de-Siècle Culture* [Oxford: Oxford University Press, 1986], p. 290).

102. Eliza Haywood, *The Female Spectator* (London, 1745), vol. 1, p. 298; also Charles-Louis de Secondat, baron de la Brède et de Montesquieu, *The Spirit of the Laws*, trans. Thomas Nugent (1750; New York: Hafner Press, 1949), pp. 258–259.

103. David Hume, *A Treatise on Human Nature*, ed. L. A. Selby-Bigge (Oxford, 1888), book III, part 2, sect. 12. See also Jean-Jacques Rousseau, *Lettre à M. d'Alembert sur les spectacles*, ed. M. Fuchs (Geneva: Droz, 1948), pp. 114, 117.

104. Sarah Trimmer did not go to see the pig because she believed that great cruelty must have been used in teaching it things so foreign to its nature. No animal, she declared, is capable of mastering the human sciences (*Fabulous Histories; or, The History of the Robins* [1788; London, 1821], pp. 50–52).

105. Thomas Taylor, *A Vindication of the Rights of Brutes* (London, 1792), especially 13, 19.

106. "Essay of the Learned Martinus Scriblerus, Concerning the Origin of Sciences," in [Swift], *Miscellanies in Prose and Verse*, vol. 3, pp. 98–116. See also M. F. Ashley Montagu, "Tyson's Orang-Outang, Sive Homo Sylvestris and Swift's Gulliver's Travels," *Publications of the Modern Language Association of America* 59 (1944): 84–89.

107. Nicolas-Edme Restif de la Bretonne, "Lettre d'un singe, aux animaux de son espèce," in *La découverte australe* (Leipzig, 1781), vol. 3, pp. 1–138.

108. E. T. A. Hoffmann, "Nachricht von einem gebildeten jungen Mann," in *Sämtliche Werke*, ed. Carl von Maassen (Munich: Müller, 1912), vol. 1, pp. 396–406.

109. Wilhelm Hauff, "Der Affe als Mensch" (1827), in *Sämtliche Werke* (Munich: Winkler-Verlag, 1970), vol. 2, pp. 153–170.

110. Thomas Love Peacock, *Melincourt* (Philadelphia, 1817), especially vol. 1, pp. 57, 182.

111. This essay served as a companion piece to *An Essay Towards the Character of Her Late Majesty Caroline, Queen Consort of Great Britain* (London, 1738). See G. S. Rousseau, "Madame Chimpanzee," in *Enlightenment Crossings* (Manchester: University of Manchester Press, 1991), pp. 198–209.

Eliza Haywood provided much natural history (and also astronomy) in her *Female Spectator* but her interests were limited to small creatures—bees, butterflies, caterpillars, flies, even worms. Though Haywood's volumes were published only seven years after Madame Chimpanzee was shown in London, there was no mention of her. One might have thought that Madame Chimpanzee would have attracted a woman biographer, as was the case with the wild girl of Champagne. See Madame Hecquet, *Histoire d'une jeune fille sauvage* (Paris, 1755); this work is sometimes attributed to Charles de La Condamine.

112. Julia Douthwaite, "The History and Fictions of the Wild Girl of Champagne," paper presented to the American Society for Eighteenth-Century Studies, April 1991.

113. Peacock, *Melincourt*, vol. 1, pp. 9, 44.

114. Hester Hastings, *Man and Beast in French Thought of the Eighteenth Century* (Baltimore: Johns Hopkins University Press, 1936), p. 10.

115. Donna Haraway, *Primate Visions: Gender, Race, and Nature in the World of Modern Science* (New York: Routledge, 1989), especially pp. 304–315. See also *Science* 260 (16 April 1993): 420–429.

4. The Anatomy of Difference

1. Suicide, self mutilation, insanity, and abortions were common among black slaves; at least one of the blacks whom Soemmerring dissected had committed suicide. Wolfram Schäfer, "Von 'Kammermohren,' 'Mohren'-Tambouren und 'Ost-Indianern,'" *Hessische Blätter für Volks- und Kulturforschung* 23 (1988): 35–79, especially n. 132. See also Urs Bitterli, *Die Entdeckung des schwarzen Afrikaners* (Zurich: Atlantis, 1970). There is currently much controversy about whether a significant number of Africans inhabited Frederick's Chinese village (see, for example, Schäfer, "Von 'Kammermohren,'" and Sigrid Oehler-Klein, "Samuel Thomas Soemmerrings Neuroanatomie als Bindeglied zwischen Physiognomik und Anthropologie," in *Die Natur des Menschen: Probleme der Physischen Anthropologie und Rassenkunde, 1750–1850*, ed. Gunter Mann, Jost Benedum, and Werner Kümmel [Stuttgart: Gustav Fischer Verlag, 1990], p. 58 n. 8). While eighteenth-century sources speak of a Chinese colony populated with Africans, recent historians, using the Chatoul Rechnungen held at the Staats-Archiv in Marburg, have been able to document only a few Africans living there. This controversy, however, seems unresolvable; my queries at archives in Kassel revealed that documents from this colony were destroyed in World War II.

2. Käthe Heinemann, "Aus der Blütezeit der Medizin am Collegium illustre Carolinum zu Kassel," *Zeitschrift des Vereins für hessische Geschichte und Landeskunde* 71 (1960): 85–96, especially 90. See also Klaus Mross, "Ernst Gottfried Baldinger (1738–1804), gelehrter Arzt der Aufklärungszeit, und sein Schüler Samuel Thomas Soemmerring," in *Samuel Thomas Soemmer-*

ring und die Gelehrten der Goethezeit, ed. Gunter Mann and Franz Dumont (Stuttgart: Gustav Fischer Verlag, 1985), p. 258.

3. This book was expanded and republished one year later as *Über die körperliche Verschiedenheit des Negers vom Europäer* (Frankfurt, 1785). Soemmerring changed the title of his book from "Mohren" to "Neger" without explanation. He continued to revise the book until about 1817 but never published a new edition (see his manuscript in the Senckenbergische Bibliothek, Frankfurt, Lfd. Nr. 2). The book was never translated.

4. Paul Edwards and James Walvin, *Black Personalities in the Era of the Slave Trade* (Baton Rouge: Louisiana State University Press, 1983), pp. 18–19; Folarin Shyllon, *Black People in Britain, 1555–1833* (Oxford: Oxford University Press, 1977), p. 4. See also Shelby McCloy, *The Negro in France* (Lexington: University of Kentucky Press, 1961); James Walvin, *Black and White: The Negro and English Society, 1555–1945* (London: Penguin Press, 1973); Hans Debrunner, *Presence and Prestige: Africans in Europe* (Basil: Basler Afrika Bibliographen, 1979); David Dabydeen, *Hogarth's Blacks: Images of Blacks in Eighteenth-Century English Art* (Athens, Ga.: University of Georgia Press, 1987); and G. S. Rousseau and Roy Porter, eds., *Exoticism in the Enlightenment* (Manchester: Manchester University Press, 1990).

5. In addition to the works cited separately, see also Henry Home, Lord Kames, *Sketches of the History of Man* (Edinburgh, 1774); Johann Caspar Lavater, *Physiognomische Fragmente, zur Beförderung der Menschenkenntniß und Menschenliebe* (Leipzig, 1775–1778); Christoph Meiners, *Grundriß der Geschichte der Menschheit* (1785; Lemgo, 1793) and *Geschichte des weiblichen Geschlechts* (Hanover, 1788–1800); Immanuel Kant, *Anthropologie in pragmatischer Hinsicht* (1798; Frankfurt and Leipzig, 1799); Jacques Moreau de la Sarthe, *Histoire naturelle de la femme* (Paris, 1803); Wilhelm von Humboldt "Über den Geschlechtsunterschied und dessen Einfluss auf die organische Natur," in *Werke*, ed. Andreas Flitner and Klaus Giel (Stuttgart: J. G. Cotta, 1960), vol. 1, pp. 268–295 and "Plan einer vergleichenden Anthropologie," Ibid., pp. 337–375; Julien-Joseph Virey, *De la femme* (Paris, 1823) and *Histoire naturelle du genre humain* (Paris, 1880).

6. For studies of race see, for example, Maragaret Hodgen, *Early Anthropology in the Sixteenth and Seventeenth Centuries* (Philadelphia: University of Pennsylvania Press, 1964); Philip D. Curtin, *The Image of Africa: British Ideas and Actions, 1780–1850* (Madison: University of Wisconsin Press, 1964); David Brion Davis, *The Problem of Slavery in Western Culture* (Oxford: Oxford University Press, 1966); George Stocking, Jr., *Race, Culture, and Evolution: Essays in the History of Anthropology* (New York: Free Press, 1968); also his *Bones, Bodies, Behavior: Essays on Biological Anthropology* (Madison: University of Wisconsin Press, 1988); Winthrop D. Jordan, *White over Black: American Attitudes toward the Negro, 1550–1812* (Chapel Hill: University of North Carolina Press, 1968); and Nancy Leys Stepan, *The Idea of Race in Science: Great Britain, 1800–1960* (Hamden, Conn.: Archon Books, 1982). For studies of sexual differences, see Elizabeth Fee, "Nineteenth-Century Craniology: The Study of the Female Skull," *Bulletin of the History of Medicine* 53 (1979): 415–

433; Esther Fischer-Homberger, *Krankheit Frau und andere Arbeiten sur Medizingeschichte der Frau* (Bern: Hans Huber Verlag, 1979); Londa Schiebinger, *The Mind Has No Sex? Women in the Origins of Modern Science* (Cambridge, Mass.: Harvard University Press, 1989); Ludmilla Jordanova, *Sexual Visions: Images of Gender in Science and Medicine between the Eighteenth and Twentieth Centuries* (Madison: University of Wisconsin Press, 1989); Thomas Laqueur, *Making Sex: Body and Gender from the Greeks to Freud* (Cambridge, Mass.: Harvard University Press, 1990). For studies of sex and race, see, for example, Nancy Leys Stepan, "Race and Gender: The Role of Analogy in Science," *Isis* 77 (June 1986): 261–277; Elizabeth Spelman, *Inessential Woman: Problems of Exclusion in Feminist Thought* (Boston: Beacon Press, 1988); Bell Hooks, *Black Looks: Race and Representation* (Boston: South End Press, 1992); Henry Louis Gates, Jr., ed., *"Race," Writing, and Difference* (Chicago: University of Chicago Press, 1986); Kathy Peiss and Christina Simmons, eds., *Passions and Power: Sexuality in History* (Philadelphia: Temple University Press, 1989); David Goldberg, ed., *Anatomy of Racism* (Minneapolis: University of Minnesota Press, 1990); Dominick La Capra, ed., *The Bounds of Race: Perspectives on Hegemony and Resistance* (Ithaca: Cornell University Press, 1991); and Evelyn Brooks Higginbotham, "African-American Women's History and the Metalanguage of Race," *Signs: Journal of Women in Culture and Society* 17 (1992): 251–274.

7. Michel Foucault, *Discipline and Punish: The Birth of the Prison*, trans. Alan Sheridan (New York: Pantheon, 1977), p. 193.

8. These collections of skeletons and skulls, pickled genitalia and fetuses served professional interests and also attracted the curious. Royalty and local nobility (including queens and ladies) came to visit. See the catalogue of Johann Blumenbach's collection, *On the Natural Varieties of Mankind*, trans. Thomas Bendyshe (1865; New York: Bergman, 1969), pp. 155–161. The late eighteenth century also saw the rise of physical anthropology, though the sharp distinction between ethnology (with its greater attention to language and culture) and physical anthropology (with its more single-minded perusal of physical characteristics) was not as marked in the eighteenth century as it would be later.

9. Samuel Thomas von Soemmerring, *Vom Baue des menschlichen Körpers* (Frankfurt, 1791–1796).

10. Though sex made up one of his categories of analysis, Blumenbach treated it only briefly and did not attach to it the significance that others did at this time. Johann Blumenbach, *Geschichte und Beschreibung der Knochen des menschlichen Körpers* (Göttingen, 1786), pp. 81–83. Blumenbach chose not to focus on sexual difference in an environment where the question was hotly debated. Ernst Brandes, his brother-in-law and administrator at the University in Göttingen where Blumenbach taught, wrote *Über die Weiber* (Leipzig, 1787), an extremely misogynist book. Christoph Meiners, another of Blumenbach's colleagues, also wrote a four-volume history unfriendly to women (*Geschichte des weiblichen Geschlechts*). At the same time, Blumenbach's colleague, August Schlözer, championed the intellectual development of his daughter, Dorothea, who became the first woman Ph.D. in Germany in 1787.

11. Jakob Ackermann, *Über die körperliche Verschiedenheit des Mannes vom Weiber ausser Geschlechtstheilen*, trans. Joseph Wenzel (Koblenz, 1788), p. 5. Johann Döllinger, "Versuch einer Geschichte der menschlichen Zeugung," in Arthur Meyer, *Human Generation: Conclusions of Burdach, Döllinger and von Baer* (Stanford: Stanford University Press, 1956), p. 42.

12. Blumenbach, *On the Natural Varieties of Mankind*, p. 108. In this period, dissections were commonly done on orphans, prostitutes with three or more convictions, and criminals (*Erneurte Medicinalordnung vom 21. December 1767*, pp. 477–478). Buffon similarly suggested that class influenced skin color: "Arabian princesses and ladies are extremely handsome, beautiful, and fair because they are always protected from the sun, but common women are blackened by it" (*Histoire naturelle, générale et particulière* [Paris, 1749–1804], vol. 3, p. 426).

13. Blumenbach, *On the Natural Varieties of Mankind*, p. 306.

14. Richard Lewontin, *Human Diversity* (New York: Scientific American Books, 1982), pp. 11–134. Anthony Appiah, "The Uncompleted Argument: DuBois and the Illusion of Race," *"Race," Writing, and Difference*, ed. Gates, p. 21.

15. [François Bernier], "Nouvelle division de la terre, par les differentes espèces ou races d'hommes qui l'habitent . . . " *Journal des savants* 12 (1684): 148–155.

16. Carl Linnaeus, *Systema naturae per regna tria naturae*, 10th ed. (Stockholm, 1758), pp. 21–23. See also Jan Pieterse, *White on Black: Images of Africa and Blacks in Western Popular Culture* (New Haven: Yale University Press, 1992), p. 18.

17. George Stocking, Jr., *Victorian Anthropology* (New York: Free Press, 1987), p. 26.

18. Petrus Camper, *The Works of the Late Professor Camper on the Connexion between the Science of Anatomy and the Arts of Drawing, Painting, Statuary, etc.*, trans. T. Cogan (London, 1794), p. 21. The conservative Christoph Meiners stressed that "no nation is so similar in all its members that it can be represented by one skull." Cited in Johann Blumenbach, *Beyträge zur Naturgeschichte* (Göttingen, 1790), p. 74.

19. Wilfrid Blunt, *The Compleat Naturalist: A Life of Linnaeus* (London: William Collins Sons & Co., 1971), p. 157.

20. Charles White, *An Account of the Regular Gradation in Man and Different Animals and Vegetables* (London, 1796), p. 134.

21. [Theodor von Hippel], *Über die bürgerliche Selbstständigkeit der Weiber*, in *Sämmtliche Werke* (Berlin, 1828), vol. 6, p. 35. Even today, an Islamic judge is required to wear a beard (*Guardian*, 9 August 1991).

22. Pliny the Elder, *Natural History*, trans. H. Rackham (Cambridge, Mass.: Harvard University Press, 1942), VII, lix, p. 649.

23. Philippus Camerarius, *The Walking Librarie; or, Meditations and Observations Historical, Natural, Moral, Political, and Poetical*, trans. John Molle (London, 1621), pp. 121–127. Augustin Frangé, *Mémoires pour servir à l'histoire de la barbe de l'homme* (Liège, 1774). William Lawrence also commented on the beard as a mark of masculinity (*Lectures on Physiology, Zo-*

ology, and the Natural History of Man [London, 1819], p. 317). See also Charles Darwin, The Descent of Man and Selection in Relation to Sex (1871; London: John Murray, 1913), p. 885.

24. Charles de Rochefort, Histoire naturelle et morale des îles Antilles de l'Amérique, 2d ed. (Rotterdam, 1665), p. 440.

25. Giles Constable, "Introduction on Beards in the Middle Ages," Burchardi, ut Videtur, Abbatis Bellevallis, Apologia de barbis, ed. R. B. C. Huygens, Corpus Christianorum 62 (1985): 47–130.

26. James Burnet, Lord Monboddo, Of the Origin and Progress of Language (Edinburgh, 1773–1792), vol. 1, p. 276.

27. Bernier, "Nouvelle division de la terre." See also Georges Gusdorf, Dieu, la nature, l'homme au siècle des lumières (Paris: Payot, 1972), p. 362.

28. Richard Bradley, A Philosophical Account of the Works of Nature (London, 1721), p. 169.

29. Richard McCausland, "Particulars Relative to the Nature and Customs of the Indians of North-America," Philosophical Transactions of the Royal Society of London 76 (1786): 229–235.

30. Charles-Louis de Secondat, Baron de Montesquieu, The Spirit of the Laws, trans. Thomas Nugent (1750; New York: Hafner Press, 1949), pp. 237–238.

31. Rochefort, Histoire naturelle et morale, p. 440.

32. Butler and Thayendanega cited in McCausland, "Nature and Customs of the Indians of North-America," pp. 231–232.

33. Blumenbach, On the Natural Varieties of Mankind, pp. 271–272. See also Cod. Ms. Blumenbach. IX. c., Niedersächsische Staats- und Universitätsbibliothek, Göttingen. For European attitudes toward native Americans, see Lee Huddleston, Origins of the American Indians: European Concepts, 1492–1729 (Austin: University of Texas Press, 1967); Lewis Hanke, Aristotle and the American Indians: A Study in Race Prejudice in the Modern World (London: Hollis and Carter, 1959); Hugh Honour, The New Golden Land: European Images of America from the Discoveries to the Present Time (New York: Pantheon Books, 1975); and Fredi Chiappelli, ed., First Images of America: The Impact of the New World on the Old (Berkeley and Los Angeles: University of California Press, 1976).

34. Ackermann, Über die körperliche Verschiedenheit, p. 18n. In the eighteenth century, this link was made without explanation. For medical theories linking beards and menstruation, see Joan Cadden, The Meanings of Sexual Difference in the Middle Ages: Medicine, Natural Philosophy, and Culture (Cambridge: Cambridge University Press, 1992).

35. Helkiah Crooke, Mikrokosmographia, A Description of the Body of Man (London, 1615), p. 71. Immanuel Kant, Beobachtungen über das Gefühl des Schönen und Erhabenen, in Kants Werke, ed. Wilhelm Dilthey (Berlin, 1900–1919), vol. 2, pp. 229–230. The beard was a common symbol of virility; see Gabriel Jouard, Nouvel essai sur la femme considérée comparativement à l'homme (Paris, 1804), p. 8. Critics of Olympe de Gouges's L'esclavage des noirs also used the symbolic value of the beard in their attack: "She forgets the weakness of her sex; in order to produce a great dramatic work it is necessary

to bear a beard on the chin" (cited in Olivier Blanc, *Olympe de Gouges* [Paris: Syros, 1981], p. 75). On the subsequent history of anthropologists' assessment of beardless women, see Cynthia Russett, *Sexual Science: The Victorian Construction of Womanhood* (Cambridge, Mass.: Harvard University Press, 1989), pp. 74–75.

36. Blumenbach, *On the Natural Varieties of Mankind*, pp. 173–174.

37. Bernier, "Nouvelle division de la terre." Buffon also devoted much attention to beauty. See also Jean Lavater, *Essai sur la physiognomonie* (The Hague, 1783), vol. 2, pp. 143–145.

38. Meiners, *Grundriß der Geschichte der Menschheit*, pp. 89–90. Meiners used other characteristics to distinguish peoples, such as size, strength, fat, color, hair, and beard, but he was best known at this time for his remarks on beauty.

39. Humboldt, cited in Lawrence, *Lectures*, p. 280. On "the blush of modesty," see Ruth Yeazell, *Fictions of Modesty: Women and Courtship in the English Novel* (Chicago: University of Chicago Press, 1991), pp. 65–80.

40. Buffon, *Histoire naturelle*, vol. 3, p. 461. On Buffon, see Jacques Roger, *Buffon: Un Philosophe au Jardin du Roi* (Paris: Fayard, 1989). William Lawrence and James Prichard also gave relativist arguments in the early nineteenth century.

41. Johann Blumenbach, *Beyträge zur Naturgeschichte* (Göttingen, 1806–1811), p. 73. Friends of Africans described Africans as "sable" or "ebony," thus avoiding the sinister connotations of blackness, a term that conjured up visions of sin, death, mourning, melancholy, and evil in the Christian West.

42. Bernier, "Nouvelle division de la terre."

43. Hugh Honour, *The Image of the Black in Western Art* (Cambridge, Mass.: Harvard University Press, 1979), vol. 4, part 1, p. 51. See also Henri Grégoire, *De la littérature des nègres, ou Recherches sur leurs facultés intellectuelles, leurs qualités morales et leur littérature* (Paris, 1808); and Laura Brown, "The Romance of Empire: Oroonoko and the Trade in Slaves," in *The New Eighteenth Century: Theory/Politics/English Literature*, ed. Felicity Nussbaum and Laura Brown (London: Methuen, 1987), pp. 41–61.

44. This is Camper's claim; Hans Kunst claimed they painted from African models (*L'Africain dans l'art européen* [Bad Godesberg: Inter Nationes, 1967], plate 26).

45. Blumenbach, *On the Natural Varieties of Mankind*, pp. 141–142. Grégoire listed Europeans who attested to the beauty of blacks (*De la littérature des nègres*, pp. 29–30). Hans Debrunner interestingly suggests that this woman, Pauline Hippolyte de Buisson, whom Blumenbach found exquisitely beautiful, made Blumenbach a champion of Africans. Debrunner, however, gives no evidence to substantiate his claim (*Presence and Prestige*, p. 143).

46. Le Maire cited in Blumenbach, *On the Natural Varieties of Mankind*, p. 144.

47. Byran Edwards, *The History, Civil and Commercial, of the British Colonies in the West Indies* (1793; Philadelphia, 1806), vol. 2, pp. 227–233. On Edwards, see David Brion Davis, *The Problem of Slavery in the Age of Revolution: 1700–1823* (Ithaca: Cornell University Press, 1975), pp. 185–186.

48. Cited in Honour, *The Image of the Black in Western Art*, vol. 4, pt. 2, p. 10.

49. *Caucasian* first appeared in the 1795 edition of Blumenbach's *De generis humani varietate nativa* (*On the Natural Varieties of Mankind*) and included Finns, Asians west of the Ob River, the Caspian Sea, and the Ganges, along with the people of North Africa—nearly all the inhabitants of the world known to the ancient Greeks and Romans.

50. Blumenbach, *On the Natural Varieties of Mankind*, p. 269. Thomas Huxley charged much later that this Georgian skull was not average but distinctly brachycephalic (*Man's Place in Nature and Other Anthropological Essays* [1896; New York: Greenwood Press, 1968], p. 244).

51. White, *Account of the Regular Gradation*, p. 100; James Prichard, *Researches into the Physical History of Man* (1813; Chicago: University of Chicago Press, 1973), pp. 233–239.

52. Blumenbach, *On the Natural Varieties of Mankind*, p. 269. In his notebook, Blumenbach had copied out Delisle, Chardin, and Winckelmann's opinions (Cod. Ms. Blumenbach V, Bl. 23, Niedersächsische Staats- und Universitätsbibliothek, Göttingen). It was generally agreed that these were the most beautiful and elegant people. See Buffon, *Histoire naturelle*, vol. 3, pp. 433–434; Camper, *Works*, p. 19; and Johann Winckelmann, *Reflections Concerning the Imitation of the Grecian Artists in Painting and Sculpture* (1755; Glasgow, 1766), p. 20.

53. Jean Chardin, *Voyages du Chevalier Chardin en Perse* (1686; Amsterdam, 1735), vol. 1, p. 171. Cod. Ms. Blumenbach, V, 23, Niedersächsische Staats- und Universitätsbibliothek, Göttingen.

54. Buffon, *Histoire naturelle*, vol. 3, p. 528. Also Winckelmann, *Reflections*, p. 4.

55. Martin Bernal, *Black Athena: The Afroasiatic Roots of Classical Civilization* (New Brunswick: Rutgers University Press, 1987), p. 219. Herder placed human origins in the mountains of Asia, though he does not give an exact location (Johann Gottfried Herder, *Outlines of a Philosophy of the History of Man*, trans. T. Churchill [London, 1800], pp. 259–264); William Lawrence located the origins of humankind in Tibet (*Lectures*, p. 256).

56. *Les six voyages de Jean Baptiste Tavernier . . . en Turquie, en Perse, et aux Indes* (Paris, 1679); also Davis, *The Problem of Slavery in Western Culture*, pp. 41–43; and *the Encyclopedia of Islam* (Leiden: E. J. Brill, 1960–1978), vol. 1, pp. 35–37, and vol. 4, pp. 345–346.

57. Bernier, "Nouvelle division de la terre," pp. 154–155. Buffon also reported that the Turks carried off women from Georgia and Circassia to serve as their wives and concubines. Buffon noted that the traffic in women "selected by merchants on account of their beauty" was not confined to white women alone. Fine women "of all complexions" were taken into Persia; the whites coming from Poland, Muscovy, Circassia, and Georgia, the tawny women from Mongolia, and the blacks from Melinda and from around the Red Sea (*Histoire naturelle*, vol. 3, p. 422). See also Bernard Lewis, *Race and Color in Islam* (New York: Harper & Row, 1970), pp. 64–65.

58. M. de Thevenot, *Relations d'un voyage fait au Levant* (Paris, 1665), part 2, p. 38.

59. In one instance, Blumenbach referred to Noah's ark coming to rest in the mountains of Armenia, though the language he used distanced him from the

biblical view (*Decas collectionis suae craniorum diversarum gentium* [Göttingen, 1808], explanation to plate XLI). In this plate he suggested that the Armenians might have been the earliest humans, "assuming that we accept" that the inhabitants of the earth go back to the mountainous regions of Armenia after Noah's flood. In his *On the Natural Varieties of Mankind*, however, where he introduced the term *Caucasian*, Blumenbach did not offer this explanation. Dr. Frank Dougherty, editor of Blumenbach's correspondence, is of the opinion that Blumenbach intended to pay tribute to the biblical tradition but without stating it specifically in order not to appear old-fashioned. I thank Dr. Dougherty for his thoughts on this matter. See also his "Der Begriff der Naturgeschichte nach J. F. Blumenbach anhand seiner Korrespondenz mit Jean-André DeLuc," *Berichte zur Wissenschaftsgeschichte* 9 (1986): 95–107, and his "Christoph Meiners und Johann Friedrich Blumenbach im Streit um den Begriff der Menschenrasse," in *Die Natur des Menschen*, ed. Mann, Benedum, Kümmel, pp. 107–108.

60. Georges Charachidzé, *Prométhée ou le Caucase: Essai de mythologie contrastive* (Paris: Flammarion, 1986).

61. Blumenbach had acquired the skull in a roundabout way from the Russian anatomist Hiltebrandt. According to Blumenbach's account, the Georgian female had been taken captive by the Russians, and brought to Muscovy. There she died suddenly, and Hiltebrandt examined her body. Struck by the extreme elegance of her skull, he carefully preserved it before sending it to Baron von Asch in St. Petersburg, who sent it on to Blumenbach (*On the Natural Varieties of Mankind*, p. 162). See also Frank Dougherty, *Commercium Epistolicum J. F. Blumenbachii: Aus einem Briefwechsel des klassischen Zeitalters der Naturgeschichte (Katalog)* (Göttingen: Hubert & Co., 1984), pp. 148–149.

62. Samuel Thomas von Soemmerring, *Tabula sceleti feminini juncta descriptione* (Utrecht, 1796).

63. Lawrence, *Lectures*, p. 337.

64. Ibid., pp. 454–455; Prichard, *Researches* (1813), pp. 41–43. Also Samuel Stanhope Smith, *An Essay on the Causes of the Variety of Complexion and Figure in the Human Species* (1787; Cambridge, Mass.: Harvard University Press, 1965), p. 109.

65. Darwin, *Descent of Man*, p. 894.

66. Prichard, *Researches* (1813), pp. 41–43.

67. Darwin emphasized that ideals of beauty tended to exaggerate natural traits. Races with scanty beards, for example, enhanced their beauty by plucking them completely, while races with heavy beards gloried in them (*Descent of Man*, pp. 915, 923).

68. Camper attributed this attitude to both the ancients (Herodotus, Hippocrates, Aristotle, Pliny) and the moderns (Vesalius, Haller, and Buffon). Camper, *Works*, pp. 22, 60. The midwife, Jane Sharp, attributed this to mothers, not midwives (*The Midwives Book* [London, 1671], p. 368).

69. Blumenbach, *On the Natural Varieties of Mankind*, p. 232. This was something he continued to investigate. In 1797, when Friedrich Konrad Hornemann was sent into Africa by the Association for Promoting the Discovery of

the Interior Parts of Africa, Blumenbach asked for firsthand observations about whether Africans flattened their children's noses. He also asked in his list of forty-five queries if African women gave birth more easily than other women. See Hans Plischke, *Johann Friedrich Blumenbachs Einfluss auf die Entdeckungsreisenden seiner Zeit* (Göttingen: Vandenhoeck & Ruprecht, 1937), pp. 81–82. Buffon similarly attributed the characteristically flat African nose (and big belly) to the practice among African women of carrying their children on their backs. The jerk of the gait caused the child's nose to strike repeatedly against the mother's back; and the child, to avoid these blows, pushed its head and its stomach forward (*Histoire naturelle*, vol. 3, pp. 458–459).

70. Peter Kolb, *The Present State of the Cape of Good Hope*, trans. Guido Medley (London, 1731), vol. 1, pp. 310–311. Jemima Kindersley also reported that the Hottentots broke the noses of their infants (*Letters from the Island of Teneriffe, Brazil, the Cape of Good Hope, and the East Indies* [London, 1777], p. 68).

71. Blumenbach, *On the Natural Varieties of Mankind*, pp. 116, 240. Among the many reports, see de Rochefort, *Histoire naturelle et morale*, p. 441. In the sixteenth century, the Catholic church had attempted to stop native Peruvian women from shaping the heads of their children. Blumenbach, *On the Natural Varieties of Mankind*, p. 242 n. 3.

72. Jean-Jacques Rousseau, *Emile, ou De l'éducation* (1762), in *Oeuvres complètes*, ed. Bernard Gagnebin and Marcel Raymond, vol. 4 (Paris: Gallimard, 1959–1969), p. 253.

73. Jordan, *White over Black*, pp. 12, 242. For a discussion of maternal impressions, see Sander Gilman, *Sexuality: An Illustrated History* (New York: John Wiley & Sons, 1989), pp. 106–109; and Barbara Stafford, *Body Criticism: Imaging the Unseen in Enlightenment Art and Medicine* (Cambridge, Mass.: MIT Press, 1991), pp. 306–311.

74. François Leguat, *Voyage et avantures [sic] de François Leguat* (London, 1707), vol. 2, pp. 156–157. Kolb reported that the Hottentots removed the left testicle so males could run faster (*Present State of the Cape of Good Hope*, vol. 1, pp. 112–113); Thunberg reported that they did so to prevent women from bearing twins (C. P. Thunberg, "An Account of the Cape of Good Hope" [1795], in John Pinkerton, *A General Collection of the Best and Most Interesting Voyages and Travels in all Parts of the World* [London, 1808], vol. 16, p. 141); and Daniel Beeckman suggested they did so in the hope that women would bear more males (*A Voyage to and from the Island of Borneo* [London, 1718], p. 185).

75. Buffon, *Histoire naturelle*, vol. 3, pp. 469–470. Not all environmentalists were friends of Africans; Smith and Virey, for example, were racists.

76. Ibid., vol. 3, pp. 458–459.

77. Ottobah Cugoano, *Thoughts and Sentiments of the Evil and Wicked Traffic of the Slavery and Commerce of the Human Species* (London, 1787), pp. 29, 31–32. This work coincided with the founding of the London Committee for the Abolition of the Slave Trade, and some scholars have suggested that it was not written by Cugoano but by white abolitionists. From existing records it is im-

possible to say exactly how the piece was authored. Keith Sandiford has suggested that the book most likely was written and approved by Cugoano, with assistance from a collaborator or collaborators (*Measuring the Moment: Strategies of Protest in Eighteenth-Century Afro-English Writing* [London: Associated University Presses, 1988], p. 97). Cugoano apologized in the introduction for his lack of education (as was characteristic of European women in this period).

78. Olaudah Equiano, *The Life of Olaudah Equiano, or Gustavus Vassa, the African*, ed. Henry Louis Gates, Jr. (1789; New York: Mentor, 1987), pp. 23–24.

79. Blumenbach, *On the Natural Varieties of Mankind*, pp. 116, 232–233.

80. Buffon, *Histoire naturelle*, vol. 5, p. 251.

81. Edward Long, *The History of Jamaica* (London, 1774), vol. 2, p. 478.

82. Lawrence, *Lectures*, p. 351. Elsewhere in this text he conceded that races other than Caucasians might have shaped their heads to accentuate "natural defects" that they considered beautiful (p. 368).

83. Camper, *Works*, chap. 2, especially p. 25, also pp. 63–64.

84. Samuel Thomas von Soemmerring, *Vom Baue des menschlichen Körpers* (Frankfurt, 1791–1796), vol. 1, p. 87.

85. Camper, *Works*, p. 22; Soemmerring, *Über die körperliche Verschiedenheit des Negers vom Europäer*, p. 3 and preface.

86. Ibid., p. 2. Stepan, *The Idea of Race in Science*, pp. xviii–xix; also Stocking, *Race, Culture, and Evolution*, pp. 29–31. Skin was increasingly viewed as an unreliable marker of race. It was widely reported, for example, that during pregnancy the areola of even the fairest (European) woman turned as black as that of the blackest Negro (see Petrus Camper, *Dissertation physique de M. Pierre Camper* [1786; Utrecht, 1791], p. 16).

87. Fischer-Homberger, *Krankheit Frau*, pp. 85–105.

88. Schiebinger, *Mind Has No Sex?* chap. 7.

89. McCloy, *Negro in France*, p. 39.

5. Theories of Gender and Race

1. Cited in Charles Hardy, *The Negro Question in the French Revolution* (Menasha, Wisc.: George Banta Publishing Co., 1919), p. 15. Condorcet expressed similar sentiments in his "Lettres d'un bourgeois de New Haven à un citoyen de Virginie" (1787), in *Oeuvres de Condorcet*, ed., A. Condorcet O'Connor and M. F. Arago (Paris, 1847), vol. 9, pp. 15–19.

2. Cited in Jane Abray, "Feminism in the French Revolution," *American Historical Review* 80 (1975): 48.

3. Marie-Jean-Antoine-Nicolas de Caritat, marquis de Condorcet, "Sur l'admission des femmes au droit de cité" (1790), in *Oeuvres* (Stuttgart: F. Frommann, 1968), vol. 10, p. 129. See Maurice Bloch and Jean Bloch, "Women and the Dialectics of Nature in Eighteenth-Century French Thought," in *Nature, Culture and Gender*, ed. Carol P. MacCormack and Marilyn Strathern (Cambridge: Cambridge University Press, 1980), pp. 25–41; Steven Rose, Leon Kamin, and

Richard Lewontin, *Not in Our Genes: Biology, Ideology and Human Nature* (New York: Pantheon, 1984), pp. 63–81; Christine Fauré, *Democracy without Women: Feminism and the Rise of Liberal Individualism in France*, trans. Claudia Gorbman and John Berks (Bloomington: Indiana University Press, 1991); and Michèle Crampe-Casnabet, "Saisie dans les oeuvres philosophiques (XVIIIᵉ siècle)," in *Histoire des femmes en Occident*, ed. Natalie Davis and Arlette Farge (Paris: Plon, 1991), vol. 3, pp. 327–358.

4. See again chapter 4, note 6.

5. Arthur Lovejoy, *The Great Chain of Being: A Study of the History of an Idea* (1933; Cambridge, Mass.: Harvard University Press, 1964). Winthrop D. Jordan, *White over Black: American Attitudes toward the Negro, 1550–1812* (Chapel Hill: University of North Carolina Press, 1968), pp. 217–228.

6. William Smellie, *The Philosophy of Natural History* (Edinburgh, 1790), vol. 1, pp. 521–522. See also Charles White, *An Account of the Regular Gradation in Man and in Different Animals and Vegetables* (London, 1796).

7. See also Samuel Thomas von Soemmerring, *Über die körperliche Verschiedenheit des Negers vom Europäer* (Frankfurt, 1785), p. xiv.

8. Reported in Petrus Camper, *The Works of the Late Professor Camper on the Connexion between the Science of Anatomy and the Arts of Drawing, Painting, Statuary, etc.,* trans. T. Cogan (London, 1794), p. 32, though this was not his opinion.

9. One of the best discussions is found in Jordan, *White over Black*, pp. 215–265.

10. See Thomas Laqueur, *Making Sex: Body and Gender from the Greeks to Freud* (Cambridge, Mass.: Harvard University Press, 1990); and also Londa Schiebinger, *The Mind Has No Sex? Women in the Origins of Modern Science* (Cambridge, Mass.: Harvard University Press, 1989), chaps. 7, 8.

11. As Soemmerring wrote in his preface, he had studied several (*mehere*) males and one female. Soemmerring supplemented his own specimens with parts from other anatomists' collections, occasionally referring, for example, to a female African skull that one of his colleagues had prepared two years earlier. He had five complete African skulls (four male and one female) in his own collection (*Über die körperliche Verschiedenheit des Negers vom Europäer*, pp. xvii, 50). Two illustrations drawn for this book were also of males (these portraits were never published). Soemmerring's papers, Senckenbergische Bibliothek, Frankfurt, Lfd. Nr. 2, fig. 3 and 4. He also had a drawing of a female African among his papers.

12. Soemmerring, *Über die körperliche Verschiedenheit des Negers vom Europäer*, p. 34. From records from the Chatoul Rechnungen held at the StaatsArchiv in Marburg, we know that women were among the Africans living at Wilhelmshöhe.

13. The catalogue of Soemmerring's collection done by Rudolph Wagner indicates that he had four male Africans and one black female reportedly from Java among his twenty-five skeletons. It does not list the skeleton from the Kassel female ("Katalog des Präparate welche sich in dem von Soemmerring angelegten anatomischen Museum befanden," in Rudolph Wagner, *Samuel*

Thomas von Soemmerring's Leben und Verkehr mit seinen Zeitgenossen   *253*
[Leipzig, 1844], vol. 1, pp. lxxx–lxxxv).

14. Letter from Merck to Soemmerring, 13 August 1784, in ibid., p. 288.

15. Even though Soemmerring raised the issue of sexual subordination in his book on race (*Über die körperliche Verschiedenheit des Negers vom Europäer*, p. ix), he did not treat the issue of sexual differences among Africans.

16. Jean-Jacques Rousseau, *Emile, ou De l'éducation* (1762), in *Oeuvres complètes*, ed. Bernard Gagnebin and Marcel Raymond (Paris: Gallimard, 1959–1969), vol. 4; Pierre Roussel, *Système physique et moral de la femme, ou Tableau philosophique de la constitution, de l'état organique, du tempérament, des moeurs, & des fonctions propres au sexe* (Paris, 1775); Jakob Ackermann, *Über die körperliche Verschiedenheit des Mannes vom Weiber ausser Geschlechtstheilen*, trans. Joseph Wenzel (Koblenz, 1788); and Jacques Moreau de la Sarthe, *Histoire naturelle de la femme* (Paris, 1803).

17. Julien-Joseph Virey, *De la femme* (Paris, 1823). Virey's *Histoire naturelle du genre humain* (Paris, 1800) makes some reference to women.

18. Elizabeth Spelman, *Inessential Woman: Problems of Exclusion in Feminist Thought* (Boston: Beacon Press, 1988), pp. 37–56.

19. Soemmerring listed one partial skeleton and a skull of African females in his extensive private collection, consisting of 1,462 specimens preserved in alcohol, 2,439 dried preparations, and more than 200 skulls of people of various nations, remarkable or sick individuals (Ignaz Döllinger, *Gedächtnißrede auf Samuel Thomas von Soemmerring* [Munich, 1830], pp. 14–15). See also "Präparate, welche Herr Hofrath liess," *Medicinisches Journal*, ed. Ernst Gottfried Baldinger, 4 (1787): 14–23. Eighteenth-century anatomists' collections were, indeed, extensive; a Mr. Van Butchel kept his first wife embalmed at his home (Petrus Camper, "Petri Camperi itinera in Angliam, 1748–85," *Opuscula selecta Neerlandicorum de arte medica* 15 (1939): 205. See also Johann Blumenbach's partial catalogue prefacing the third edition of his *On the Natural Varieties of Mankind*, trans. Thomas Bendyshe (1795; New York: Bergman, 1969). Seventy-one of the eighty-two skulls listed are male.

20. Georges-Louis Leclerc, comte de Buffon, *Histoire naturelle, générale et particulière* (Paris, 1749–1804), vol. 3, "Variétés dans l'espèce humaine," and vol. 4, supplément.

21. Pierre Boulle, "Coloured People in Paris on the Eve of the French Revolution," in *L'image de la Révolution française*, ed Michel Vovelle (New York: Pergamon Press, 1990), vol. 4, p. 2467. See also Paul Edwards and James Walvin, *Black Personalities in the Era of the Slave Trade* (Baton Rouge: Louisiana State University Press, 1983), p. 19.

22. White, *An Account of the Regular Gradation*, chart, p. 45.

23. Genevieve Lloyd, *The Man of Reason: "Male" and "Female" in Western Philosophy* (Minneapolis: University of Minnesota Press, 1984).

24. Camper, *Works*, p. 50.

25. Ibid., p. 19. Camper included among the beautiful people, the inhabitants of

"the northern parts of the Mogul empire and of Persia, the Armenians, the Turks, Georgians, Migrelians, Circassians, and the inhabitants of Europe in general."

26. William Lawrence, *Lectures on Physiology, Zoology, and the Natural History of Man* (London, 1819), p. 168.

27. Petrus Camper, "Redevoering over den Oorsprong en de Kleur der Zwarten," *De Rhapsodist* 2 (1772): 393.

28. Camper, *Works*, p. 17.

29. Stephen Jay Gould, "Petrus Camper's Angle: The Grandfather of Scientific Racism has Gotten a Bum Rap," *Natural History* (July 1987): 12–16; Robert Visser, *The Zoological Work of Petrus Camper (1722–1789)* (Amsterdam: Rodopi, 1985); and Miriam Meijer, "The Anthropology of Petrus Camper," paper read before the American Society for Eighteenth-Century Studies, April 1991.

30. Blumenbach, *On the Natural Varieties of Mankind*, pp. 150–151.

31. Johann Blumenbach, *Abbildungen naturhistorischer Gegenstände* (Göttingen, 1810), no. 51.

32. Petrus Camper, "De l'orang-outang et de quelques autres espèces de singes," in *Oeuvres de Pierre Camper* (Paris, 1803), vol. 1, pp. 47–48. Among his collection of skulls of different nations (eight in all), he identified one as female—that of a Hottentot (*Works*, p. 8). We also know from Soemmerring's work that the "Celebean" was female (Samuel Thomas von Soemmerring, *Vom Baue des menschlichen Körpers* [Frankfurt, 1791–1796], vol. 1, p. 71). No sex was given for the other six, though we know from Camper's notes that the "Calmuck" was male.

33. This propensity for craniologists to favor the male is also evident in Friedrich Tiedemann's carefully documented "On the Brain of the Negro, compared with that of the European and the Orang-Outang." For the *Ethiopian race* he compared the skulls of thirty-eight males and three females; for the *Mongolian Race* eighteen males and two females; for the *American Race* twenty-four males and three females; and so on (*Philosophical Transactions of the Royal Society of London* [1836]: 497–527, especially 519).

34. Male skulls, however, outnumbered female skulls by a wide margin in his monumental *Decas collectionis suae craniorum diversarum gentium* (Göttingen, 1790–1828).

35. Lawrence also used Blumenbach's Georgian head and Jewish girl to exemplify the Caucasian formation (*Lectures*, p. 338). Virey reproduced Blumenbach's skulls, choosing to compare only the Georgian and Ethiopian (which he labeled "Negro"; it was also female). See his *Histoire naturelle du genre humain*, vol. 2, p. 136.

36. Johann Blumenbach, *Beyträge zur Naturgeschichte* (Göttingen, 1806–1811), pp. 63–66. In an earlier work, Blumenbach had used cameo scenes that he considered representative of life among each of his five human varieties: the Caucasians (male and female) lounged in a harem; the Mongolians drank tea; an Ethopian family sat by their hut, the mother nursing a child; the Americans were again portrayed in a family scene, the mother with a young child at her knee, the father with hunting gear; and a Malaysian family was shown on their

farm surrounded by chickens and pigs (*Beyträge zur Naturgeschichte* [Göttingen, 1790]).

37. Schiebinger, *Mind Has No Sex?* pp. 197, 209, 212, and 214.

38. For Blumenbach, as for many of his era, the skull epitomized racial diversity, revealing "the principle physical characters of humanity." Blumenbach wrote proudly of his vast skull collection: "When viewing this collection hopefully no one will say with the Cynic Menippus—when he arrived in the underworld—that they all look alike." Blumenbach, *Beyträge zur Naturgeschichte* (1806–1811), p. 66.

39. Buffon, *Histoire naturelle*, vol. 3, pp. 459–460; Edward Long, *The History of Jamaica* (London, 1774), vol. 2, p. 380; White, *An Account of the Regular Gradation*, pp. 71–72. Maria Nugent, *Lady Nugent's Journal (1801–1815)*, ed. Frank Cundall (London: Adam & Charles Black, 1907), p. 94.

40. Barbara Bush, *Slave Women in Caribbean Society, 1650–1838* (Bloomington: Indiana University Press, 1990), p. 15.

41. Petrus Camper, *Vermischte Schriften* (Lingen, 1801), pp. 342–343. In the 1780s, Camper measured the Negro pelvis at 125 degrees (these measurements were added by the editor from Camper's notebooks).

42. Camper, *Works*, pp. 61–63. The subjects measured were reported in Soemmerring, *Über die körperliche Verschiedenheit des Negers vom Europäer*, p. 35. Camper also compared pelvic proportions reported by Albrecht Dürer and in "the Antonius," which I take to be another well-known European piece of statuary.

43. Camper, *Works*, pp. 60–61.

44. Soemmerring, *Über die körperliche Verschiedenheit des Negers vom Europäer*, pp. 34–35.

45. White, *An Account of the Regular Gradation*, p. 72; cited in James Prichard, *Researches into the Physical History of Mankind* (London, 1841), vol. 1, p. 323.

46. Moritz Weber, *Die Lehre von den Ur- und Racen-Formen der Schädel und Becken des Menschen* (Düsseldorf, 1830), p. 5.

47. Willem Vrolik, *Considérations sur la diversité des bassins de différentes races humaines* (Amsterdam, 1826), p. 11.

48. See, for example, Soemmerring, *Über die körperliche Verschiedenheit des Negers vom Europäer*, pp. 67–69; Lawrence, *Lectures*, p. 462.

49. Havelock Ellis, cited in Sander Gilman, *Sexuality: An Illustrated History* (New York: John Wiley & Sons, 1989), p. 295.

50. Schiebinger, *Mind Has No Sex?* pp. 212–213; Nancy Leys Stepan, "Race and Gender: The Role of Analogy in Science," *Isis* 77 (June 1986): 261–277; and Cynthia Russett, *Sexual Science: The Victorian Construction of Womanhood* (Cambridge, Mass.: Harvard University Press, 1989).

51. Sander Gilman, *Difference and Pathology: Stereotypes of Sexuality, Race and Madness* (Ithaca: Cornell University Press, 1985), p. 83.

52. Blumenbach, *On the Natural Varieties of Mankind*, p. 151.

53. Camper, *Works*, p. 20; Virey, *Histoire naturelle du genre humain*, vol. 1, p. 317.

54. See Gloria Hull, Patricia Bell Scott, and Barbara Smith, eds., *All the Women Are White, All the Blacks Are Men, But Some of Us Are Brave: Black Women's Studies* (Old Westbury, New York: Feminist Press, 1982). One sees these assumptions expressed over and over again today (see Spelman, *Inessential Woman*, pp. 114–115).

55. Barbara Bush, "White 'Ladies,' Coloured 'Favourites' and Black 'Wenches'; Some Considerations on Sex, Race and Class Factors in Social Relations in White Creole Society in the British Caribbean," *Slavery and Abolition* 2 (1981): 244–262, especially 249; Hazel Carby, *Reconstructing Womanhood: The Emergence of the Afro-American Woman Novelist* (New York: Oxford University Press, 1987), pp. 20–39; and Evelyn Brooks Higginbotham, "African-American Women's History and the Metalanguage of Race," *Signs: Journal of Women in Culture and Society* 17 (1992); 251–274, especially 262–266.

56. See Jordan, *White over Black*; and James Walvin, *Black and White: The Negro and English Society, 1555–1945* (London: Penguin Press, 1973); among others.

57. Thomas Herbert, *Some Yeares Travel into Africa and Asia* (London, 1638), p. 17. See also "Cowley's Voyage Round the Globe," in William Hacke, *A Collection of Original Voyages* (London, 1699), p. 35; and Edward Cooke, *A Voyage to the South Sea* (London, 1712), vol. 2, p. 70. See also R. W. Frantz, "Swift's Yahoos and the Voyagers," *Modern Philology* 29 (1931–1932): 49–57, especially 53.

58. [Marie-Jean-Antoine-Nicolas de Caritat, marquis de Condorcet], "Réflexions sur l'esclavage des nègres" (1781), in *Oeuvres de Condorcet*, ed. A. Condorcet O'Connor and M. F. Arago (Paris, 1847), vol. 7, p. 82.

59. Bernadette Bucher, *Icon and Conquest: A Structural Analysis of the Illustrations of de Bry's Great Voyages*, trans. Basia Miller Gulati (1977; Chicago: University of Chicago Press, 1981).

60. Only de Rochefort suggested that throwing a breast over the shoulder was a desirable trait (Charles de Rochefort, *Histoire naturelle et morale des îles Antilles de l'Amérique*, 2d ed. (Rotterdam, 1665), p. 441.

61. William Towerson, cited in Walvin, *Black and White*, p. 22. Also François Leguat, *Voyage et avantures [sic] de François Leguat* (London, 1707), vol. 2, p. 159.

62. Buffon, *Histoire naturelle*, vol. 3, p. 407; Blumenbach, *On the Natural Varieties of Mankind*, p. 247 n. 5; C. P. Thunberg, "An Account of the Cape of Good Hope" (1795), in John Pinkerton, *A General Collection of the Best and Most Interesting Voyages and Travels in all Parts of the World* (London, 1808), vol. 16, pp. 29–30; and Samuel Stanhope Smith, *An Essay on the Causes of the Variety of Complexion and Figure in the Human Species* (1787; Cambridge, Mass.: Harvard University Press, 1965), p. 82. Lithgow (1614) remarked on the unsightly breasts of Irish women, comparing them to the money bags of an East-India merchant—well tanned and large (ibid., p. 83). See also Lawrence's summary of descriptions of African women's breasts (*Lectures*, pp. 416–417).

63. Ibid., p. 359.
64. Thunberg, "An Account of the Cape of Good Hope," in Pinkerton, *A General Collection of . . . Voyages*, vol. 16, pp. 29–30. Richard Ligon, *A True and Exact History of the Island of Barbados* (London, 1657), p. 51; also Thomas Winterbottom, *An Account of the Native Africans* (1803; London: Frank Cass & Co., 1969), vol. 2, p. 264. Carl Linnaeus, *Systema naturae per regna tria naturae*, 10th ed. (Stockholm, 1758), p. 22.
65. Blumenbach, *On the Natural Varieties of Mankind*, pp. 247–248.
66. Smith, *An Essay on the Causes of the Variety . . . in the Human Species*, p. 82.
67. Hermann Ploss, Max Bartels, and Paul Bartels, *Woman: An Historical Gynecological and Anthropological Compendium*, ed. Eric Dingwall (St. Louis: C. V. Mosby Company, 1936), pp. 327–336, especially 330.
68. Linnaeus, *Systema naturae*, 10th ed., pp. 22, 24. Winthrop Jordan mistranslated *sinus pudoris* as: "Women's bosom a matter of modesty" (*White over Black*, p. 221); Frank Spencer also translated it incorrectly as "women without shame" (*Ecce Homo: An Annotated Bibliographic History of Physical Anthropology* [New York: Greenwood Press, 1986], p. 78); and most recently, Pieterse has it wrong—"the bosoms of women are distended" (Jan Pieterse, *White on Black: Images of Africa and Blacks in Western Popular Culture* [New Haven: Yale University Press, 1992], p. 40). In his "Anthropomorpha" Linnaeus claimed that female troglodytes had these hanging folds of skin (Carl Linnaeus, "Anthropomorpha," respondent C. E. Hoppius [1760] in *Amoenitates academicae* [Erlangen, 1789], vol. 6, description of figure 4).
69. John Ovington, *A Voyage to Suratt in the Year 1689* (London, 1696), p. 497.
70. Blumenbach, *On the Natural Varieties of Mankind*, p. 250 n. 4; Voltaire, *Lettres d'Amabed*, letter 4, *Oeuvres complètes de Voltaire* (Paris: Garnier Frères, 1879), vol. 21, pp. 458–459.
71. François Le Vaillant, *Voyage de François Le Vaillant dans l'intérieur de l'Afrique* (1790; Paris, 1798), vol. 2, p. 351.
72. Peter Kolb, *The Present State of the Cape of Good Hope*, trans. Guido Medley (London, 1731), vol. 1, p. 118.
73. John Barrow, *Reisen in das Innere von Südafrika in den Jahren, 1797 und 1798* (1801; Berlin, 1802), p. 310.
74. Blumenbach, *On the Natural Varieties of Mankind*, pp. 249–250; Blumenbach, *Handbuch der Naturgeschichte*, p. 64. He may have changed his mind later on; Cuvier remarked that Blumenbach sent drawings of an excessively long specimen to Banks (Georges Cuvier, "Extrait d'observations faites sur le cadavre d'une femme connue à Paris et à Londres sous le nom de Vénus Hottentotte," *Mémoires du Muséum d'Histoire Naturelle* 3 [1817]: 268).
75. John Hawkesworth, *An Account of the Voyages Undertaken by the Order of His Present Majesty for Making Discoveries in the Southern Hemisphere* (London, 1773), vol. 3, p. 792.
76. Ibid.; Barrow, *Reisen in das Innere von Südafrika*, p. 309.
77. Le Vaillant, *Voyage*, vol. 2, pp. 351–353; see also Virey, *De la femme*, p. 30; and Moreau de la Sarthe, *Histoire naturelle de la femme*, p. 525.

78. Le Vaillant, *Voyage*, vol. 2, pp. 352–353.
79. Barrow, *Reisen in das Innere von Südafrika*, pp. 309–310.
80. Le Vaillant, *Voyage*, vol. 2, pp. 349, 351, 353.
81. François Le Vaillant, *Travels from the Cape of Good-Hope into the Interior Parts of Africa*, trans. Elizabeth Helme (London, 1790), preface.
82. Barrow, *Reisen in das Innere von Südafrika*, p. 311.
83. Le Vaillant, *Voyage*, vol. 2, p. 351.
84. Sander Gilman, "Black Bodies, White Bodies: Toward an Iconography of Female Sexuality in Late Nineteenth-Century Art, Medicine, and Literature," in *"Race," Writing, and Difference*, ed. Henry Louis Gates, Jr. (Chicago: University of Chicago Press, 1986), pp. 223–261.
85. Cuvier, "Extrait d'observations," pp. 259–274. See also J. Müller, "Über die äusseren Geschlechtstheile der Buschmänninnen," *Müllers Archiv* (1836): 319–345.
86. My account of her life has been taken from Percival Kirby, "The Hottentot Venus," *Africana Notes and News* 6 (1949): 55–62; and "More About the Hottentot Venus," ibid., 10 (1953): 124–134. See also Edwards and Walvin, *Black Personalities*, pp. 171–182; and Stephen Jay Gould, *The Flamingo's Smile: Reflections in Natural History* (New York: Norton & Company, 1985), pp. 291–305; Gilman, *Difference and Pathology*, pp. 83–88; and Anne Fausto-Sterling, *Making a Difference: Biology and the Social/Scientific Construction of Sexuality* (in preparation).
87. Richard Altick, *The Shows of London* (Cambridge, Mass.: Harvard University Press, 1978), pp. 268–273.
88. Henri de Blainville, "Sur une femme de la race hottentote," *Bulletin des sciences, par la Société Philomatique de Paris* (1816): 183–190, especially 183.
89. Etienne Geoffroy Saint-Hilaire and Frédéric Cuvier, *Histoire naturelle des mammifères, avec des figures originales enluminées, dessinées d'après des animaux vivants* (Paris, 1819), plates 115 and 116.
90. De Blainville, "Sur une femme de la race hottentote," pp. 183–190.
91. Leguat, *Voyage et avantures* [sic] *de François Leguat*, vol. 2, p. 159.
92. For Cuvier's account of Bartmann's genitalia, see "Extrait d'observations," pp. 265–266.
93. Virey, *De la femme*, p. 31.
94. Cuvier, "Extrait d'observations," p. 266. William Hunter also had a wax cast of the external genitalia of an African woman among the specimens in his anatomical museum.
95. In his *Le règne animal*, Cuvier asserted that "the negro race" resembled apes ([Paris, 1817], vol. 1, p. 95).
96. In the nineteenth century, the skins of Africans were sometimes taken after death and stuffed for display in natural history museums. The anatomist Bonn at Amsterdam was noted for his beautiful skin collection. See Hans Debrunner, *Presence and Prestige: Africans in Europe* (Basil: Basler Afrika Bibliographen, 1979), p. 145.

97. On this point, see also Gilman, *Sexuality*, p. 293.
98. Ernst Kantorowicz, *The King's Two Bodies: A Study in Medieval Political Theology* (Princeton: Princeton University Press, 1957). See also Pierre Boulle, "In Defense of Slavery: Eighteenth-Century Opposition to Abolition and the Origins of a Racist Ideology in France," in *History from Below*, ed. Frederick Krantz (Oxford: Basil Blackwell, 1988), pp. 219–246.
99. Soemmerring, *Über die körperliche Verschiedenheit des Negers vom Europäer*, preface.
100. Jean Tarrade, *Le commerce colonial à la fin de l'Ancien Régime* (Paris: Presses Universitaires de France, 1972); Hardy, *The Negro Question in the French Revolution*, p. 1.
101. The *gens de couleur*, however, did not represent the interest of blacks—free or slave. On different occasions, free blacks demanded separate representation for themselves (rhetorically opposing their racial purity to the bastard origins of the citizens of color). David Geggus, "Racial Equality, Slavery, and Colonial Secession during the Constituent Assembly," *The American Historical Review* 94 (1989): 1290–1308, especially 1298. Hardy's *The Negro Question in the French Revolution* provides a detailed account of the National Assembly proceedings. See also Pierre Pluchon, *Nègres et Juifs au XVIIIe siècle: Le racisme au siècle des Lumières* (Paris: Tallandier, 1984); and Julien Raymond, *Observations sur l'origine et les progrès du préjugé des colons blancs contre les hommes de couleur* (Paris, 1791).
102. Long, *History of Jamaica*, vol. 2, pp. 260–261, 321. David Brion Davis, *The Problem of Slavery in Western Culture* (Oxford: Oxford University Press, 1966), p. 278; Geggus, "Racial Equality, Slavery, and Colonial Secession," p. 1297.
103. Gabriel Debien, *Les colons de Saint-Dominique et la révolution* (Paris: Colin, 1953); Cyril James, *The Black Jacobins: Toussaint L'Ouverture and the San Domingo Revolution* (New York: Dial Press, 1938); and David Brion Davis, *The Problem of Slavery in the Age of Revolution: 1770–1823* (Ithaca: Cornell University Press, 1975), pp. 142–146.
104. Hardy, *The Negro Question in the French Revolution*, p. 80.
105. Richard Cobb and Colin Jones, eds. *Voices of the French Revolution* (Topsfield, Mass.: Salem House Publishers, 1988), p. 136; also Hardy, *The Negro Question in the French Revolution*, p. 78.
106. "Heroic manhood" is Dorinda Outram's term from *The Body and the French Revolution: Sex, Class and Political Culture* (New Haven: Yale University Press, 1989).
107. William Lawrence, a raving racist, was opposed to slavery on the grounds that superior beings should not oppress the weak and ignorant (*Lectures*, p. 364).
108. On the meaning of fraternity, see Marcel David, *Fraternité et Révolution française, 1789–1799* (Paris: Aubier, 1987).
109. Hugh Honour, *The Image of the Black in Western Art* (Cambridge, Mass.: Harvard University Press, 1979), vol. 4, pt. 1, p. 55.
110. For a discussion of William Blake, see Albert Boime, *Art in an Age of Revo-*

lution: 1750–1800 (Chicago: University of Chicago Press, 1987), vol. 1, pp. 308–370.

111. Darline Levy, Harriet Applewhite, and Mary Johnson, eds., *Women in Revolutionary Paris, 1789–1795* (Urbana: University of Illinois Press, 1979), pp. 213–217.

112. Cited in Joan Landes, *Women and the Public Sphere in the Age of the French Revolution* (Ithaca: Cornell University Press, 1988), p. 145.

113. Abray, "Feminism in the French Revolution," p. 58. For accounts of women during the French Revolution, see also Landes, *Women and the Public Sphere in the Age of the French Revolution*; Outram, *The Body and the French Revolution*; Dominique Godineau, *Citoyennes tricoteuses: Les femmes du peuple à Paris pendant la Révolution française* (Aix-en-Provence: Alinea, 1988), pp. 264–265; and Lynn Hunt, *The Family Romance and the French Revolution* (Berkeley and Los Angeles: University of California Press, 1992).

114. Convention Nationale, *Journal des débats et des décrets*, no. 258–286 (June 1793): 51–52; Convention Nationale, *Archives parlementaires* 66 (4 June 1793): 56–57; *Boston Magazine* in Cobb and Jones, *Voices of the French Revolution*, p. 212.

115. Abray, "Feminism in the French Revolution," p. 54.

116. Olympe de Gouges, *Les droits de la femme* (Paris, 1791), p. 14. On de Gouges, see Olivier Blanc, *Olympe de Gouges* (Paris: Syros, 1981). De Gouges's play, "L'Esclavage des Nègres," had been forced from the stage by colonists.

117. Abray, "Feminism in the French Revolution," p. 56.

118. Darline Levy and Harriet Applewhite, "Women of the Popular Classes in Revolutionary Paris, 1789–1795," in *Women, War, and Revolution*, ed. Carol Berkin and Clara Lovett (New York: Holmes & Meier, 1980), p. 25.

119. Lynn Hunt, *Politics, Culture, and Class in the French Revolution* (Berkeley and Los Angeles: University of California Press, 1984), p. 94. Also Maurice Agulhon, *Marianne into Battle: Republican Imagery and Symbolism in France, 1789–1880*, trans. Janet Lloyd (1979; Cambridge: Cambridge University Press, 1981), pp. 11–37.

120. Long, *History of Jamaica*, vol. 2, p. 280. Colonial white women, too, were admonished to "render the island more populous." Hazel Carby has discussed the differences in definitions of motherhood for southern white women and slave women (*Reconstructing Womanhood*, pp. 29–31).

121. [Condorcet], "Réflexions sur l'esclavage des nègres," p. 88. New laws protected pregnant and nursing mothers, while economic incentives encouraged reproduction. In the British West Indies, for example, female slaves having six living children were exempt from hard labor, and the owner from paying taxes on that slave. The governor also suggested that a little gift be given to every "wench that was brought to bed and that all the barren ones be whipt upon a certain day every Year." Cited in Richard Sheridan, *Doctors and Slaves: A Medical and Demographic History of Slavery in the British West Indies, 1680–1834* (Cambridge: Cambridge University Press, 1985), pp. 224, 229, 239. There were also efforts to curb sexual exploitation of black women

by white planters and overseers. Arlette Gautier, "Les esclaves femmes aux Antilles françaises: 1635–1848," *Historical reflections/Réflexions historiques* 10 (1983): 409–433.

122. Long, *History of Jamaica*, vol. 2, p. 490.

123. Condorcet added that black women also often miscarried from forced labor or bad treatment ("Réflexions sur l'esclavage des nègres," p. 100).

124. Maria Sibylla Merian, *Metamorphosis insectorum Surinamensium*, ed. Helmut Decker (1705; Leipzig: Insel-Verlag A. Kippenberg, 1975), commentary to plate 45; see also commentary to plates 7, 25, and 13. See also Sheridan, *Doctors and Slaves*, pp. 244–245. For an opposing view, see Marietta Morrissey, *Slave Women in the New World: Gender Stratification in the Caribbean* (Lawrence: University Press of Kansas, 1989), pp. 111–118.

125. [Janet Schaw], *Journal of a Lady of Quality . . . 1774–1776* (New Haven: Yale University Press, 1922), p. 78.

126. Virey, *De la femme*, p. 2 n. 1.

127. Davis, *The Problem of Slavery in Western Culture*, p. 274.

128. Nugent, *Lady Nugent's Journal*, p. 94.

6. Who Should Do Science?

1. Bernal has argued further that the Greek achievement in arts and letters might best be seen as resulting from a felicitous mixing of native Europeans and colonizing Africans and Semites. Martin Bernal, *Black Athena: The Afroasiatic Roots of Classical Civilization* (New Brunswick: Rutgers University Press, 1987).

2. Heinrich von Staden, "Affinities and Elisions: Helen and Hellenocentrism," *Isis* 83 (1992): 578–595, especially 589. Both von Staden and G. E. R. Lloyd caution that looking for a single origin of Western science fails to appreciate the permeability of cultural boundaries, both ancient and modern. G. E. R. Lloyd, "Methods and Problems in the History of Ancient Science: The Greek Case," *Isis* 83 (1992): 564–577, especially 572. See also "The Challenge of Black Athena" special issue of *Arethusa* (1989).

3. See, for example, William Lawrence, *Lectures on Physiology, Zoology, and the Natural History of Man* (London, 1819), p. 340; Etienne Geoffroy Saint-Hilaire cited in Nicole et Jean Dhombres, *Naissance d'un pouvoir: Sciences et savants en France (1793–1824)* (Paris: Payot, 1989), p. 106. See also Diderot and d'Alembert's *Encyclopédie, ou Dictionnaire raisonné des sciences, des arts et des métiers* (Paris, 1751–1765), vol. 5, "Egyptiens." China was an ancient civilization favored by eighteenth-century physiocrats. The Freemasons were especially appreciative of Egyptian accomplishments.

4. Ivan Van Sertima, ed., *Blacks in Science: Ancient and Modern* (New Brunswick: Transaction Books, 1984), p. 13. Alexander von Humboldt addressed similar issues concerning pre-Colombian civilizations in the Americas. See Mary Louise Pratt, *Imperial Eyes: Travel Writing and Transculturation* (London: Routledge, 1992), p. 134.

5. Lawrence, *Lectures*, p. 340.

6. Ambroise Paré, *The Collected Works of Ambroise Paré*, trans. Thomas Johnson (1634; New York: Milford House, 1968), p. 20. Jean Bodin, the French political philosopher, also taught that the peoples of northern regions produced military power, the peoples of the southern regions produced science and religion, and the peoples of the temperate zone founded greatest empires (*The Six Books of a Commonweale*, trans. Richard Knolles [London, 1606], p. 550).

7. The influence of the theory of humors can be seen in Linnaeus's classification of humans, where he assigned a mode of governing to each race. Americans governed by customs, Europeans by laws, Asians by opinions, and Africans by caprice (Carl Linnaeus, *Systema naturae per regna tria naturae*, 10th ed. [Stockholm, 1758], p. 38).

8. Aristotle, *Politics*, VII, 6.

9. Georges-Louis Leclerc, comte de Buffon, *Histoire naturelle, générale et particulière* (Paris, 1749–1804), vol. 3, p. 528. Also Johann Winckelmann, *Reflections Concerning the Imitation of the Grecian Artists in Painting and Sculpture* (1755; Glasgow, 1766), p. 4.

10. Dhombres, *Naissance d'un pouvoir*, pp. 93–149.

11. Johann Blumenbach, "Observations on some Egyptian Mummies opened in London," *Philosophical Transactions of the Royal Society of London* 84 (1794): pt. 2, 177–195.

12. Constantin-François Volney, *Voyage en Syrie et en Egypte* (1787; Paris: Mouton & Co., 1959), pp. 62–64.

13. Christoph Meiners, "De veterum Aegyptiorum origine," *Commentationes Societatis Scientiarum Regiae Gottingensis* 10 (1791): 57–79; Winckelmann, cited in Blumenbach, "Observations on some Egyptian Mummies," p. 193.

14. Georges Cuvier, "Extrait d'observations faites sur le cadavre d'une femme connue à Paris et à Londres sous le nom de Vénus Hottentotte," *Mémoires du Muséum d'Histoire Naturelle* 3 (1817): 272–273.

15. Lawrence, *Lectures*, pp. 341–342.

16. Edward Long, *The History of Jamaica* (London, 1774), vol. 2, p. 355.

17. Blumenbach, "Observations on some Egyptian Mummies," pp. 177–195. Soemmerring also concluded that ancient Egypt had had a mixed population. Of the four mummy heads he examined, he described two as European and one as African (Samuel Thomas von Soemmerring, *Vom Baue des menschlichen Körpers* [Frankfurt, 1791–1796], vol. 1, p. 74).

18. Johann Blumenbach, *Beyträge zur Naturgeschichte* (Göttingen, 1790), pp. 85, 91.

19. Von Staden pointed out how historical selectivity has produced such a view. Heinrich von Staden, "Affinities and Elisions," p. 584. See also Francesca Rochberg, "Introduction" to special section on the Cultures of Ancient Science, ibid., pp. 547–553.

20. Londa Schiebinger, *The Mind Has No Sex? Women in the Origins of Modern Science* (Cambridge, Mass.: Harvard University Press, 1989), pp. 102–104.

21. François-Marie Arouet de Voltaire, *Dictionnaire philosophique* (1764; Amsterdam, 1789), vol. 5, p. 255.
22. Blumenbach, *On the Natural Varieties of Mankind*, p. 81. On African men and women, see Henry Louis Gates, Jr., *Figures in Black: Words, Signs, and the "Racial" Self* (New York: Oxford University Press, 1989), pp. 3–24.
23. We hear about Bettisia Gozzadini, who lectured in law at the University of Bologna in 1296. Novella d'Andrea replaced her deceased father as professor of canon law at the University of Bologna in the fourteenth century. In 1678, Elena Cornaro Piscopia became the first woman to receive the doctorate of philosophy at Padua. Maria Agnesi of Milan became well known for her work in differential and integral calculus. Laura Bassi taught physics at the University of Bologna for forty-eight years. Dorothea Erxleben became the first woman ever to receive a medical degree in Germany in 1754. See my *The Mind Has No Sex?* pp. 12–17, 250–257.
24. Johann Blumenbach, "Observations on the Bodily Conformation and Mental Capacity of the Negroes," *Philosophical Magazine* 3 (1799): 141–146, especially 145. This library was auctioned off in Göttingen in 1840.
25. On Amo, see *Antonius Guilielmus Amo, Afer aus Axim in Ghana: Dokumente, Autographe, Belege* (Halle: Martin Luther Universität, 1968); Burchard Brentjes, *Anton Wilhelm Amo: Der schwarze Philosoph in Halle* (Leipzig: Koehler & Amelang, 1976); also Blumenbach, "Observations on the Bodily Conformation and Mental Capacity of the Negroes"; Henri Grégoire, *De la littérature des nègres, ou Recherches sur leurs facultés intellectuelles, leurs qualités morales et leur littérature* (Paris, 1808), pp. 198–202; Paulin Hountondji, *African Philosophy: Myth and Reality*, trans. Henri Evans (London: Hutchinson University Library for Africa, 1983), chap. 5; and Gates, *Figures in Black*, pp. 11–12. Blumenbach's information about Amo apparently came from the philosopher Hollmann who had instructed Amo in philosophy at Wittenberg (Bentjes, *Amo*, p. 72).
26. On Wheatley, see Gates's excellent discussion, *Figures in Black*, pp. 61–79.
27. Hans Debrunner identifies her as Pauline Hippolyte de Buisson (*Presence and Prestige: Africans in Europe* [Basil: Basler Afrika Bibliographen, 1979], p. 143).
28. Hans-Konrad Schmutz, "Friedrich Tiedemann und Johann Friedrich Blumenbach: Anthropologie und Sklavenfrage," in *Die Natur des Menschen: Probleme der Physischen Anthropologie und Rassenkunde, (1750–1850)*, ed. Gunter Mann, Jost Benedum, and Werner Kümmel (Stuttgart: Gustav Fischer Verlag, 1990), p. 358.
29. There were also experiments in elementary- and secondary-school education: Wilberforce established a school for Africans at Clapham, near London; African children from Coesnon's college in Paris were examined by members of the French National Institute. Grégoire, *De la littérature des nègres*, pp. 176–177.
30. Folarin Shyllon, *Black People in Britain, 1555–1833* (Oxford: Oxford University Press, 1977), p. 48.
31. In addition to Amo, a Sultan Achmet from India matriculated at Halle in 1733

and Salomon Negri from Damascus in 1701 (*Antonius Guilielmus Amo*, p. 296).

32. Ibid., pp. 9–10.

33. Ibid., pp. 125 and 134.

34. Schiebinger, *Mind Has No Sex?* chap. 9.

35. Long, *History of Jamaica*, vol. 2, pp. 475–485.

36. David Hume, "Of National Characters," in *The Philosophical Works*, ed. Thomas Green and Thomas Grose (London, 1886), vol. 4, p. 252 n. 1.

37. The Berlin Academy was unusual in having women of high rank, such as Catherine the Great, as honorary members in the eighteenth and nineteenth centuries. The first woman to be elected for her scientific merit was Lise Meitner in 1949. Italian academies also admitted some women in the eighteenth century. Emilie du Châtelet, for example, who was denied membership in French scientific academies, was honored with membership in Italian academies.

38. An African of fortune and a friend of many well-known men of science, Williams was admitted to the meetings of the Royal Society and even proposed as a member (*Gentlemen's Magazine* 42 [1771]:595). Blumenbach had a copy of this article among his papers (Cod. Ms. Blum IXb, B1. 36, p. 48, Niedersächsische Staats- und Universitätsbibliothek, Göttingen).

39. I thank Mary Sampson, archivist at the Royal Society, for helping to clarify this matter.

40. M. Argo, "Notices nécrologiques," *Comptes Rendus* (1836): 96–101. Alfred Lacroix, "Notice historique sur les membres et correspondants de l'Académie des Sciences ayant travaillé dans les colonies françaises des Mascareignes et de Madagascar au XVIIIᵉ siècle et au début du XIXᵉ," *Mémoires de l'Académie des Sciences* 62 (17 December 1934): 82–85.

41. Grégoire, *De la littérature des nègres*, pp. 207–208.

42. Lacroix, "Notice historique sur les membres et correspondants de l'Académie des Sciences," p. 82. The Académie des Sciences in Paris was unable to tell me if any persons of African descent had become members since the 1930s.

43. Brentjes, *Anton Wilhelm Amo*, p. 71.

44. Claude-Nicolas Le Cat, *Traité de la couleur de la peau humaine* (Amsterdam, 1765).

45. Joan Landes, *Women and the Public Sphere in the Age of the French Revolution* (Ithaca: Cornell University Press, 1988), pp. 23–28; Schiebinger, *Mind Has No Sex?* pp. 30–32; and Dena Goodman, "Enlightenment Salons: The Convergence of Female and Philosophic Ambitions," *Eighteenth-Century Studies* 22 (1989): 329–350.

46. Claire de Durfort, duchesse de Duras, *Ourika*, ed. Claudine Herrmann (Paris: Des Femmes, 1979), p. 38.

47. David Geggus, "Racial Equality, Slavery, and Colonial Secession during the Constituent Assembly," *The American Historical Review* 94 (1989): 1290–1308, especially 1297.

48. Shelby McCloy, *The Negro in France* (Lexington: University of Kentucky Press, 1961), pp. 38–39.

49. Richard Sheridan, *Doctors and Slaves: A Medical and Demographic History of Slavery in the British West Indies, 1680–1834* (Cambridge: Cambridge University Press, 1985), pp. 49–50.

50. *De Jure Maurorum in Europa* (1729), discussed in *Wöchentliche Hallische Nachrichten* 12 (1729), reprinted in *Antonius Guilielmus Amo*, pp. 5–6. His standard works, *De humanae mentis apatheia* (Wittenberg, 1734), *Ideam distinctam* (Wittenberg, 1734), and *Tractatus de arte sobrie et accurate philosophandi* (Halle, 1738), sound familiar themes: What is sensation? Does the faculty of sense belong to mind? How do we acquire distinct ideas? See also Hountondji, *African Philosophy*, p. 111. The same was true of women's writings in this period; see my *Mind Has No Sex?* pp. 270–271.

Nature's Body Wronged

1. For the exceptional case of Marie Thiroux d'Arconville, see Londa Schiebinger, *The Mind Has No Sex? Women in the Origins of Modern Science* (Cambridge, Mass.: Harvard University Press, 1989), pp. 195–200.

2. David E. Allen, *The Naturalist in Britain: A Social History* (1976; Harmondsworth, Middlesex: Penguin Books, 1978), pp. 28–29. The Bibliothèque Nationale in Paris holds the catalogues of some thirty-five natural history collections auctioned off in the eighteenth century. Five of these collections belonged to women. See, for example, P. Remy, *Catalogue d'une collection de très belles coquilles, madrepores, stalactiques, . . . de Madame Bure* (Paris, 1763).

3. See Renée-Paule Guillot, "La vraie 'Bougainvillée': La première femme qui fit le tour du monde," *Historama* 1 (1984): 36–40.

4. Richard Ligon, *A True and Exact History of the Island of Barbados* (London, 1657), pp. 120–121.

5. Eliza Haywood, *The Female Spectator* (London, 1745), vol. 2, p. 243.

6. Kindersley claimed they guarded her in order to prevent her from becoming acquainted with any of their women (without saying why). Jemima Kindersley, *Letters from the Island of Teneriffe, Brazil, the Cape of Good Hope, and the East Indies* (London, 1777), pp. 25–26. See also Ketaki Kushari Dyson, *A Various Universe: A Study of the Journals and Memoirs of British Men and Women in the Indian Subcontinent, 1765–1856* (Delhi and New York: Oxford University Press, 1978), pp. 124–126.

7. Johann Blumenbach, *On the Natural Varieties of Mankind*, trans. Thomas Bendyshe (1795; New York: Bergman, 1969), p. 212 n. 2.

8. On Merian, see Margarete Pfister-Burkhalter, *Maria Sibylla Merian, Leben und Werk 1647–1717* (Basel: GS-Verlag, 1980); and Elisabeth Rücker, "Maria Sibylla Merian," *Fränkische Lebensbilder* 1 (1967): 221–247; Rücker, *Maria Sibylla Merian* (Nuremberg: Germanisches Nationalmuseum, 1967); and Schiebinger, *Mind Has No Sex?* pp. 68–79.

9. Wilfrid Blunt, *The Compleat Naturalist: A Life of Linnaeus* (London: William Collins Sons & Co., 1971), p. 117.

266 10. Maria Merian, *Metamorphosis insectorum Surinamensium*, ed. Helmut Decker (1705; Leipzig: Insel-Verlag A. Kippenberg, 1975), commentary to plate no. 36.

11. Ibid., p. 38.

12. Schiebinger, *Mind Has No Sex?*

13. Ibid., chaps. 2 and 3.

14. Maria Riddell, *Voyages to the Madeira, and Leeward Caribbean Isles with Sketches of the Natural History of these Islands* (Edinburgh, 1792), preface.

15. Ibid., p. 82. Others, including Byran Edwards, also recorded this use. On Riddell, see Janet Todd, ed., *A Dictionary of British and American Women Writers, 1660–1800* (London: Methuen & Co. Ltd., 1984), s.v. "Riddell."

16. Hans Ludendorff, "Zur Frühgeschichte der Astronomie in Berlin," *Vorträge und Schriften der Preussischen Akademie der Wissenschaften* 9 (1942): 15. See also my account of Winkelmann in *Mind Has No Sex?* pp. 82–98.

17. [Marie-Anne de Roumier Robert], *La Voix de la nature, ou Les aventures de Madame la marquise de * * * * (Amsterdam, 1763); Françoise de Graffigny, *Lettres d'une péruvienne* (n.p., 1747); Olympe de Gouges, *Réflexions sur les hommes nègres* (Paris, 1788); and de Gouges, *L'esclavage des noirs, ou L'heureux naufrage* (Paris, 1792). On Robert, see Erica Harth, *Cartesian Women: Versions and Subversions of Rational Discourse in the Old Regime* (Ithaca: Cornell University Press, 1992), pp. 179–184.

18. Cited in Mary Louise Pratt, *Imperial Eyes: Travel Writing and Transculturation* (London: Routledge, 1992), pp. 31–32.

19. Foucher d'Obsonville, *Essais philosophiques sur les moeurs de divers animaux étrangers* (Paris, 1783), pp. 372–373.

20. Hans Sloane, *A Voyage to the Islands Madera . . .* (London, 1707), vol. 1, p. xlvi.

21. Foucher d'Obsonville, *Essais philosophiques*, p. 365.

22. Isert, cited in Pratt, *Imperial Eyes*, p. 96.

23. Adult males average about five feet in height, the adult female about four feet (Robert and Ada Yerkes, *The Great Apes: A Study of Anthropoid Life* [New Haven: Yale University Press, 1929], p. 199).

24. Edward Tyson, *Orang-Outang, sive Homo Sylvestris; or, The Anatomy of a Pygmie Compared with that of a Monkey, an Ape, and a Man* (London, 1699), p. 15.

25. Thomas Boreman, *A Description of Some Curious and Uncommon Creatures* (London, 1739), p. 25. See also William Bosman, "A New and Accurate Description of the Coast of Guinea" (London, 1705), in John Pinkerton, *A General Collection of the Best and Most Interesting Voyages and Travels in all Parts of the World* (London, 1808), vol. 16, p. 440.

26. Michel Foucault, *The Order of Things: An Archaeology of the Human Sciences* (1966; New York: Vintage Books Edition, 1973), p. 130. Also Pratt, *Imperial Eyes*, pp. 29, 35–37.

27. Alice Stroup, *A Company of Scientists: Botany, Patronage, and the Community at the Seventeenth-Century Parisian Royal Academy of Sciences* (Berkeley and Los Angeles: University of California Press, 1990).

28. Carl Linnaeus, *Critica botanica* (Leiden, 1737), no. 229.

29. Michel Adanson, *Familles des plantes* (Paris, 1763), vol. 1, p. clxxiii. On this point, see Joseph Needham, Lu Gwei-Djen, and Huang Hsing-Tsung, *Science and Civilization in China* (Cambridge: Cambridge University Press, 1986), vol. 6, pt. 1, pp. 19, 168.

30. Mary Astell in *Letters of Lady Mary Wortley Montagu Written during her Travels in Europe, Asia, and Africa* (1763; London, 1789), preface. See also Joseph Lew, "Lady Mary's Portable Seraglio," *Eighteenth-Century Studies* 24 (1991): 432–450.

31. Lansdown Guilding, "Observations on the Work of Maria Sibilla Merian on the Insects, etc., of Surinam," *The Magazine of Natural History* 7 (1834): 356, 362, 369–371.

32. Sloane, *A Voyage to the Islands of Madera . . .* , vol. 2, p. 49.

33. See J. T. Noonan, *Contraception: A History of Its Treatment by the Catholic Theologians and Canonists* (Cambridge, Mass.: Belknap Press of Harvard University Press, 1965); also John Riddle, *Contraception and Abortion from the Ancient World to the Renaissance* (Cambridge, Mass.: Harvard University Press, 1992).

34. Gunnar Heinsohn and Otto Steiger, *Die Vernichtung der Weisen Frauen* (Herbstein: März Verlag, 1985).

Bibliography

Abir-Am, Pnina, and Dorinda Outram, eds. *Uneasy Careers and Intimate Lives: Women in Science, 1789–1979.* New Brunswick: Rutgers University Press, 1987.

Abray, Jane. "Feminism in the French Revolution." *American Historical Review* 80 (1975): 43–62.

Ackermann, Jakob. *Über die körperliche Verschiedenheit des Mannes vom Weiber ausser Geschlechtstheilen.* Trans. Joseph Wenzel. Koblenz, 1788.

Allen, David, E. *The Naturalist in Britain: A Social History.* 1976; Harmondsworth, Middlesex: Penguin Books, 1978.

Anel le Robours, Marie-Angelique. *Avis aux mères qui veulent nourrir leurs enfans.* 3d ed. Paris, 1775.

Antonius Guilielmus Amo, Afer aus Axim in Ghana: Dokumente, Autographe, Belege. Halle: Martin Luther Universität, 1968.

Arber, Agnes. *Herbals: Their Origin and Evolution, a Chapter in the History of Botany, 1470–1670.* 3d ed. Cambridge: Cambridge University Press, 1986.

Aristotle. *Historia animalium.* In *The Works of Aristotle.* Trans. D'arcy Thompson. Oxford: Clarendon Press, 1910.

———. *Generation of Animals.* Trans. A. L. Peck. Cambridge, Mass.: Harvard University Press, 1953.

Barrow, John. *Reisen in das Innere von Südafrika in den Jahren, 1797 und 1798.* 1801; Berlin, 1802.

Beckles, Hilary. *Natural Rebels: A Social History of Enslaved Black Women in Barbados.* New Brunswick: Rutgers University Press, 1989.

Beeckman, Daniel. *A Voyage to and from the Island of Borneo.* London, 1718.

Bendyshe, Thomas. "The History of Anthropology." *Memoirs Read Before the Anthropological Society of London* (1865): 335–458.

270   Bernal, Martin. *Black Athena: The Afroasiatic Roots of Classical Civilization*. New Brunswick: Rutgers University Press, 1987.

[Bernier, François.] "Nouvelle division de la terre, par les differentes espèces ou races d'hommes qui l'habitent . . ." *Journal des savants* 12 (1684): 148–155.

Blainville, Henri de. "Sur une femme de la race hottentote." *Bulletin des sciences, par la Société Philomatique de Paris* (1816): 183–190.

Blanc, Olivier. *Olympe de Gouges*. Paris: Syros, 1981.

Blumenbach, Johann. *Handbuch der Naturgeschichte*. Göttingen, 1779.

———. *Geschichte und Beschreibung der Knochen des menschlichen Körpers*. Göttingen, 1786.

———. *Beyträge zur Naturgeschichte*. Göttingen, 1790.

———. *Decas collectionis suae craniorum diversarum gentium*. Göttingen, 1790–1828.

———. "Observations on some Egyptian Mummies opened in London." *Philosophical Transactions of the Royal Society of London* 84 (1794): pt. 2, 177–195.

———. *Beyträge zur Naturgeschichte*. Göttingen, 1806–1811.

———. *Abbildungen naturhistorischer Gegenstände*. Göttingen, 1810.

———. *On the Natural Varieties of Mankind*. Trans. Thomas Bendyshe. 1865; New York: Bergman, 1969.

Blunt, Wilfrid. *The Compleat Naturalist: A Life of Linnaeus*. London: William Collins Sons & Co., 1971.

Bontius, Jacob. *Historiae naturalis & medicae Indiae Orientalis libri sex*. Amsterdam, 1658.

[Boreman, Thomas.] *A Description of Some Curious and Uncommon Creatures*. London, 1739.

Bradley, Richard. *A Philosophical Account of the Works of Nature*. London, 1721.

Brentjes, Burchard. *Anton Wilhelm Amo: Der schwarze Philosoph in Halle*. Leipzig: Koehler & Amelang, 1976.

Broberg, Gunnar. *Homo Sapiens L.: Studier i Carl von Linnés naturuppfattning och människolära*. Stockholm: The Swedish History of Science Society, 1975.

———. "*Homo sapiens*: Linnaeus's Classification of Man." In *Linnaeus: The Man and His Work*. Ed. Tore Frängsmyr. Berkeley and Los Angeles: University of California Press, 1983.

———, ed. *Linnaeus: Progress and Prospects in Linnaean Research*. Stockholm: Almquist & Wiksell International, 1980.

Bucher, Bernadette. *Icon and Conquest: A Structural Analysis of the Illustrations of de Bry's Great Voyages*. Trans. Basia Miller Gulati. 1977; Chicago: University of Chicago Press, 1981.

Buffon, Georges-Louis Leclerc, comte de. *Histoire naturelle, générale et particulière*. 44 vols. Paris, 1749–1804.

Burrell, Harry. *The Platypus*. Sydney: Angus & Robertson Limited, 1927.

Bush, Barbara. "White 'Ladies,' Coloured 'Favourites' and Black 'Wenches'; Some Considerations on Sex, Race and Class Factors in Social Relations in White Creole Society in the British Caribbean." *Slavery and Abolition* 2 (1981): 244–262.

———. *Slave Women in Caribbean Society, 1650–1838*. Bloomington: Indiana University Press, 1990.

Bynum, Caroline. *Jesus as Mother: Studies in the Spirituality of the High Middle* 271
Ages. Berkeley and Los Angeles: University of California Press, 1982.

Cadden, Joan. *The Meanings of Sexual Difference in the Middle Ages: Medicine, Natural Philosophy, and Culture.* Cambridge: Cambridge University Press, 1992.

Cadogan, William. *An Essay upon Nursing and the Management of Children.* London, 1748.

Camerarius, Philippus. *The Walking Librarie; or, Meditations and Observations Historical, Natural, Moral, Political, and Poetical.* Trans. John Molle. London, 1621.

Camerarius, Rudolph. *De sexu plantarum epistola.* Tübingen, 1694.

Camper, Petrus. *Dissertation physique de M. Pierre Camper.* 1786; Utrecht, 1791.

———. *The Works of the Late Professor Camper on the Connexion between the Science of Anatomy and the Arts of Drawing, Painting, Statuary, etc.* Trans. T. Cogan. London, 1794.

———. *Vermischte Schriften.* Lingen, 1801.

———. "De l'orang-outang et de quelques autres espèces de singes." In vol. 1 of *Oeuvres de Pierre Camper.* Paris, 1803.

———. "Petri Camperi itinera in Angliam, 1748–85." *Opuscula selecta Neerlandicorum de arte medica* 15 (1939).

Carby, Hazel. *Reconstructing Womanhood: The Emergence of the Afro-American Woman Novelist.* New York: Oxford University Press, 1987.

Cavendish, Margaret, Duchess of Newcastle. *Philosophical Letters.* London, 1664.

Chardin, Jean. *Voyages du Chevalier Chardin en Perse.* 4 vols. 1686; Amsterdam, 1735.

Cobb, Richard, and Colin Jones, eds. *Voices of the French Revolution.* Topsfield, Mass.: Salem House Publishers, 1988.

Cohen, William. *The French Encounter with Africans: White Responses to Blacks, 1530–1880.* Bloomington: Indiana University Press, 1980.

Condorcet, Marie-Jean-Antoine-Nicolas de Caritat, Marquis de. "Eloge de M. de Linné." *Histoire de l'Académie Royale des Sciences.* Paris, 1778.

———. "Réflexions sur l'esclavage des nègres" (1781). In vol. 7 of *Oeuvres de Condorcet.* Ed. A. Condorcet O'Connor and M. F. Arago (Paris, 1847).

———. "Sur l'admission des femmes au droit de cité" (1790). In vol. 10 of *Oeuvres* (Stuttgart: F. Frommann, 1968).

Cooke, Edward. *A Voyage to the South Sea.* 2 vols. London, 1712.

Crooke, Helkiah. *Mikrokosmographia, A Description of the Body of Man.* London, 1615.

Cugoano, Ottobah. *Thoughts and Sentiments of the Evil and Wicked Traffic of the Slavery and Commerce of the Human Species.* London, 1787.

Curtin, Philip D. *The Image of Africa: British Ideas and Actions, 1780–1850.* Madison: University of Wisconsin Press, 1964.

Cuvier, Georges. *Leçons d'anatomie comparée.* Paris, 1800–1805.

———. "Extrait d'observations faites sur le cadavre d'une femme connue à Paris et à Londres sous le nom de Vénus Hottentotte." *Mémoires du Muséum d'Histoire Naturelle* 3 (1817): 259–274.

———. *Le règne animal.* 4 vols. Paris, 1817.

Dabydeen, David. *Hogarth's Blacks: Images of Blacks in Eighteenth-Century English Art.* Athens, Ga.: The University of Georgia Press, 1987.

Darwin, Charles. *The Descent of Man and Selection in Relation to Sex.* 1871; London: John Murray, 1913.

Darwin, Erasmus. *The Loves of the Plants* (1789). Part II of *The Botanic Garden: A Poem in Two Parts.* New York: Garland Publishing, Inc., 1978.

———. *Zoonomia; or, The Laws of Organic Life.* 2 vols. London, 1794.

———. *A Plan for the Conduct of Female Education in Boarding Schools.* London, 1797.

———. *The Letters of Erasmus Darwin.* Ed. Desmond King-Hele. Cambridge: Cambridge University Press, 1981.

Daudin, Henri. *De Linné à Jussieu: Méthodes de la classification.* Paris: Félix Alcan, 1926.

Davis, David Brion. *The Problem of Slavery in Western Culture.* Oxford: Oxford University Press, 1966.

———. *The Problem of Slavery in the Age of Revolution: 1770–1823.* Ithaca: Cornell University Press, 1975.

Davis, Natalie, and Arlette Farge, eds. *Histoire des femmes en Occident.* Paris: Plon, 1991.

Debrunner, Hans. *Presence and Prestige: Africans in Europe.* Basil: Basler Afrika Bibliographen, 1979.

Delaporte, François. *Nature's Second Kingdom: Explorations of Vegetality in the Eighteenth Century.* Trans. Arthur Goldhammer. 1979; Cambridge, Mass.: MIT Press, 1982.

Dhombres, Nicole and Jean. *Naissance d'un pouvoir: Sciences et savants en France (1793–1824).* Paris: Payot, 1989.

Dictionarium Britannicum. Ed. G. Gordon, P. Miller, and N. Bailley. London, 1730.

Dictionnaire classique d'histoire naturelle. Paris, 1825.

Duchet, Michèle. *Anthropologie et histoire au siècle des lumières: Buffon, Voltaire, Rousseau, Helvétius, Diderot.* Paris: François Maspero, 1971.

Dudley, Edward, and Maximillian Novak, eds. *The Wild Man Within: An Image in Western Thought from the Renaissance to Romanticism.* Pittsburgh: University of Pittsburgh Press, 1972.

Duras, Claire de Durfort, duchesse de. *Ourika.* Ed. Claudine Herrmann. 1824; Paris: Des Femmes, 1979.

Edwards, Paul, and James Walvin. *Black Personalities in the Era of the Slave Trade.* Baton Rouge: Louisiana State University Press, 1983.

Encyclopédie, ou Dictionnaire raisonné des sciences, des arts et des métiers. Paris, 1751–1765.

Equiano, Olaudah. *The Life of Olaudah Equiano, or Gustavus Vassa, the African.* Ed. Henry Louis Gates, Jr. 1789; New York: Mentor, 1987.

Farley, John. *Gametes and Spires: Ideas about Sexual Reproduction, 1750–1914.* Baltimore: Johns Hopkins University Press, 1982.

Fauré, Christine. *Democracy without Women: Feminism and the Rise of Liberal In-*

dividualism in France. Trans. Claudia Gorbman and John Berks. Bloomington: *273*
Indiana University Press, 1991.

Fausto-Sterling, Anne. *Myths of Gender: Biological Theories about Women and Men*. New York: Basic Books, 1985.

Fildes, Valerie. *Breasts, Bottles and Babies: A History of Infant Feeding*. Edinburgh: Edinburgh University Press, 1986.

————. *Wet Nursing: A History from Antiquity to the Present*. Oxford: Basil Blackwell, 1988.

————, ed. *Women as Mothers in Pre-Industrial England*. London: Routledge, 1990.

Fischer-Homberger, Esther. *Krankheit Frau und andere Arbeiten zur Medizingeschichte der Frau*. Bern: Hans Huber Verlag, 1979.

Foucher d'Obsonville, (name unknown). *Essais philosophiques sur les moeurs de divers animaux étrangers*. Paris, 1783.

Fox Keller, Evelyn. *A Feeling for the Organism: The Life and Work of Barbara McClintock*. New York: W. H. Freeman, 1983.

————. *Reflections on Gender and Science*. New Haven: Yale University Press, 1985.

Frängsmyr, Tore, ed. *Linnaeus: The Man and His Work*. Berkeley and Los Angeles: University of California Press, 1983.

Furet, François, and Mona Ozouf, eds. *A Critical Dictionary of the French Revolution*. Trans. Arthur Goldhammer. Cambridge, Mass.: Harvard University Press, 1989.

Gates, Henry Louis, Jr. *Figures in Black: Words, Signs, and the "Racial" Self*. New York: Oxford University Press, 1989.

————, ed. *"Race," Writing, and Difference*. Chicago: University of Chicago Press, 1986.

Gautier, Arlette. "Les esclaves femmes aux Antilles françaises: 1635–1848." *Historical reflections/Réflexions historiques* 10 (1983): 409–433.

Geggus, David. "Racial Equality, Slavery, and Colonial Secession during the Constituent Assembly." *The American Historical Review* 94 (1989): 1290–1308.

Gelphi, Barbara. *Shelley's Goddess: Maternity, Language, Subjectivity*. New York: Oxford University Press, 1992.

Geoffroy, Claude. "Observations sur la structure et l'usage des principales parties des fleurs." *Mémoires de l'Académie Royale des Sciences* (1711): 210–230.

Geoffroy Saint-Hilaire, Etienne, and Frédéric Cuvier. *Histoire naturelle des mammifères, avec des figures originales enluminées, dessinées d'après des animaux vivants*. Paris, 1819.

Gilibert, J. E. "Dissertation sur la dépopulation, causée par les vices, les préjugés et les erreurs des nourrices mercénaires." In vol. 2 of *Les chefs-d'oeuvres de Monsieur de Sauvages*. Lyon, 1770.

Gill, Theodor. "The Story of a Word—Mammal." *Popular Science Monthly* 61 (1902): 434–438.

Gilman, Sander. *Difference and Pathology: Stereotypes of Sexuality, Race and Madness*. Ithaca: Cornell University Press, 1985.

————. *Sexuality: An Illustrated History*. New York: John Wiley & Sons, 1989.

Gouges, Olympe de. *Réflexions sur les hommes nègres*. Paris, 1788.

————. *Les droits de la femme*. Paris, 1791.

Gould, Stephen Jay. "Chimp on the Chain." *Natural History* (December 1983): 18–26.

————. *The Flamingo's Smile: Reflections in Natural History*. New York: Norton & Company, 1985.

————. "Freudian Slip." *Natural History* 96 (1987): 14–19.

————. "Petrus Camper's Angle: the Grandfather of Scientific Racism has Gotten a Bum Rap." *Natural History* (July 1987): 12–16.

Grégoire, Henri. *De la littérature des nègres, ou Recherches sur leurs facultés intellectuelles, leurs qualités morales et leur littérature*. Paris, 1808.

Gregory, William. "The Orders of Mammals." *Bulletin of the American Museum of Natural History* 27 (1910).

Grew, Nehemiah. *The Anatomy of Plants*. London, 1682.

Hacke, William. *A Collection of Original Voyages*. London, 1699.

Haeckel, Ernst. *Das Menschen-Problem und die Herrentiere von Linné*. Frankfurt: Neuer Frankfurter Verlag, 1907.

Hanke, Lewis. *Aristotle and the American Indians: A Study in Race Prejudice in the Modern World*. London: Hollis and Carter, 1959.

Haraway, Donna. *Primate Visions: Gender, Race, and Nature in the World of Modern Science*. New York: Routledge, 1989.

Harding, Sandra. *The Science Question in Feminism*. Ithaca: Cornell University Press, 1986.

————. *Whose Science? Whose Knowledge? Thinking from Women's Lives*. Ithaca: Cornell University Press, 1991.

Harding, Sandra, and Jean O'Barr, eds. *Sex and Scientific Inquiry*. Chicago: University of Chicago Press, 1987.

Hardy, Charles. *The Negro Question in the French Revolution*. Menasha, Wis.: George Banta Publishing Co., 1919.

Hawkesworth, John. *An Account of the Voyages Undertaken by the Order of His Present Majesty for Making Discoveries in the Southern Hemisphere*. 4 vols. London, 1773.

Heller, John. *Studies in Linnaean Method and Nomenclature*. Frankfurt: Peter Lang, 1983.

Herbert, Thomas. *Some Yeares Travel into Africa and Asia*. London, 1638.

Hodgen, Margaret. *Early Anthropology in the Sixteenth and Seventeenth Centuries*. Philadelphia: University of Pennsylvania Press, 1964.

Hollander, Anne. *Seeing through Clothes*. New York: Penguin Books, 1975.

Home, Henry, Lord Kames. *Sketches of the History of Man*. Edinburgh, 1774.

Honour, Hugh. *The New Golden Land: European Images of America from the Discoveries to the Present Time*. New York: Pantheon Books, 1975.

————. *The Image of the Black in Western Art*. 4 vols. Cambridge, Mass.: Harvard University Press, 1979.

Hooks, Bell. *Black Looks: Race and Representation*. Boston: South End Press, 1992.

Hountondji, Paulin. *African Philosophy: Myth and Reality*. Trans. Henri Evans. London: Hutchinson University Library for Africa, 1983.

Hubbard, Ruth. *The Politics of Women's Biology*. New Brunswick: Rutgers University Press, 1990.

Huddleston, Lee. *Origins of the American Indians: European Concepts, 1492–1729*. Austin: University of Texas Press, 1967.

Hull, Gloria, Patricia Bell Scott, and Barbara Smith, eds. *All the Women Are White, All the Blacks Are Men, But Some of Us Are Brave: Black Women's Studies*. Old Westbury, New York: Feminist Press, 1982.

Hunt, Lynn. *Politics, Culture, and Class in the French Revolution*. Berkeley and Los Angeles: University of California Press, 1984.

———. *The Family Romance of the French Revolution*. Berkeley and Los Angeles: University of California Press, 1992.

———, ed. *Eroticism and the Body Politic*. Baltimore: Johns Hopkins University Press, 1991.

Hunter, John. *Essays and Observations on Natural History, Anatomy, Physiology, Psychology, and Geology*. Ed. Richard Owen. London, 1861.

Huxley, Thomas. *Man's Place in Nature and Other Anthropological Essays*. 1896; New York: Greenwood Press, 1968.

Jackson, Benjamin. *Linnaeus*. London: H. F. & G. Witherby, 1923.

Janson, H. W. *Apes and Ape Lore in the Middle Ages and the Renaissance*. London: The Warburg Institute, 1952.

Jones, Vivien, ed. *Women in the Eighteenth Century: Constructions of Femininity*. New York: Routledge, 1990.

Jordan, Winthrop D. *White over Black: American Attitudes toward the Negro, 1550–1812*. Chapel Hill: University of North Carolina Press, 1968.

Jordonova, Ludmilla. *Sexual Visions: Images of Gender in Science and Medicine between the Eighteenth and Twentieth Centuries*. Madison: University of Wisconsin Press, 1989.

———, ed. *Languages of Nature*. New Brunswick: Rutgers University Press, 1986.

Jouard, Gabriel. *Nouvel essai sur la femme considérée comparativement à l'homme*. Paris, 1804.

Kant, Immanuel. *Anthropologie in pragmatischer Hinsicht*. 1798; Frankfurt and Leipzig, 1799.

Kemp, T. S. *Mammal-like Reptiles and the Origin of Mammals*. London: Academic Press, 1982.

Kermack, D. M., and K. A. Kermack. *The Evolution of Mammalian Characters*. London: Croom Helm, 1984.

Kessler, Suzanne. "The Medical Construction of Gender: Case Management of Intersexed Infants." *Signs: Journal of Women in Culture and Society* 16 (1990): 3–26.

Kevles, Bettyann. *Females of the Species: Sex and Survival in the Animal Kingdom*. Cambridge, Mass.: Harvard University Press, 1986.

Kindersley, Jemima. *Letters from the Island of Teneriffe, Brazil, the Cape of Good Hope, and the East Indies*. London, 1777.

King-Hele, Desmond. *Erasmus Darwin*. New York: Charles Scribner's Sons, 1963.

———. *Doctor of Revolution: The Life and Genius of Erasmus Darwin*. London: Faber & Faber, 1977.

Kirby, Percival. "The Hottentot Venus." *Africana Notes and News* 6 (1949): 55–62.

———. "More about the Hottentot Venus." *Africana Notes and News* 10 (1953): 124–134.

Kirchhoff, Heinz. "Die künstlerische Darstellung der weiblichen Brust als Attribut der Weiblichkeit und Fruchtbarkeit als auch der Spende der Lebenskraft und der Weisheit." *Geburtshilfe und Frauenheilkunde* 50 (1990): 234–243.

Kolb, Peter. *The Present State of the Cape of Good Hope*. Trans. Guido Medley. 2 vols. 1731.

Koyré, Alexandre. *From the Closed World to the Infinite Universe*. Baltimore: Johns Hopkins Press, 1957.

La Capra, Dominick, ed. *The Bounds of Race: Perspectives on Hegemony and Resistance*. Ithaca: Cornell University Press, 1991.

Lacroix, Alfred. "Notice historique sur les membres et correspondants de l'académie des sciences ayant travaillé dans les colonies françaises des Mascareignes et de Madagascar au XVIIIᵉ siècle et au début du XIXᵉ." *Mémoires de l'Académie des Sciences* 62 (17 December 1934): 1–87.

La Mettrie, Julien Offray de. *L'homme plante*. Potsdam, 1748.

Landes, Joan. *Women and the Public Sphere in the Age of the French Revolution*. Ithaca: Cornell University Press, 1988.

Laqueur, Thomas. *Making Sex: Body and Gender from the Greeks to Freud*. Cambridge, Mass.: Harvard University Press, 1990.

Larson, James. *Reason and Experience: The Representation of Natural Order in the Work of Carl von Linné*. Berkeley and Los Angeles: University of California Press, 1971.

Lawrence, William. *Lectures on Physiology, Zoology, and the Natural History of Man*. London, 1819.

Le Cat, Claude-Nicolas. *Traité de l'existance du fluide des nerfs*. Berlin, 1765.

———. *Traité de la couleur de la peau humaine*. Amsterdam, 1765.

Leguat, François. *Voyage et avantures* [sic] *de François Leguat*. 2 vols. London, 1707.

Lepenies, Wolf. *Das Ende der Naturgeschichte: Wandel kultureller Selbstverständlichkeiten in den Wissenschaften des 18. und 19. Jahrhunderts*. Frankfurt: Suhrkamp, 1978.

Le Vaillant, François. *Voyage de François Le Vaillant dans l'intérieur de l'Afrique*. 1790; Paris, 1798.

———. *Travels from the Cape of Good-Hope into the Interior Parts of Africa*. Trans. Elizabeth Helme. London, 1790.

Levy, Darline, Harriet Applewhite, and Mary Johnson, eds. *Women in Revolutionary Paris, 1789–1795*. Urbana: University of Illinois Press, 1979.

Lewin, Roger. *Human Evolution*. 2d ed. Boston: Blackwell Scientific Publications, 1989.

Lewontin, Richard. *Human Diversity*. New York: Scientific American Books, 1982.

Ligon, Richard. *A True and Exact History of the Island of Barbados*. London, 1657.

Lindemann, Mary. "Love For Hire: The Regulation of the Wet-Nursing Business in Eighteenth-Century Hamburg." *Journal of Family History* 6 (1981): 379–395.

Linnaeus, Carl. *Praeludia sponsaliorum plantarum*. In vol. 1 of *Smärre Skrifter af Carl von Linné*. Ed. N. H. Lärjungar and T. Fries. Uppsala: Almquist & Wiksell, 1908.

———. *Systema naturae* (1735). Ed. M. S. J. Engel-Ledeboer and H. Engel. Nieuw-koop: B. de Graaf, 1964.

———. *Fauna Svecica*. Stockholm, 1746.

———. *Species plantarum*. Stockholm, 1753.

———. *Systema naturae per regna tria naturae*. 10th ed. Stockholm, 1758.

———. "Nutrix noverca." Respondent F. Lindberg. In vol. 3 of *Amoenitates academicae* (1752). Erlangen, 1787.

———. "Anthropomorpha." Respondent C. E. Hoppius. In vol. 6 of *Amoenitates academicae* (1760). Erlangen, 1789.

Long, Edward. *The History of Jamaica*. 3 vols. London, 1774.

Longino, Helen. *Science as Social Knowledge: Values and Objectivity in Scientific Inquiry*. Princeton: Princeton University Press, 1990.

Lovejoy, Arthur. *The Great Chain of Being: A Study of the History of an Idea*. 1933; Cambridge, Mass.: Harvard University Press, 1964.

———. "Monboddo and Rousseau." *Modern Philology* 30 (1932–1933): 275–296.

Lyon, John, and Phillip Sloan. *From Natural History to the History of Nature: Readings from Buffon and His Critics*. Notre Dame: University of Notre Dame Press, 1981.

Macfarlane, Alan. *The Origins of English Individualism: The Family, Property and Social Transition*. Cambridge: Cambridge University Press, 1979.

Maier, Michael. *Atalanta fugiens*. Oppenheim, 1618.

Mann, Gunter, Jost Benedum, and Werner Kümmel, eds. *Die Natur des Menschen: Probleme der Physischen Anthropologie und Rassenkunde, (1750–1850)*. Stuttgart: Gustav Fischer Verlag, 1990.

Mann, Gunter, and Franz Dumont, eds. *Samuel Thomas Soemmerring und die Gelehrten der Goethezeit*. Stuttgart: Gustav Fischer Verlag, 1985.

McCausland, Richard. "Particulars Relative to the Nature and Customs of the Indians of North-America." *Philosophical Transactions of the Royal Society of London* 76 (1786): 229–235.

McCloy, Shelby. *The Negro in France*. Lexington: University of Kentucky Press, 1961.

McNeil, Maureen. *Under the Banner of Science: Erasmus Darwin and His Age*. Manchester: Manchester University Press, 1987.

Meiners, Christoph. *Grundriß der Geschichte der Menschheit*. 1785; Lemgo, 1793.

———. *Geschichte des weiblichen Geschlechts*. 4 vols. Hanover, 1788–1800.

Melzer, Sara, and Leslie Rabine. *Rebel Daughters: Women and the French Revolution*. New York: Oxford University Press, 1992.

Merchant, Carolyn. *The Death of Nature: Women, Ecology, and the Scientific Revolution*. San Francisco: Harper & Row, 1980.

Merian, Maria Sibylla. *Metamorphosis insectorum Surinamensium*. Ed. Helmut Decker. 1705; Leipzig: Insel-Verlag A. Kippenberg, 1975.

278   Merrick, Jeffrey. "Royal Bees: The Gender Politics of the Beehive in Early Modern Europe." *Studies in Eighteenth-Century Culture* 18 (1988): 7–37.

Monboddo, James Burnet, Lord. *Of the Origin and Progress of Language*. 6 vols. Edinburgh, 1773–1792.

Montagu, M. F. Ashley. *Edward Tyson and the Rise of Human and Comparative Anatomy in England*. Philadephia: American Philosophical Society, 1943.

Montesquieu, Charles-Louis de Secondat, baron de. *The Spirit of the Laws*. Trans. Thomas Nugent. 1750; New York: Hafner Press, 1949.

Moreau de la Sarthe, Jacques. *Histoire naturelle de la femme*. Paris, 1803.

Morrissey, Marietta. *Slave Women in the New World: Gender Stratification in the Caribbean*. Lawrence: University Press of Kansas, 1989.

Morton, A. G. *History of Botanical Science: An Account of the Development of Botany from Ancient Times to the Present Day*. New York: Academic Press, 1981.

Moscucci, Ornella. *The Science of Woman: Gynaecology and Gender in England, 1800–1929*. Cambridge: Cambridge University Press, 1990.

Neumann, Erich. *Die Grosse Mutter*. Zurich: Rhein Verlag, 1956.

Nugent, Maria. *Lady Nugent's Journal (1801–1815)*. Ed. Frank Cundall. London: Adam & Charles Black, 1907.

Nussbaum, Felicity, and Laura Brown, eds. *The New Eighteenth Century: Theory/Politics/English Literature*. New York: Methuen, 1987.

O'Malley, C. D., and H. W. Magoun. "Early Concepts of the Anthropomorpha." *Physis: Rivista di storia della scienza* 4 (1962): 39–63.

Outram, Dorinda. *The Body and the French Revolution: Sex, Class and Political Culture*. New Haven: Yale University Press, 1989.

Ovington, John. *A Voyage to Suratt in the Year 1689*. London, 1696.

Paré, Ambroise. *The Collected Works of Ambroise Paré*. Trans. Thomas Johnson. London 1634; New York: Milford House, 1968.

Pateman, Carole. *The Sexual Contract*. Stanford: Stanford University Press, 1988.

Peacock, Thomas Love. *Melincourt*. Philadephia, 1817.

Perrault, Claude. *Mémoires pour servir à l'histoire naturelle des animaux*. Paris, 1676.

Pieterse, Jan. *White on Black: Images of Africa and Blacks in Western Popular Culture*. New Haven: Yale University Press, 1992.

Pinkerton, John. *A General Collection of the Best and Most Interesting Voyages and Travels in all Parts of the World*. 17 vols. London, 1808–1814.

Pliny the Elder. *Natural History*. Trans. H. Rackham. Cambridge, Mass.: Harvard University Press, 1942.

Ploss, Hermann, Max Bartels, and Paul Bartels. *Woman: An Historical Gynecological and Anthropological Compendium*. Ed. Eric Dingwall. 3 vols. St. Louis: C. V. Mosby Company, 1936.

Polwhele, Richard. *The Unsex'd Females; a Poem*. 1798; New York, 1800.

Pratt, Mary Louise. *Imperial Eyes: Travel Writing and Transculturation*. London: Routledge, 1992.

Prévost, Antoine. *Histoire générale des voyages*. 25 vols. The Hague, 1747–1780.

Prichard, James. *Researches into the Physical History of Man*. 1813; Chicago: University of Chicago Press, 1973.

————. *Researches into the Physical History of Mankind.* 4th ed. 5 vols. London, 1841.

Proctor, Robert. *Value-Free Science? Purity and Power in Modern Knowledge.* Cambridge, Mass.: Harvard University Press, 1991.

Pulteney, Richard. *A General View of the Writings of Linnaeus.* 2d ed. London, 1805.

Raulin, Joseph. *De la conservation des enfans.* 3 vols. Paris, 1768.

Ray, John. *Synopsis methodica: Animalium quadrupedum et serpentini generis.* London, 1693.

Raynal, Guillaume-Thomas. *Histoire philosophique et politique des établissements et du commerce des Européens dans les deux Indies.* 1770; The Hague, 1774.

Restif de la Bretonne, Nicolas-Edme. *La découverte australe.* 4 vols. Leipzig, 1781.

Riddell, Maria. *Voyages to the Madeira, and Leeward Caribbean Isles with Sketches of the Natural History of these Islands.* Edinburgh, 1792.

Rochefort, Charles de. *Histoire naturelle et morale des îles Antilles de l'Amérique.* 2d ed. Rotterdam, 1665.

Rossiter, Margaret. *Women Scientists in America: Struggles and Strategies to 1940.* Baltimore: Johns Hopkins University Press, 1982.

Rousseau, G. S., and Roy Porter, eds. *Exoticism in the Enlightenment.* Manchester: Manchester University Press, 1990.

Rousseau, Jean-Jacques. "Discours sur l'origine et les fondements de l'inégalité parmi les hommes." In vol. 3 of *Oeuvres complètes*, ed. Bernard Gagnebin and Marcel Raymond, 1755; Paris: Gallimard, 1959–1969.

————. *Emile, ou De l'éducation* (1762). In vol. 4 of *Oeuvres complètes*, ed. Bernard Gagnebin and Marcel Raymond. Paris: Gallimard, 1959–1969.

Roussel, Pierre. *Système physique et moral de la femme, ou Tableau philosophique de la constitution, de l'état organique, de tempérament, des moeurs, & des fonctions propres au sexe.* Paris, 1775.

Russett, Cynthia. *Sexual Science: The Victorian Construction of Womanhood.* Cambridge, Mass.: Harvard University Press, 1989.

Sachs, Julius von. *Geschichte der Botanik vom XVI. Jahrhundert bis 1860.* Munich, 1876.

Sala-Molins, Louis. *Le code noir, ou Le calvaire de Canaan.* Paris: Presses Universitaires de France, 1987.

Savage, Thomas. "Notice Describing the External Character and Habits of a New Species of Troglodytes (*T. gorilla*, Savage)." *Proceedings of the Boston Society of Natural History* 2 (1848): 245–247.

[Schaw, Janet.] *Journal of a Lady of Quality . . . 1774–1776.* New Haven: Yale University Press, 1992.

Schiebinger, Londa. *The Mind Has No Sex? Women in the Origins of Modern Science.* Cambridge, Mass.: Harvard University Press, 1989.

————. "Why Mammals Are Called Mammals: Gender Politics in Eighteenth-Century Natural History." *American Historical Review* 98 (1993): 382–411.

————. "The Gendered Ape: Early Representations of Primates in Europe." In *A Question of Identity: Women, Science, and Literature*, ed. Marina Benjamin. New Brunswick: Rutgers University Press, 1993.

280 Schmidt-Linsenhoff, Viktoria, ed. *Sklavin oder Bürgerin: Französische Revolution und neue Weiblichkeit, 1760–1830*. Frankfurt: Jonas Verlag, 1989.

Senior, Nancy. "Aspects of Infant Feeding in Eighteenth-Century France." *Eighteenth-Century Studies* 16 (1983): 367–388.

Seward, Anna. *Memoirs of the Life of Dr. Darwin*. Philadelphia, 1804.

Sharp, Jane. *The Midwives Book*. London, 1671.

Sheridan, Richard. *Doctors and Slaves: A Medical and Demographic History of Slavery in the British West Indies, 1680–1834*. Cambridge: Cambridge University Press, 1985.

Shteir, Ann. "Linnaeus's Daughters: Women and British Botany." In *Women and the Structure of Society*. Ed. Barbara Harris and Jo Ann McNamara. Durham: Duke University Press, 1984.

———. "Botany in the Breakfast Room: Women in Early Nineteenth-Century British Plant Study." In *Uneasy Careers and Intimate Lives: Women in Science, 1789–1979*. Ed. Pnina G. Abir-Am and Dorinda Outram. New Brunswick: Rutgers University Press, 1987.

Shyllon, Folarin. *Black People in Britain, 1555–1833*. Oxford: Oxford University Press, 1977.

Siegesbeck, Johann. *Verioris brevis sciagraphia*. St. Petersburg, 1737.

Skinner, Henry. *The Origin of Medical Terms*. Baltimore: Williams & Wilkins Company, 1949.

Sloane, Hans. *A Voyage to the Islands Madera. . . .* London, 1707.

Smellie, William. "Botany." *Encyclopaedia Britannica*. Edinburgh, 1771.

———. *The Philosophy of Natural History*. 2 vols. Edinburgh, 1790.

Smith, James E., ed. *The Correspondence of Linnaeus*. 2 vols. London, 1821.

Smith, Samuel Stanhope. *An Essay on the Causes of the Variety of Complexion and Figure in the Human Species*. 1787; Cambridge, Mass.: Harvard University Press, 1965.

Soemmerring, Samuel Thomas von. *Über die körperliche Verschiedenheit des Mohren vom Europäer*. Frankfurt, 1784.

———. *Über die körperliche Verschiedenheit des Negers vom Europäer*. Frankfurt, 1785.

———. *Vom Baue des menschlichen Körpers*. 5 vols. Frankfurt, 1791–1796.

———. *Tabula sceleti feminini juncta descriptione*. Utrecht, 1796.

Spelman, Elizabeth. *Inessential Woman: Problems of Exclusion in Feminist Thought*. Boston: Beacon Press, 1988.

Spencer, Frank. *Ecce Homo: An Annotated Bibliographic History of Physical Anthropology*. New York: Greenwood Press, 1986.

Stafford, Barbara. *Body Criticism: Imaging the Unseen in Enlightenment Art and Medicine*. Cambridge, Mass.: MIT Press, 1991.

Stafleu, Frans A. *Linnaeus and the Linnaeans: The Spreading of Their Ideas in Systematic Botany, 1735–1789*. Utrecht: A. Oosthoek's Uitgeversmaatschappy, 1971.

Stearn, W. T. "The Background of Linnaeus's Contributions to the Nomenclature and Methods of Systematic Biology." *Systematic Zoology* 8 (1959): 4–22.

Stedman, John. *Narrative of a Five Years' Expedition against the Revolted Negroes of Surinam.* 1796; Baltimore: Johns Hopkins University Press, 1988.

Stepan, Nancy Leys. *The Idea of Race in Science: Great Britain 1800–1960.* Hamden, Conn.: Archon Books, 1982.

———. "Race and Gender: The Role of Analogy in Science." *Isis* 77 (June 1986): 261–277.

Stocking, George, Jr. *Race, Culture, and Evolution: Essays in the History of Anthropology.* New York: Free Press, 1968.

———. *Victorian Anthropology.* New York: Free Press, 1987.

———. *Bones, Bodies, Behavior: Essays on Biological Anthropology.* Madison: University of Wisconsin, 1988.

Stone, Lawrence. *The Family, Sex and Marriage in England, 1500–1800.* New York: Harper & Row, 1977.

———. *Road to Divorce: England 1530–1987.* Oxford: Oxford University Press, 1990.

Stroup, Alice. *A Company of Scientists: Botany, Patronage, and the Community at the Seventeenth-Century Parisian Royal Academy of Sciences.* Berkeley and Los Angeles: University of California Press, 1990.

Sussman, George. *Selling Mothers' Milk: The Wet-Nursing Business in France, 1715–1914,* Urbana: University of Illinois Press, 1982.

Taylor, Thomas. *A Vindication of the Rights of Brutes.* London, 1792.

Thomas, Keith. *Man and the Natural World: A History of the Modern Sensibility.* New York: Pantheon Books, 1983.

Thornton, Robert. *A New Illustration of the Sexual System of Carolus von Linnaeus.* London, 1799–1807.

———. *The Temple of Flora.* 1799; Boston: New York Graphic Society, 1981.

Thunberg, C. P. "An Account of the Cape of Good Hope" (1795). In vol. 16 of John Pinkerton, *A General Collection of the Best and Most Interesting Voyages and Travels in All Parts of the World.* London, 1808.

Tiedemann, Friedrich. "On the Brain of the Negro, compared with that of the European and the Orang-Outang." *Philosophical Transactions of the Royal Society of London* (1836): 497–527.

Tinland, Franck. *L'homme sauvage, Homo ferus et Homo sylvestris, de l'animal à l'homme.* Paris: Payot, 1968.

Trew, Christoph. *Vermehrtes und verbessertes Blackwellisches Kraüter-Buch.* Nuremberg, 1750.

Trumbach, Randolph. *The Rise of the Egalitarian Family: Aristocratic Kinship and Domestic Relations in Eighteenth-Century England.* New York: Academic Press, 1978.

Tulp, Nicolaas. *Observationum medicarum libri tres.* Amsterdam, 1641.

Tyson, Edward. *Orang-Outang, sive Homo Sylvestris; or, The Anatomy of a Pygmie Compared with that of a Monkey, an Ape, and a Man.* London, 1699.

Vaillant, Sébastien. *Discours sur la structure des fleurs.* Leiden, 1718.

Valmont de Bomare, Jacques-Christophe. *Dictionnaire raisonné universel d'histoire naturelle.* Lyon, 1791.

Van Sertima, Ivan, ed. *Blacks in Science: Ancient and Modern*. New Brunswick: Transaction Books, 1984.

Virey, Julien-Joseph. *Histoire naturelle du genre humain*. 3 vols. Paris, 1800.

————. *De la femme*. Paris, 1823.

Visser, Robert. *The Zoological Work of Petrus Camper (1722–1789)*. Amsterdam: Rodopi, 1985.

Volney, Constantin-François. *Voyage en Syrie et en Egypte*. 1787; Paris: Mouton & Co., 1959.

Von Staden, Heinrich. "Affinities and Elisions: Helen and Hellenocentrism." *Isis* 83 (1992): 578–595.

Wagner, Rudolph. *Samuel Thomas von Soemmerring's Leben und Verkehr mit seinen Zeitgenossen*. Leipzig, 1844.

Wakefield, Priscilla. *Introduction to Botany*. London, 1796.

————. *Instinct Displayed*. 1816; London, 1821.

Walvin, James. *Black and White: The Negro and English Society, 1555–1945*. London: Penguin Press, 1973.

Warner, Marina. *Alone of All Her Sex: The Myth and the Cult of the Virgin Mary*. New York: Alfred A. Knopf, 1976.

————. *Monuments and Maidens: The Allegory of the Female Form*. New York: Atheneum, 1985.

Weber, Moritz. *Die Lehre von den Ur- und Racen-Formen der Schädel und Becken des Menschen*. Düsseldorf, 1830.

White, Charles. *An Account of the Regular Gradation in Man and in Different Animals and Vegetables*. London, 1796.

Winckelmann, Johann. *Reflections Concerning the Imitation of the Grecian Artists in Painting and Sculpture*. 1755; Glasgow, 1766.

Witkowski, Gustave-Jules. *Les seins dans l'histoire*. Paris: A. Maloine, 1903.

Wolker, Robert. "Tyson and Buffon on the Orang-utan." *Studies on Voltaire and the Eighteenth Century* 155 (1976): 2301–2319.

————. "Perfectible Apes in Decadent Cultures: Rousseau's Anthropology Revisited." *Daedelus* 107 (1978): 107–134.

Yeazell, Ruth. *Fictions of Modesty: Women and Courtship in the English Novel*. Chicago: University of Chicago Press, 1991.

Yerkes, Robert, and Ada. *The Great Apes: A Study of Anthropoid Life*. New Haven: Yale University Press, 1929.

Index

Africans, 64, 90, 98, 127, 129, 133, 136, 141–142; compared to apes, 5, 140, 145, 149, 156, 158, 161, 169, 171, 188, 198, 211, 258n95; in Europe, 115–116, 143, 148, 177–178; in European colonies, 173–174, 175, 179, 181, 183; learned, 191, 193–196; objects of anthropological study, 5, 91, 95, 115–120, 138–139, 144–147, 149–150, 156–159. *See also* Amo, Anton Wilhelm; Capitein, Jacobus Elisa; Cugoano, Ottobah; Equiano, Olaudah; "Hottentot Venus"; Lislet-Geoffroy, Jean-Baptiste; Ourika; Wheatley, Phillis; Williams, Francis

Aldrovandi, Ulisse, 43

Allegorical figures, 57 (fig. 2.2), 58 (fig. 2.3), 61 (fig. 2.4), 63 (fig. 2.5), 72–73 (fig. 2.7), 128 (fig. 4.2), 176 (fig. 5.7), 178 (fig. 5.8), 180 (fig. 5.9), 182 (fig. 5.10)

Alston, Charles, 29

Altmann, Jeanne, 114

Amazons, 34, 60

Amman, John, 30

Amo, Anton Wilhelm: studies at the Universities of Halle and Wittenberg, 191, 192–193, 196, 263n25; *De jure Maurorum in Europa*, 200

Anel le Robours, Marie-Angelique, 68

Apes, 56, 233n1, 235n18; ability to speak, 82–84; bone in penis of, 76, 89, 96 (fig. 3.5); cultured, 85, 87–88, 108–112; display affections, 84, 87, 101; erect posture of, 84–85, 237n39; female characteristics of, 88–94; gendered, 5, 75–76, 94–106; male and sexual relations with women, 94–98; modesty in, 5, 99–101; reason in, 81–82, 227n52; and virility of male, 5, 76, 96–98. *See also* César de Malaca; Madame Chimpanzee; Oran Haut-ton, Sir

Aristotle, 1, 38, 40, 44, 45, 53, 74, 76, 81, 88, 89, 91, 98, 99, 117, 147, 186, 204, 225n35, 228n55; classification of, 42–43; on milk, 48, 56. *See also* Apes

Augustine of Hippo, 60, 75, 81

Baer, Karl Ernst von, 21

Banks, Joseph, 187, 206